DECISIONS

The spiritual path is a path of decisions. The sexual life is a lifetime of decisions. We are souls with free wills, invited to choose. We think of choices as decisions about what is right or wrong. A deeper essence of each choice is: Does it, in the long run, enhance *life* or *death*? With each choice we may move toward attunement with good and an enhancement of life within ourselves—physically, mentally, spiritually—or we may move toward manifesting evil and construction of patterns that eventually lead to death. We are invited to choose!

Bantam Books by Herbert B. Puryear, Ph.D.
Ask your bookseller for the books you have missed

THE EDGAR CAYCE PRIMER
REFLECTIONS ON THE PATH
SEX AND THE SPIRITUAL PATH

SEX AND THE SPIRITUAL PATH

Based on the Edgar Cayce Readings

Herbert B. Puryear, Ph.D.

BANTAM BOOKS
TORONTO • NEW YORK • LONDON • SYDNEY • AUCKLAND

This low-priced Bantam Book
has been completely reset in a type face
designed for easy reading, and was printed
from new plates. It contains the complete
text of the original hard-cover edition.
NOT ONE WORD HAS BEEN OMITTED.

SEX AND THE SPIRITUAL PATH

A Bantam Book / published by arrangement with
A. R. E. Press

PRINTING HISTORY

A. R. E. edition published December 1980
Bantam edition / May 1986

ISBN 0-553-25635-1

Published simultaneously in the United States and Canada

Bantam Books are published by Bantam Books, Inc. Its trademark, consisting of the words "Bantam Books" and the portrayal of a rooster, is Registered in U.S. Patent and Trademark Office and in other countries. Marca Registrada. Bantam Books, Inc., 666 Fifth Avenue, New York, New York 10103.

PRINTED IN THE UNITED STATES OF AMERICA

O 0 9 8 7 6 5 4 3 2 1

. . . how much greater is
a day in the house of the Lord—
or a moment in His presence—
than a thousand years
in carnal forces? (262-57)

This book is dedicated
to Jesus,
and to my friends,
in whose love and forgiveness
I rejoice!

Contents

Preface ix

Acknowledgments xi

Introduction xiii

1 Sex! and How It Got That Way 1

2 Your Spiritual Path 16

3 The Body Is the Temple 44

4 Mind Is the Builder 68

5 Sex and the Individual 96

6 Sex In Relationships 141

7 Decisions, Decisions, Decisions 192

Appendix 223

Preface

The great and special privilege of my life has been to be able to study and work with the Edgar Cayce readings. I consider myself to be a student and a seeker. Thus in approaching a topic such as this, I write about it because of its importance, not because I am an expert on the subject. What I have tried to do is to present to other students what the readings say about sex in a context true to the greater thrust of the readings and indeed true to the greater meaning of life.

The readings instruct us to re-examine our purposes, attitudes, choices and activities regarding sex. They call us to measure these by standards more truly loving than our society or even we, as seekers on the path, are generally willing to employ. These challenging statements from the readings are like precious gems which I have tried to place in unobtrusive settings that will highlight and not detract from the quality of the gems themselves.

Acknowledgments

I am especially appreciative of the help from several people who have made this project possible. Mae Gimbert St. Clair, Bob Zindorf, Caroline King and Kiiri Tamm enabled me to have immediate access to all of the relevant readings. Dee Shambaugh, Marilyn Peterson, Diana Barrentine and Norine Stella enabled me to put my reflections and arrangements into several drafts and final form. I appreciate the patience and editorial contributions of Ken Skidmore and his staff and the cooperative response of John Van Auken and the staff of the A.R.E. Press.

I am appreciative of the amazing work of Edgar Cayce, his wife Gertrude and his son Hugh Lynn Cayce and of Gladys Davis Turner, who enabled this work to be established, and of Charles Thomas Cayce, under whose leadership it grows in viability and outreach.

Introduction

So much has been written, discussed and debated about sex that one may ask if anything further can be said. It seems, however, that the new openness about sex has raised more questions than it has answered. This questioning has posed special problems for those on the spiritual path.

Most of what has been written has been from the viewpoint of our contemporary society. Much of the literature deals specifically with clinical considerations; some reflects the moralistic bias of the Bible's inferred views on sex; some is based on popular polls presenting statistical data. Spiritual considerations of sex have tended to come out of the monastic traditions of the West or the yogic traditions of the East. Yet another viewpoint may be needed.

The Edgar Cayce readings give a perspective on sex, as they do on many topics, which is uniquely holistic. The readings deal with sex from the perspectives of soul purposes, mental attitudes, and practical and physical considerations. The spirit of the readings, as always, is to give what is helpful and hopeful.

It is not my purpose in writing this book to present "everything you always wanted to know about sex" from the Edgar Cayce readings. Rather it is to offer my understanding of the readings perspective on sex in the context of the greater understanding this information gives to the meaning and purpose of life and the journey of the soul. This book is addressed to you who are on the spiritual path who have questions about sex or sexual problems, to help you integrate what you know about the path with your immediate concerns about sexuality.

I am writing from the perspectives first of a pilgrim on the path; second, as a student and enthusiast of the Edgar Cayce readings; third, as a partner in a marriage of 29 years; and fourth, as a clinical psychologist with 22 years of counseling experience.

Further, I seek to help each individual to begin to discover that which for him is his own unique spiritual path and to begin to make decisions about sexual influences in his life that are in accord with his own decisions about his spiritual path.

SEX AND THE SPIRITUAL PATH

1

Sex! and How It Got That Way

The Greater Influence

. . . there is no soul but what the sex life becomes the greater influence in the life. Not as always in gratification in the physical act, but rather that that finds expression in the creative abilities of the body itself. 911-2

There is presently in our society a new openness about sex which has the potential for being very healthy. However, much of it is an overreaction to the repressive attitudes about sex of an earlier period; and just as the pendulum had swung to one extreme in the repressive attitude, now it is swinging to the opposite extreme in the imbalanced and excessive attitudes of the new liberality. To achieve the balance, we must value and retain openness of attitude while moving to a healthier and more spiritually based understanding of the problems and opportunities of sex. A balanced perspective must consider the nature and purpose of man as a soul in the earth plane.

Someone asked Edgar Cayce, "Am I devoting enough time to soul development?" The source of the readings replied that soul development should take precedence over all things. How do our concerns about sex fit into this priority? We are fearful that soul development will limit and frustrate our sexual expression. The Edgar Cayce readings, while remaining true to the priority of the spiritual life, also consistently reflect an attitude toward human behavior that is non-condemning and understanding. We may expect in this information an attitude toward sex that is, on the one hand, deeply realistic with respect to the human condition and, on the other hand, highly spiritual in perspective.

The Nature of Man

Let us consider the nature of man as it is pictured in the philosophy of the Cayce readings. The first premise is the Oneness of all force. The readings regard all things, seen and unseen, as expressions of the One Force, the Spirit which is the life and substance of the one reality of all dimensions. We, as souls, are spiritual beings and are part of that One Force.

At present we are caught up in a three-dimensional awareness. Because we are in three dimensions, we conceptualize reality as three dimensional in trying to understand ourselves, the world about us, and the God-force. We understand the Divine as a Trinity in the Father, the Son and the Holy Spirit. And we, as children of God, made in His image, also reflect triune qualities. We have not only aspects of the Father, Son and Holy Spirit within ourselves, but also a triune consciousness—the conscious, subconscious and superconscious. We manifest in a triune form with physical bodies, mental bodies and spiritual bodies.

The spiritual body is the soul; as such it was created, and will continue to exist without sex. But to understand sex and how it came to be "the greater influence" in our three-dimensional existence, we must consider how we came into the earth plane and came to be known as man with male and female forms.

A Cosmic View of the Story of Man

From the beginning all souls were perfect and one with God; created out of His desire for companionship, we were co-creators with Him.

The first cause was, that the created would be the companion for the Creator; that it, the creature, would—through its manifestations in the activity of that given unto the creature—show itself to be not only worthy of, but companionable to, the Creator. 5753-1

In the beginning, when there was the creating, or the calling of individual entities into being, we were made to be the companions with the Father-God.

1567-2

This period has been poetically characterized as the time "when the morning stars sang together as they announced the glory of the coming of man." (1857-2) We were given access to the life force, minds with which to build, and wills to choose how we would use it. (These are the attributes of the soul.) As co-creators with God, we had the opportunity for unlimited experiencing, for manifesting creatively and for sharing those creations and exeriences one with another.

There were some, however, a group of us, who out of the spirit of wanting to manifest without regard to the creations of others, began to develop the spirit of rebellion. We chose to manifest out of harmony with other creators. This development might be called "the fall in heaven." Several references in the Bible describe this situation: see Genesis 3:5 (the story of Adam and Eve, who were told, " . . . ye shall be as gods"); Ezekiel 28 (the admonitions to the King of Tyre, who was told that he was in Eden, perfect in all of his ways, until fault was found in him who said "I am a god!"); and Isaiah 14 (the fall of the Day Star, Lucifer, who said, "I will make myself like the Most High"). The spirit of *God* is expressed in the term "let *us*"; the spirit of rebellion, that led to our fall, is characterized by the term "*I* will!" (Let us keep in mind that this original fall or rebellion occurred when we were still in spirit form before our incarnation in the earth plane.)

Note carefully the deep concern with which the readings address this basic problem and its solution:

Then we must know from whence we came; how, why; and whence we go—and why.

In God's own purpose, Spirit is His presence then. For the Spirit of God moved and that which is in matter came into being, for the opportunities of His associates, His companions, His sons, His daughters. These are ever spoken of as One.

Then there came that as sought for self-indulgence, self-glorification; and there was the beginning of warring among themselves for activity—*still* in Spirit.

Then those that had made selfish movements moved into that which was and is *opportunity*, and there came life into same.

Then what was the Spirit that moved that made rebellion? The Spirit of God or the Spirit of Self?

This becomes self-evident even when we look about us in our own experience day by day. They that have the Spirit of God have the Spirit of truth, have the Spirit of Christ, have the Spirit of construction.

They that have the Spirit of rebellion have the Spirit of hate, the Spirit of confusion; and seek self-glory rather than peace, harmony and understanding.

Thus as has been indicated, the Spirit pushed into matter—and became what we see in our three-dimensional world as the kingdoms of the earth; the mineral, the vegetable, the animal—a three-dimensional world.

And that which beareth witness is the Spirit of Truth, the Spirit of Light. For He said, "Let there be light; and there was light."

Then indeed there is no power that emanates that is not from God.

Then what is this Spirit of rebellion, what is this Spirit of hate? What is this Spirit of self-indulgence? What is this Spirit that makes men afraid?

***Selfishness!* Allowed, yes, of the Father. For, as given, He has not willed that the souls should perish but**

that we each should know the truth—and the truth would make us free. Of what? Selfishness!

Then we should each know that the sin which lies at our door is ever the sin of selfishness, self-glory, self-honor.

Hence as the Master has said, unless we become even as He, we may not in *any* wise enter in.

Enter to what? To the consciousness that our Father would that we be even as that Spirit of truth manifested by the Son of Righteousness, that—even as those souls—took on flesh in this three-dimensional world; becoming a part, a parcel of what? Those kingdoms of which the earth is a part; or that by their very presence is in existence.

Hence we find He had come, is come, ever has come into the experience that He might through love—not force, not hate, not by command but by edification and justification—bring that soul that is dominated by the Spirit to understanding.

Thus we find His intervention in man's attempt throughout the eons of time and space. For these (time and space) become portions of this three-dimensional plane. And what is the other? Time, space, patience!

For God has shown and does show us day by day, even as His Son gave, that in patience we become aware of our souls, of our identity, of our being each a corpuscle, as it were, in the great body, in the heart of, our God. And He has not willed otherwise.

Then what is the Spirit of God? *Patience, time and space* in the material understanding.

This then is our first premise; that God *is*—in the material experience of man—*time, space, patience!* 262-114

Let us understand that sex was not the reason for the fall, but rebellion in the spirit plane that manifested in the earth plane. And the problems in relation to sex were logical consequences of the spiritual rebellion, because both involved the misuse of creative energy.

The division into sexes in the animal and plant kingdoms was an ongoing part of the evolutionary development in the earth plane before the souls of man entered.

Thus the problem of sex for the soul is not the physical fact of sex but rather the mental orientation toward carnal desires. The physical manifestations in the evolutionary developments in the earth plane were a part of an ongoing manifestation of the spirit of one God. However, even though the earth and the development of life upon it was for man's experiencing, it was not for him to project himself into that evolutionary development and make modifications of it in accord wih carnal desires but rather with universal law. Thus the beginning problem and the problem to this day is not physicality but rather carnality. It is not experiencing the earth plane that is the problem, but rather it is the desiring of the carnal mind that draws us into the earth plane again and again.

Thus, we were a wave of souls who had fallen in awareness from harmony with the Whole. We came into this solar system, then into the three-dimensional sphere of the planet Earth. The readings say that the earth was created for us to experience as a fact of creation, but not as a place of permanent tenancy. But because of our special attraction to the activities in the earth, we became involved and subsequently identified with the various life forms here. Finally we so invested our consciousnesses into these forms, that we forgot where we came from and where we should be going. This was a self-created entrapment.

The nature of this entrapment is relevant to our consideration of sex, because the attributes of co-creator remained with us in some measure. We began to experiment with the various forms that had already been evolving. We began to build through the creative power of our minds the combinations of forms that may be seen even to this day in certain artistic depictions and mythological creatures.

These, then, are the manners in which the *entities*, those *beings*, those *souls*, in the beginning partook of, or developed. Some brought about monstrosities, as those of its (that entity's) association by its projection with its association with beasts of various characters. Hence those

of the . . . satyr, and the like; those of the sea, or mermaid; those of the unicorn, and those of the various forms . . . 364-10

We built or projected combinations of features of different species, so as to make the centaur, minotaur, humanoid forms with hooves, claws or tails of animals or birds, or human bodies with the heads of birds. These, according to the readings, are not just the imaginations of the creators of myths, but rather depictions of the actual state of affairs as it existed in the earth plane hundreds of thousands of years ago. This problem continued in physical expression as recently as 12,000 years ago.

As has been indicated, in that particular experience there were still those who were physically entangled in the animal kingdom with appendages, with cloven hooves, with four legs, with portions of trees, with tails, with scales, with those various things that thought forms (or evil) had so indulged in as to separate the purpose of God's creation of man, as man—not as animal but as man. And the animal seeks only gratifying of self, the preservation of life, the satisfying of appetites. With infinity injected in same brought the many confused activities or thoughts that we know now as appetities. Yes, a dog may learn to smoke! Yes, a horse may learn to eat sugar! But these are not natural inclinations—rather man's influence upon these activities by associations!

All these forms, then, took those activities in the physical beings of individuals. 2072-8

Thought Forms

Our souls abused the One force and the minds given us.

As to their forms in the physical sense, these were much rather of the nature of thought forms, or able to push out of themselves in that direction in which its development took shape in thought—much in the way

and manner as the amoeba would in the waters of a stagnant bay, or lake, in the present. As these took form, by the gratifying of their own desire for that as builded or added to the material conditions, they became hardened or set—much in the form of the existent human body of the day, with that of color as partook of its surroundings much in the manner as the chameleon in the present. 364-3

There were two special problems associated with these thought-form projections: First, they were not independent creations, apart and aside from the soul, but rather they became a part of the emanations of the soul itself. These became enmeshing and entangling, obscuring the soul's continuing awareness of its greater reality. Thus as the soul became immersed in its own thought forms, it became more continually cut off from an awareness of and attunement with the higher dimensions and its original source of Oneness with the Universe and the Infinite. Furthermore, these thought forms were especially involved with sex activities. The propagation of these lower forms began to impinge on the manifestations of other aspects of creation.

Adam and Eve to the Rescue

With the entrapment of the first wave of souls in thought-form projections, we may say in a sense that God had a problem. How was He to get through to His children who had invested their consciousnesses so deeply in forms that kept them from their awareness of Oneness with Him?

Seeing the entrapment of the first group, He sent a second wave of souls to enable the entrapped souls to begin to remember who they were and to allow themselves to be freed from the thought forms in which they had become "lost."

Then, as the sons of God came together and saw in the earth the unspeakable conditions becoming more and

more of self-indulgence, self-glorification, the ability to procreate through the very forces of their activity, we find that our Lord, our Brother, *chose* to measure up, to earn, to *attain* that companionship for man with the Father through the overcoming of *self* in the physical plane. 262-115

This stage is the period recounted in the Bible as the entry of Adam and Eve into the earth plane. From the legend of Lilith and Amilius comes the separation of Eve from Adam. This division was to assure success in the mission so that the Sons of God (the second wave) would not become involved with the sons and daughters of men (the first wave).

Let us study this development carefully. The story has strong implications for us today in the purpose and choosing of a mate!

Q-1. How is the legend of Lilith connected with the period of Amilius?

A-1. In the beginning, as was outlined, there was presented that that became as the Sons of God, in that male and female were as in one, with those abilities for those changes as were able or capable of being brought about. In the changes that came from those *things*, as were of the projections of the abilities of those entities to project, this as a being came as the companion; and when there was that turning to the within, through the sources of creation, as to make for the helpmeet of that as created by the first cause, or of the Creative Forces that brought into being that as was made, *then*—from out of self—was brought that as was to be the helpmeet, *not* just companion of the body. Hence the legend of the associations of the body during that period before there was brought into being the last of the creations, which was not of that that was *not* made, but the first of that that *was* made, and a helpmeet to the body, that there might be no change in the relationship of the *Sons* of God *with* those relationships of the sons and daughters of men.

In this then, also comes that as is held by many who

have reached especially to that understand of how *necessary*, then, becomes the *proper* mating of those souls that may be the *answers* one to another of that that may bring, through that association, that companionship, into being that that may be the more helpful, more sustaining, more the well-*rounded* life or experience of those that are a *portion* one of another. Do not misinterpret, but knowing that all are *of* one—yet there are those divisions that make for a *closer* union, when there are the proper relationships brought about. 364-7

At this point two major lines developed—the Sons and Daughters of God and the sons and daughters of men—both manifesting in male and female expression.

Q-2. How long did it take for the division into male and female?

A-2. That depends upon which, or what branch or *line* is considered. When there was brought into being that as of the projection of that created *by* that created, this took a period of evolutionary—or, as would be in the present year, fourscore and six years. That as brought into being as was of the creating *of* that that became a portion of, *of* that that was already created by the *Creator, that* brought into being as *were* those of the forces in nature itself. God said, "Let there be light" and there *was* light! God said, "Let there be life" and there *was* life!

Q-3. Were the thought forms that were able to push themselves out of themselves inhabited by souls, or were they of the animal kingdom?

A-3. That as created by that *created*, of the animal kingdom. That created as by the Creator, with the soul.

Q-4. What was meant by the Sons of the Highest in Atlantis and the second coming of souls to the earth, as mentioned in a life reading [2802-1] given through this channel?

A-4. In this period of age, as was seen—There is fault of words here to *project* that as actually *occurs* in the *formations* of that as comes about! There was, with

the *will* of that as came into being through the correct channels, of that as created by the Creator, that of the *continuing* of the souls in its projection and projection—see? while in that as was *of* the offspring, of that as pushed itself *into* form to *satisfy, gratify,* that of the desire of that known as carnal forces of the *senses,* of those created, there continued to be the war one with another, and there were then—*from* the other *sources* (worlds) the continuing entering of those that *would* make for the keeping of the balance, as of the first purpose of the Creative Forces, as it magnifies itself in that given sphere of activity, of that that had been *given* the *ability* to *create* with its *own* activity—see? and hence the second, or the *continued* entering of souls into that known as the earth's plane during this period, for that activity as was brought about. 364-7

Adam was a single individual; at the same time he is also said to have projected into the earth in five places at once. Thus "Adam" might also be a generic term for the whole wave of souls that entered at this time to be of aid to the first group.

The ones that became the most *useful* were those as would be classified (or called in the present) as the *ideal* stature, that was of both male and female (as those separations had been begun); and the most ideal (as would be called) was Adam, who was in that period when he (Adam) appeared as five in one . . . 364-11

Now let us keep in mind the difference in the first wave projecting in Atlantis and the second wave associated with the five projections of Adam.

Q-5. Was Atlantis one of the five points at which man appeared in the beginning, being the home of the red race?

A-5. One of the five points. As has been given, in what is known as Gobi, India, in Carpathia [?], or in that known as the Andes, and that known as in the western

plain of what is now called America—the five places. In their presentation, as we find, these—in the five places, as *man* (Let's get the difference in that as first appeared in what is known as Atlantis, and that as *man* appearing from those projections in the five places—and, as has been given, from their environ took on that as became necessary for the meeting of those varying conditions under which their individualities and personalities began to put on form)—one in the white, another in the brown, another in the black, another in the red. 364-9

The creation of Adam and Eve provided a structure, a vehicle, which was suited for survival and propagation on the earth plane and had the potential for attuning to the God Force. It, therefore, comprised elements of existing patterns on the earth plane and also replicated the universe in miniature.

Thus there was brought into the earth plane a unique creation which was not a product of evolution. The readings say this happened quickly, as man measures time. Spirit forces borrowed the most advanced evolutionary characteristics from those animals exhibiting the greatest adaptability to life in the earth plane. Yet Adam and Eve bore the image of God, a model of the universe.

"God said, we will make man." Then man—the creation in itself, that combining all of the forms of creation so far created, that that same force might understand by having passed through that same creation as was necessary to bring up to that dividing point between man and animal and plant, and mineral kingdom—was *given* then the will, and the soul, that it might make itself One with that creation. 900-340

With the entry of Adam and Eve and the development of *Homo sapiens* as the ultimate vehicle for the reawakening of the entrapped souls, there were set boundaries and limitations: no soul could enter and work in the earth plane except in human form; and no human body would continue to live except as an expression of an indwelling soul. We may think of this arrangement as a quarantine imposed by the higher forces, or we may think of it as protective constraints of a loving Father.

The Implementation of the Plan

The *image* of God in man is the *law* or pattern of the Whole written on the soul. (This is discussed in Deuteronomy 30, Jeremiah 31, Hebrews 10 and Romans 10.) As we mobilize this image in application in our lives, we manifest health in our physical bodies and love in our relationships with those about us. This was God's idea, His promise in creating Adam and Eve, so that we need not know the conflict, disharmony and disease of the animal forms we created.

Although the plan itself was adequate, our response as rebellious souls was not immediate. The unfoldment of the plan only began with the soul named Amilius, who projected as Adam. (Remember, imprinted on him was the pattern of the Universe, our way back to Oneness.) This soul had no physical beginning but a physical death. He later manifested, the readings say, as Enoch, who had a physical birth but no physical death, being translated or taken up by God. As Melchizedek, he had neither beginning nor ending of days, neither a physical birth nor a physical death in the earth plane.

Although this helping soul sought to reach out again and again to His fellow souls, these attempts were not receiving an adequate response. Thus the plan continued over time. Subsequently there were the manifestations as Joseph of the Old Testament, Joshua, Asaph, Jeshua and other experiences in the earth plane. The final offering was the life of the man called Jesus.

The implementation of the plan is summarized fully in the following:

Q-5. What was meant by "As in the first Adam sin entered, so in the last Adam all shall be made alive"? [Study carefully I Corinthians 15:35-50]

A-5. Adam's entry into the world in the beginning,

then, must become the savior *of* the world, as it was committed to his care, "Be thou fruitful, multiply, and *subdue* the earth!" Hence Amilius, Adam, the first Adam, the last Adam, becomes—then—that that is *given* the *power over* the earth, and—as in each soul the first to be conquered is self—then *all things*, conditions and elements, are subject unto that self! That a universal law, as may be seen in that as may be demonstrated either in gases that destroy one another by becoming elements of the same, or that in the mineral or the animal kingdom as may be found that destroy, or *become* one *with* the other. Hence, as Adam given—the *Son* of God—so he *must* become that that would be able to take the world, the earth, back to that source from which it came, and *all power* is given in his keeping in the earth, that he has overcome; self, death, hell and the grave even, become subservient unto Him *through* the conquering of self in that made flesh; for, as in the beginning was the Word, the Word *was* with God, the Word *was* God, the same was *in* the beginning. The Word came and dwelt among men, the offspring of self in a material world, and the Word *overcame* the world—and hence the world *becomes*, then, as the servant of that that overcame the world! 364-7

The incarnation of Jesus was the ultimate conclusion to the plan which had its beginning in Adam. Whereas in Adam there was given the vehicle and the pattern made in the image of God, in Jesus that pattern was lived out in fullness in the earth plane in the life of the Man who became fully obedient unto universal law. He lived and demonstrated for us a life in full attunement with Divine Oneness. In that life of obedience He overcame death completely in the resurrection of the body. Then with that resurrection, all power was given to that One, and He became the Way for every one of us, a mediator between the souls of men and the Divine Father. He established the Way through which we may enter into the awareness of God, a thought form, a pattern of love. Through it, the power and love of God can flow through us, giving us life in conformity with His image, the Law of the Universe.

Summary

The original problem of man was the soul's fall in heaven through the spirit of rebellion. That problem became projected into the experiences in the earth plane. The spirit of rebellion manifested in the expressions of sex.

Sex was a part of the ongoing life in the earth plane and, as *Homo sapiens* was developed, it became a natural part of that expression for the propagation of that species through which redemption was to be possible. However, carnal desires and related thought forms entrapped and kept souls bound to the laws of this limited dimension. The problem was not the expression of sex itself, but rather the carnality of the mind.

Once the perfect physical vehicle was established, sex became a means to enhance soul growth in the form of a challenge to the carnal mind and the rebellious spirit. Self-centeredness of those who act without concern for the needs and rights of others became the basis of the confusion about sex. On the one hand sex seems to be the cause of man's problems; on the other, it can be one of the most beautiful modes of the expression of love that approaches the Divine.

As we seek to understand the expression of sex and life on the spiritual path, we must keep separate in our thinking (1) the divine origin of sex, of the human body, and the promise offered for growing attunement with the Divine; and (2) the problem of abuse due to the rebellious spirit and the carnal mind which continue to entrap us in the earth plane.

2

Your Spiritual Path

Q-6. Am I on the Path?

A-6. This alone is with thee and thy Lord! Who *is* thy Lord? 2035-1

. . . the more important, the most important experience of this or any individual entity is to first know what *is* the ideal—spiritually. 357-13

We are, every one of us, spiritual beings gone astray from God and on a journey of return. Each of us is a pilgrim on the spiritual path. As we think of this, we may visualize a mountain with people climbing up various routes, all of whom are seeking the same summit. We may say, "Are there not many paths to that one mountaintop?" Perhaps a more appropriate analogy would be to imagine one path, the Way, with many detours that we, as unique individuals, take. We sometimes get off the path and thus delay the directness of our journey and slow the speed with which we progress toward the goal.

We are spiritual beings with *free wills* with which to choose. Choices are set for us each day; we may through these choices put ourselves in closer attunement or out of accord with the Divine.

God Is in His Heaven and All Is Right with the World?

Because of the marvelous way in which the love and grace of God is shown toward man in his erring ways, philosophies have developed which would lead us to believe that everything is going just as it should go. We make our own choices and thereby encounter a series of painful experiences, which in time become growth experiences. We learn from these, and in retrospect we may say, "You see, I needed that experience to learn this lesson!" "Therefore," we reason further, "I was *supposed* to make the choice which at the time seemed to be the wrong choice." This conclusion is untrue to our personal experiences both of ourselves and of others. Especially of others! We easily perceive how other people make wrong choices. But more seriously, we deceive ourselves by rationalizing the unnecessary consequences of our wrong choices!

A second problem with such a philosophy is that we tend to underestimate the forbearance, mercy and grace of a loving and forgiving Father. God is a God of love, and since we are His children, He seeks continually to bring us into closer harmony and accord with Him. We may say, for dramatic and illustrative purposes, that every time we choose the wrong way, God reprograms the universe so that out of the wrong choice, we may have a learning experience which may be changed from a stumbling block into a stepping-stone.

Due to His love, we may experience growth instead of retardation as a consequence of these wrong choices. Nevertheless, it should be very clear that we *can* and *do* choose wrongly. Since we can choose wrongly, then some experiences which we choose and establish for ourselves are not only undesirable, but unnecessary. We experience occasions of pain and suffering that are not needed by the soul except for the fact that we have made a choice which is out of attunement and, therefore, it must be met.

In God's love and grace, we may meet these aspects of ourselves in a manner which enables us to grow, and we should indeed be thankful for that growth. But even that is through the mercy of God, and not simply an automatic guarantee by virtue of the machinery of the Law. To the contrary! ". . . if the word spoken by angels was stedfast, and every transgression and disobedience received a just recompense of reward; How shall we escape, if we neglect so great salvation . . ." (Hebrews 2:2-3)

This type of philosophy—which says that everything is in the hands of God and thus going well—may seem particularly beautiful and spiritual. There are many forms of it today which are attractive to us because of apparent emphasis on the positive attitude. Thus, such philosophies may become all the more problematic if they lull us into complacency regarding the necessity for us to make serious choices. More and more, we must seek to make our choices in accord with high ideals and purposes and out of an attuned conscience that prefers to do the will of the Father. Misleading philosophies tend to put aside the essential nature of the fall, which was the rebellious spirit. This leads us, in turn, to fail to give the needed recognition to the continuing and abiding presence of that rebellious spirit within ourselves. We must give recognition to the fact that this problem, the rebellious spirit, continues throughout our spiritual sojourn and indeed is the final aspect of the lower self to be overcome. It must ultimately be cast into the lake of fire of God's purifying love. (See Revelation 20:10)

Signpost on the Path

If God is in His heaven and all is right with the world, then we may proceed with the assumption that wherever we are we are on the path. Sooner or later we will arrive. On the other hand, if there are choices, if there is free will, then by these choices we either put ourselves on the path or by them take detours off the path.

How can we determine whether we are on the path? Following is a map entitled "Signposts on the Path," which the pilgrim may use to discern whether or not he is on the path. This may be used specifically with respect to choices regarding sex. (See illustration.)

There is a crossroads on the path which is named Normalize. At this crossroads we may proceed ahead,

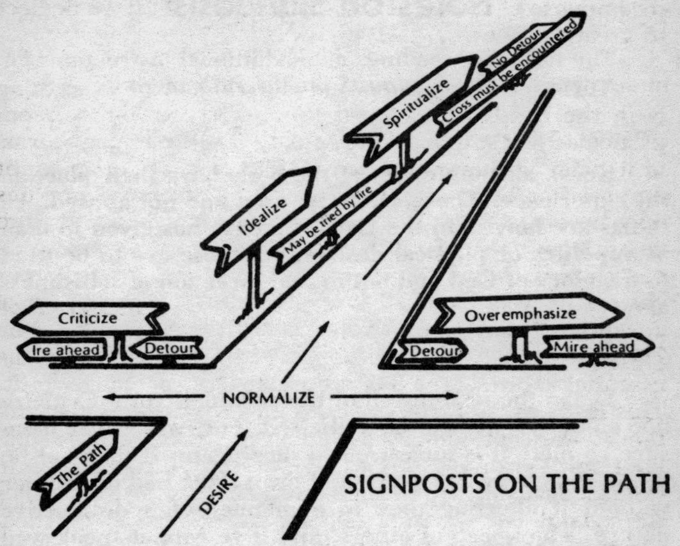

crossing Normalize and moving to Idealize and to Spiritualize. On the other hand, we may take a wrong turn and find ourselves on a detour by taking one or the other path of extremes. One of these is Criticize, which may be too severe, in which we become condemning of ourselves and others. The other extreme is called Overemphasize. On this detour we may overexaggerate the importance of our sexual expressions.

The crossroads may appear at any time! When we get off the path on either side, the first step we need to take is to move toward Normalize, then turn up the path toward Idealize to Spiritualize. A note of caution: If we get off the path on one side, we may, in seeking to return to the path, overshoot and find ourselves on another detour of the opposite extreme. Let us keep this map in mind through the rest of our consideration of the philosophy and attitude toward sex that we may gain from the Cayce readings.

Notes on Signposts

The following readings give additional instructions for understanding the *Signposts on the Path* map:

Desire

Know, all the desires of the body have their place in thy experience. These are to be used and not abused. All things are holy unto the Lord, that He has given to man as appetites or physical desires, yet these are to be used to the glory of God and not in that direction of selfishness alone. 3234-1, F.24

Criticize

Learn the lesson well of the spiritual truth; Criticize not unless ye wish to be criticized. For, with what measure ye mete it is measured to thee again. It may not be in the same way, but ye cannot even *think* bad of another without it affecting thee in a manner of a destructive nature. Think *well* of others, and if ye cannot speak well of them, don't speak! but don't think it either! Try to see self in the other's place. And this will bring the basic spiritual forces that must be the prompting influence in the experience of each soul, if it would grow in grace, in knowledge, in understanding; not only of its relationship to God, its relationship to its fellow man, but its relationship in the home and in the social life. 2936-2, F.35

. . . there are tendencies on the part of the entity to become rather severe in criticism. Not merely of others, but tending to make the same criticism of self, or to feel sorry for self—which is the severest criticism of all.

For, unless there is the ability in each entity, each soul, to appreciate self and its relationships to the Creative Forces, what opportunity is there to have others to think much of yourself also? For like begets like. These are unfailing, in spiritual, in mental and in material aspects. These change not. They are unchangeable laws. Like begets like. 3409-1, M.26

Ire

. . . don't get mad and don't cuss a body out mentally or in voice. This brings more poisons than may be created by even taking foods that aren't good. 470-37, M.54

For anger can destroy the brain as well as any disease. For it is itself a disease of the mind. 3510-1, M.36

Mire

For, what must be obliterated? Hate, prejudice, selfishness, backbiting, unkindness, anger, passion, and those things of the mire that are created in the activities of the sons of men. 5749-5

Overemphasize

. . . there are the tendencies in the present for the entity to sidetrack from the straight and narrow way. It is well that an individual be broadminded, but one can be so broadminded as to miss the purpose, the ideal. For the ideal is the straight and narrow way. The broad way oft leads to the lack of virtues of many natures. 3509-1, M.29

Q-7. Am I sexually normal?

A-7. It has been indicated for the body that the very conditions which have been necessary, for the requiring of stimuli to the various organs of the body, tend to *make* the body *over*sexed. This must be met in the same way and manner as every other condition that brings *for* the body those *harmful* conditions, or conditions that tend to make it *harder* for the ills to be passed. Not that these desires are not to be gratified to the extent that makes for the developments in a normal manner, but to gratify *any* desire in the carnal forces *of* the body—rather than in the satisfying of the spiritual life that comes of creation itself in such emotions—is to become such an one as to make for the pricks that are to be kicked against time and time again. Self well understands that such gratification has been and is conducive and inducive to those periods of torments that arise at times; while with the applications in foods, in activities, with the outlets of self mentally and physically, these associations may be brought to mean much. Cultivate the *spiritual*, the mental and physical desire, rather than those carnal desires that are gratified only for the moment. 911-7, F.24

Normalize

By the creating of a normal balance within the body for its physical and mental and spiritual well-being, we not only create a normal physical balance but then give—in the expressions of what has been indicated for the physical and mental body—an *outlet* for the beauty of sex.

Do not look upon sex as merely a *physical* expression! There is a physical expression that is beauty within itself, if it is considered from that angle; but when the mental and the spiritual are guiding, then the outlet for beauty becomes a *normal* expression of a *normal*, healthy body. 1436-1, F.27

Spiritualize

Q-8. Is it necessary to give up physical desires for spiritual development?

A-8. Rather spiritualize the physical desires as He did in the Garden. What there is shown thee as to how the physical, the spiritual, fought—as it were—one with another? "Father, let this cup pass from me." This is as every experience in the physical man when there is the fear of the loss in this or that direction. There is the constant, "Father, save me from this—from this." Yet, even as He, if there has been builded in thine experience as was in His experience—offering Himself for the world—then thou must pass through same, in making the physical desire and the will of the Father as one, that there may be the cleansing in the soul of those things that may bring the consciousness of the Oneness with the Father in whatever realm. 262-64

Q-18. So much has been written about sexual relationships between husband and wife. Is it the correct

understanding that this activity should be used only and when companions seek to build a body for an incoming entity?

A-18. Not necessarily. These depend, of course, to be sure, on the individual concept of relationships and their activities. To be sure, if the activities are used in creative, spiritual form, there is the less desire for carnal relationship; or, if there is the lack of use of constructive energies, then there is the desire for more of the carnal, physical reaction. 2072-16, F.34

Crosses

While problems arise, they have made thee strong. Be not weary, then, in well-doing. For, thou hast set thy foot on the path. Keep thy face to the light of truth in the Christ, and the shadows will fall farther and farther behind—as ye approach that throne of mercy, as ye show mercy; of love, as ye show love; of grace, as ye show and manifest grace in thy dealings with thy fellow man. 2559-1, F.40

Be not discouraged because the way seems hard at times. Know that He heareth thee. For as He hath given, "If ye will keep my law—" And what is His law? It is to love the Lord, to eschew evil—which is the whole duty of man—love thy neighbor as thyself. 1747-5, F.37

Criteria for the Path

How do I discern my spiritual path? We may suggest several criteria for evaluating this question. To be sure, an individual's own criteria are the most important; however, the following ideas are presented for consideration.

One of the clearest of the criteria for discerning whether we are solidly on the spiritual path is the willingness to move from the question, "Is it right or wrong for me to do this?" to the higher question, "What is the very best for me and all concerned?" When we ask the question, "Is it right or wrong?" we may always rationalize or find a justification or present some point of view which enables us to say, "Therefore, it's all right for me to do this." This tends to be the case with questions of right or wrong.

An example of the kind of thinking which may argue that *anything* on occasion may be right was seen several decades ago when the topic of "situation ethics" was discussed widely. Many of these discussions went like this: A type of behavior that was designated as sinful or contrary to the Ten Commandments would be considered. The question was addressed as to whether or not this was a law in some ultimate sense. Invariably, someone would devise some circumstance or situation in which it might seem to be all right or even highly desirable to act in such a way that was contrary to a Commandment. Having conceived of a difficult situation in which holding to the Commandment seemed inadequate, the person would be inclined to the conclusion that, because he had found an apparent exception, then under even more general circumstances the Commandment could not be deemed to be universal. The ultimate outcome of such discussions was a development of a more lax attitude toward the imperatives of the Commandments.

The missing ingredient from many of these discussions was the consideration of what the Edgar Cayce readings see as being the most important experience of any entity: to know what is the ideal spiritually. This ideal, when set, may become the criterion by which we may measure our adherence to our own spiritual paths. The spiritual-path question is: "What is the very best thing to do for myself and for all concerned in these particular circumstances with respect to the spiritual ideal I have set for myself?" Let us examine more fully the instructions in the readings regarding "setting the ideal."

The Spiritual Ideal

The Edgar Cayce readings clearly emphasize setting a spiritual ideal. By the word "ideal," the readings are referring to the purpose, intent, desire, motivation, incentive and "the spirit in which we do something." The word ideal must not be confused with "goal." A goal is a desired outcome; the ideal is the *spirit* in which we do anything with respect to any outcome.

There is a place, to be sure, for goal-oriented thinking. However, there is a tendency, one the goal is set—especially if it is a high and worthy goal—to allow the *end* to justify the *means*. In other words, if we set for ourselves a very high goal, especially one that promises to be of benefit to many others, we may come to think of the goal as being so important that we compromise on how we accomplish it. More importantly we may attempt to achieve the goal without retaining the qualities of spirit, of motivation and of intent that characterized the purpose of the goal itself.

For example, we may set out to build a school for children. Because we feel the establishment of the school is so important, we may act in ways that are not consistent with the spirit of the goal. As we build the school, personal ambition, a desire for financial gain or recognition, may enter. The work may continue toward accomplishing the desired goal, but it may be conducted out of motivations that are oriented primarily toward the self rather than toward the purpose. In the long run, the desire to help others is lost and we all lose.

The setting of the spiritual ideal is for the purposes (1) of quickening the proper motivation with which we seek to work and (2) of setting a criterion by which to measure our motives as we proceed. When we come to a decision point, we should make that decision and then inquire about the motivational origin of that decision. Thus we may see if the decision was based on a motive that measures up to our ideal.

The spiritual path, indeed the very nature of the spiritual, concerns itself with the quality of motivation, purpose, intent and desire that impels us in our actions. It is the spirit that counts rather than some external criterion of whether the action or the goal is valued by our society as being moral or desirable. This is one of the great stumbling blocks that we all encounter when we try to do good. When the goal is set to be of help, there comes the immediate problem of maintaining a helpful attitude and motivation through the steps that lead to the accomplishment of that goal. In an ultimate sense, the spirit in which we do whatever we do is of more consequence to our own souls and the souls of others than the specific external accomplishment.

The philosophy of the Cayce readings puts a great deal of stress on *application*. However, it is very clear that those applications which may help others are those motivated by a selfless spirit and not by the desire for self-aggrandizement. Frequently the readings admonish us to do something even if it is wrong. This statement should always be qualified by the understanding that when we act from a desire to be helpful, *then* even if the external result may seem to be wrong, progress can be made. However, this invitation (to do something even if it is wrong) is not ever intended to encourage us to do what we know is contrary to the proper motivation or to our own ideals.

What Is the Ideal?

The readings deals with both the uniqueness of the individual and with the universal qualities of the Infinite. We are told, on the one hand, that each individual must decide and choose his own ideal. On the other hand, it is indicated in the readings that there is really only one ideal.

There is one ideal—that which manifests in the earth in the Christ Jesus. *That* should be every entity's ideal—physically, mentally, materially. 2533-7

This may offer problems for some of us. Let us inquire further.

One of the most interesting and challenging aspects of the Cayce readings is the universal quality of the spirit in which the information was given. All mankind, as souls, are children of God, and all are of concern to divine Love. Nevertheless, confirmation is given to the historical events of the Bible and to the lineage from Adam through Abraham, Jacob, the children of Israel through the prophets, until the birth of Jesus of Nazareth. The readings see these events not only as having actually occurred but also as being of ultimate significance to all the souls of this system.

To my knowledge, the readings never invited any individual to get out of one religious organization and into another. However, they delineate a clear and specific relationship between the cosmic Christ and the man, Jesus of Nazareth. Those readings dealing with this concept should be studied thoroughly by anyone on the path. Any individual in any time or country, working under any religious system or set of beliefs, is a soul and a child of God. Therefore, the Divine Forces are concerned about and are trying to work with and through that unique individual. The work of the Christ through Jesus of Nazareth was of cosmic significance. There is none like Him as a concrete example and ultimate criterion of the love of God as manifested in the earth plane. He is truly our Elder Brother. As a spiritual being, He seeks to and is able to help us all. He says of Himself, "Behold, I stand at the door and knock: if anyone hears my voice and opens the door, I will come in to him . . ." (Revelation 3:20) However, we are told in the readings, He will not be the uninvited guest. Therefore, we need to set His pattern and life as our ideal, as the quality of spirit which we would have motivate our lives.

Yet, we are also instructed not to set an ideal that we have no intention of utilizing or trying to live, as a discrepancy will then develop between the two paths. For example, a businessman who claims to be a Christian may think of himself as having the Christ as his ideal; however, he may have no intention whatever of measuring his business decisions by the motivation of selfless service. He might be willing to try to measure his business activities and decisions by an idea of *fairness*. According to the readings, such a businessman would be far better off in setting what seems to be the more limiting ideal of fairness and trying in truth to measure up to that ideal, than in setting the higher and more idealistic motivation, but not endeavoring at all to measure up to the great challenge it presents.

Other Criteria

Another criterion by which to evaluate the question, "Am I on the spiritual path?" is to consider whether or not we think of ourselves as being seekers. (For Edgar Cayce, *Israel* meant "the seeker." Thus, according to the readings, the *elect* are those who seek.) The seeker has a quality of being eager to learn; therefore, the true seeker does not have to defend his present situation; he is open to growth. Being on the spiritual path means that we know that we have some growing to do and something more to learn. We must be willing to release our old ideas, our old patterns of thinking and the earlier purposes of our choices. We must know in *whom* we believe; we must grow in *what* we believe.

Regarding sex, one of the most frequently asked questions of our time is, "What is normal?" There is certainly a place in society to study what may be considered normative. This perspective may be very helpful for the specific individual in understanding himself. But a more pertinent question for people on the spiritual path is, "What is ideal? What is *my* ideal?" Specifically, with respect to sexual behavior, the challenge is to take seriously what the readings see as being the most important consideration for any entity, "What is the ideal spiritually?" The readings invite us to work on establishing that ideal and to begin to measure our lives and choices by it. Yes, they even want us to begin to bring that ideal to bear on our sexual behavior and choices!

If we have set Jesus as an ideal, we may have immediately put ourselves in a special bind, because we understand the life of Jesus of Nazareth to have been celibate. Many sources invite us to ask, "What would Jesus do?" Perhaps a much more relevant and helpful form of this question for each of us as individuals would be, "What would Jesus *have me do* under the present circumstances?" The former question inclines us to visualize the external life style of the Master in the Judean hills 2,000 years ago. The latter question brings His living spirit of love, forgiveness and understanding to bear on our immediate life circumstances. He knows the background that we bring to these circumstances and the physical, mental and spiritual needs of all individuals. He has the spirit of willingness to work with us where we are and to help us to grow step by step toward that which He would have us become.

Another criterion for being on the spiritual path is whether we are being directed by the inner spirit or by the outer circumstances of life. We may distinguish between what is spiritual and what is religious by asking whether the activity or attitude is inspired by the inner spirit or by the requirements of an external dogma or morality. This is arbitrary, to be sure, but for purposes of illustration the spiritual path may be defined as living by the promptings of the inner spirit instead of by the expectations of an externally imposed structure. We may be guided by a system, a teaching or the expectations of society or those about us. We may be guided by the expectations of the family or of a religious order, such as a monastery or a convent. To be sure, the spiritual life and the religious life are not independent of one another; however, it should be very clear that we can go through external patterns of behavior that portray piety and yet have an inner life that is far from consistent with that same spirit. The spiritual path is the path of inner guidance.

The Cayce readings say that no matter how far astray we may have gone, we may turn within and attune to the depths of our inner spirit in such a way that we may be truly guided in our choices by a sense of Oneness with the Divine. These readings are filled with extremely helpful and detailed instructions as to how to grow in greater attunement physically, mentally, spiritually with the Divine within. Instructions are given regarding the attunement of the body as the temple; how to work with our attitudes and the extraordinary importance of the mind as the builder; and spiritual practices through which we may grow in greater attunement with God.[1]

In the Cayce interpretation of John's Revelation, we are given some special insight into that mysterious portion of the book which deals with the number 666, the mark of the beast. In essence, we are told that one applicable understanding of the mark of the beast may be seen when we, as individuals, make choices in accord with the structures of man rather than with the spirit of God. There are many ways we do this, whether it be by standards imposed by society, by family, by religious groups, by church dogma. Another example may be seen in our response to arrangements or agreements that we make with others. For example, two people may agree to have lunch together on a certain day. Something may come up in which one of the people senses a call that has a higher spiritual priority. If we decide to stand by the arrangement made by man rather than by the direction of the inner spirit, that activity may be said to have the mark of the beast. As we apply this insight into a deeper understanding of our own spiritual path, we may see that one of the criteria by which we may evaluate being on the path is our willingness to bring our sexual activities and choices into accord with a true sense of the best inner guidance and attunement we can make, measured by our highest spiritual ideal, and not in accord with man-made structures.

The implications of this insight are that we must discover and set for ourselves our own unique spiritual path. The spiritual ideal is not fixed, to be sure. As we grow it may change frequently. However, the principle is that if we center ourselves and make the best attunement that we can with the highest motivation that we can mobilize, we may, through the spirit, set a course for ourselves and make choices and decisions in accord with that course. That for us becomes our own spiritual path

---

[1]For further information on meditation, the student is referred to *Meditation and the Mind of Man*.

which we may follow in our own terms and from which, *in our own terms*, we sometimes deviate.

Another criterion for measuring the intent to follow the spiritual path is the standard given by the Master Himself. He said, "By their fruits ye shall know them." Now we know that the spirit manifests in our lives in two ways. There are the *gifts* of the spirit which include healing, prophecy and those things we consider miraculous; then there are the *fruits* of the spirit, which are patience, long-suffering, kindness and brotherly love. The readings say that in the material world, only the little things count. It is as though there is nothing big we can do that is meaningful or spiritual. On the other hand, in the manifestation of the fruits of the spirit, we have the essence of growth in the spiritual life and progress on the spiritual path. We may then use these qualities of the fruits of the spirit as guides, criteria by which to judge our choices and evaluate our contemplated actions. Each sexual relationship will have some consequences on our lives and on the life of another. We may sincerely ask, "Does this relationship promise to bring forth patience, long-suffering, kindness, love?" Perhaps these notions seem too idealistic. Let us again examine the viewpoint of the readings. For example, a young man, age 26, asked:

Q-1. What is nature of experience and urges which have acted to produce the behavior of self in sexual matters, and how is this to be properly adjusted throughout?

A-1. These ye can analyze by the ways and manners indicated. This is a part of nature itself, yet it can be controlled according to that held as the ideal of the individual entity. First the concept must be in that which is of the same nature of sex itself which is creative.

Then as to whether this shall be abused or used in those directions that have been set forth and indicated, as to what you would like for others to be if there should be the choice of a mate with whom there would be the creating of a channel for another soul to enter the earth. Act in relation to the opposite sex as ye would have the

opposite sex act toward thee, if you were to be chosen as a companion. 3198-3

A young woman, age 24, was told:

Know, all the desires of the body have their place in thy experience. These are to be used and not abused. All things are holy unto the Lord, that He has given to man as appetites or physical desires, yet these are to be used to the glory of God and not in that direction of selfishness alone. 3234-1

One further example of the attitude encouraged by the readings is found in the advice given for a man, age 22. Note especially, as in the advice given to [1398], the invitation to use the spiritual ideal as a way on controlling the attitude and desires:

It is up to the entity, then, in its experience, in its associations with others, in its dealing with opportunity with others, with conditions and circumstances, to use all in a constructive way and manner and, when there are those periods when disturbance and disappointments come, to have in the spiritual ideals, the mental and mental purposes, that which will keep the body from seeking only gratifying of physical appetites. 5250-1

In considering the spiritual path and the precedence that soul development should take above all other accomplishments, we may be reminded that in *patience* we possess our souls. This may be paraphrased to say that if the experience does not teach us patience, there is no soul development. If patience is not reflected, then we may say that we have not moved further on the spiritual path. Those things then—persistency, consistency, sincerity, those qualities that indicate patience—become signposts for us as we seek to follow a path that may be truly termed spiritual. Each of us, to be sure, may have special problems properly evaluating or incorporating some of these attributes into daily living. For example, the readings ask,

"What woman is consistent and what man is sincere?" But these are also the criteria of the Master.

The Path to Grandmother's House: The Pathological Conscience

There may be attributes within us which represent themselves as conscience but which are essentially pathological. In understanding this statement, let us consider Freud's concept of man in terms of three structures: the id, the ego and the superego. The id is that primitive quality that seeks immediate gratification and immediate release of tension. When we are hungry, we want to be fed immediately. The ego is that portion of the personality which develops through experience. The ego has the job of coping and functioning in the external world. It must find ways of gaining gratification for the needs of the id without getting the whole person into trouble. The superego is the quality of conscience that grows out of the childhood experiences with the parents or parental surrogates. It is incorporated into the personality as attitudes of the parent governing sense of morality and self-worth.

Let us imagine a hungry man walking along a street, passing an open-air grocery mart. The impulse of the *id* in hunger would lead the man to grab a loaf of bread and run with it, seeking immediate gratification. The coping responsibility of the *ego* reasons with the id, keeps it under control and tries to think of ways to come up with the money. Perhaps he offers to sweep the floor for the store owner or do some other work in exchange for food. The *superego* is an aspect of conscience which would become operative if the person stole the bread, even if he were able to get away with it. A harsh superego, operating as the voice of conscience, would give the ego a very hard time in such a case, assuredly preventing him from enjoying it.

Here is another example: A mother may have a valuable and fragile lamp. She instructs her child that he must never touch the lamp; otherwise, he will be punished severely. As long as the child refrains from touching the lamp, he is being logical and realistic. However, during the developmental period of life, the values of the parent are incorporated into the child's personality. From that time, the child may never ever again be able to be comfortable touching a lamp. That is not because of any threat of punishment, but rather an internal feeling of guilt. The child might feel, "I could never touch that lamp. I just couldn't live with myself if I did such a terrible thing!" And thus, a sense of guilt and unworthiness follows no matter whether the parent is present or not. Parental and societal values endure into adulthood and do not diminish over time. The example also serves to illustrate the origin of some internalized feelings of guilt regarding sexual expression.

A special problem with the development of this type of conscience is that it may be imbalanced, even pathological. The development of the superego poses extremely important considerations for anyone on the spiritual path. We may be confronted with the pathological superego and mistake it for the true spiritual conscience. Therefore, it becomes of the utmost importance to differentiate between the superego and the true voice of conscience, the "still, small voice."

Another important problem presents itself for consideration. There are occasions when the id and the superego may combine forces and work together. In doing so, they constitute a special threat to the ego, enabling the ego to be deceived and overthrown. Here is an illustration of how this may occur: Let us psychoanalyze a well-known fairy tale, Little Red Riding Hood. Let us say that the wolf represents the id, those basic urges seeking immediate expression; Red Riding Hood represents the ego; and grandmother, the superego.

I had always wondered why it was necessary for the wolf to pretend to be the grandmother. Why, after devouring the grandmother, did not the wolf simply hide behind the door and, when Red Riding Hood entered, gobble her up, too? Why is it necessary to have the detailed deception and her half-aware responses, "Grandmother, what big teeth you have! Grandmother, what big ears you have!"

By applying a psychoanalytical approach to this story, we may find it instructive regarding an aspect of conscience. There are occasions in which the superego sides with the id's basic drive to immediate gratification. In forming this alliance, the id gains the power (which otherwise would have been impossible) to overwhelm the ego. The wolf, combining the drive of his own id in the guise of the superego (grandmother), tricked Red Riding Hood into easy vulnerability. How does this work in real life?

Here is an example—extreme, to be sure, but one which occurs on occasion. As you know, in the Bible Jesus says, "If thy right hand offend thee, cut it off." (Matthew 5:30) There are cases on record of individuals who have taken this literally and have actually severed a hand. What prompts an individual to act so destructively? It is the drive for release from tension combined with self-condemnation, supported by the "voice of God." This is an example of what may occur when the impulses of the id are supported by the pathological quality of conscience which may come from the superego.

This "conscience" has serious implications for anyone entering the spiritual life. Any time that we decide to put our lives in order, we are likely to be confronted by a noisy voice within that has a list of requirements a mile long! If I say to myself, "I'm going to resolve to begin a new life," then a voice within me says, "Good, I've been waiting for this. Now you must not drink, you must not smoke, you must not have any fun," and on and on it goes. Soon the list becomes so long, so inclusive and so unrealistic that I despair of the soundness of my new resolve. In the end, overwhelmed, I do not begin to take even the simplest steps to do better. When we speak of *turning within* and of *receiving guidance* from the voice within, we need to distinguish between that noisy and demanding conscience, which may be the pathological superego, and that gentle and encouraging conscience which is the true voice of the Divine within.

The most serious problem presented by the pathological superego is the self-condemnation that we all experience at times. We must remember always that God is a God of love and that He is never condemning in His attitude toward us. It is only we who condemn ourselves. The portion of our personality which is self-condemning is not of God. Here is an easy way to tell the pathological conscience from the "still, small voice": The superego may be loud, noisy, commanding and self-condemning. The still, small voice is always loving, encouraging, saying, "Give it another try. Keep at it! You are good. You can do it."

And concerning sexual behavior, there may especially be within us a voice of conscience that has grown out of childhood experiences. Since this is not the true voice of the spirit, its requirements may be such that we either rebel against them or we allow them to keep us in a state of self-condemnation—or both. This may divert us from the real encounter with the spirit and may even lead us to resist bringing this vital part of our lives into the light of our own spiritual understanding and ideal. Worst of all, it may lead us to a chronic self-condemnation or sense of futility whereupon we write ourselves off and stop trying.

A 47-year-old woman asked Edgar Cayce:

Q-1. Is it my fault that I am failing in every way in my home and marital relationship?

A-1. The entity is *not* failing. Do not condemn self. Condemning of self is as much of an error as condemning others. Live thine own self. Leave the results with God. Man may sow—only God may give the increase; whether in material, in mental or spiritual body. Keep self, not selfish, but selfless.

Q-12. How have I failed to use wisely what God has given me? Why am I so confused about so many things?

A-12. Do not—do not feel that ye have failed. Do not judge self. You have not failed *yet*. You only fail if you quit trying. The trying is oft counted for righteousness. Remember as He has given, "I do not condemn thee." Go, be patient, be kind, and the Lord be with thee! 3292-1

Setting the Ideal

An exercise that helps us to attune to the still, small voice is setting our ideal. The Edgar Cayce readings indicate further that to know the ideal spiritually is *the most important* experience for *any* entity! The readings suggest getting a pencil and a piece of paper, drawing three columns and labeling them, left to right, "Spiritual, Mental, Physical." In the chart given here, the exact wording of the instructions from reading 5091-3 contains a key principle for each column.

IDEALS

Spiritual	*Mental*	*Physical*
. . . thy spiritual concept of the ideal, whether it be Jesus, Buddha, mind, material, God or whatever is the word which indicates to self the ideals, spiritual.	. . . write the ideal *mental* attitude, as may arise from the concepts of the spiritual, [in] relationship to self, to home, to friends, to neighbors, to thy enemies, to things, to conditions.	. . . the ideal material . . . Not of conditions, but what has brought, what does bring into manifestation the spiritual and mental ideals. What relationships does such bring to things, to individuals, to situations? 5091-3

First, under "Spiritual," we are instructed to write one word that gives our concept of the ideal. The suggested words include *names,* such as Jesus and Buddha, and *properties* such as mind and material. What is the function of such a word which is to be our mantra? A mantra is a mind tool used in meditation for centering and for quickening the spirit. It is an invocation of the soul; it invokes the presence of the very reality of that named or called forth by it. The expression, "Speak of the devil and he will appear!" bears witness to the power of invocation. Therefore, if we select a word as a spiritual ideal, we should be sure that it is of the highest positive good.

If we set for our spiritual ideal the word *Jesus*, its use should be an invitation to the actual presence of the Spirit of the Christ. If we set a quality such as *joy* as a spiritual ideal, then, for that word to work mantrically, it should actually evoke the *spirit* of joy when we say the *word* "joy" to ourselves.

There is a further function of the word we have set as our spiritual ideal. What "ideal" truly means is that which carries for us a quality of motivation which we would like to characterize all the choices and activities we make. The key word, *motivation*, is deeply and directly related to the word spiritual. In setting a spiritual ideal, we are choosing the motivation which we want to guide our lives and by which we are willing to measure our decisions and actions.

A third function of the spiritual ideal is that it acts as a *standard*, a criterion of measurement, when we apply or fail to apply the ideal. Once we have made a decision, then we may ask ourselves, "Is this choice based on my ideal?" The ideal is not externally imposed. It is a word of our own choice. It is something to which to return, to give stability and direction to us as we proceed on the path. As we come to a choice point in our lives, if we have set our spiritual ideal, we may approach that choice point with a real measuring rod. *Remaining* on the spiritual path then becomes a matter of willingness to be guided by the motivation we have selected as our ideal.

Now let us consider the meaning of the "Mental" ideal. We have the expression, "the ideal attitude," in relation to self, home, work and friends. Having set the spiritual ideal, we begin to list in the "Mental" column things in our lives with which we are concerned. We may list self, home, friends, neighbors, enemies, things, conditions. (We may wish to make a longer list and indeed we would be well advised to work day in and day out, on the many things with which we deal.) For example, I enter "Self" under mental ideal. The my next step is to consider what is the *ideal mental attitude* in relationship to myself which derives from my spiritual ideal?

For example, I have set Jesus as my spiritual ideal and I remember that He said, "I call you not servants but brothers." Thus, I may try to generate toward myself an attitude that I am indeed a brother of the Master and write "brother to Christ." Or, if I am addressing specific aspects of self, such as my sexual life, I may remember that the Master told the woman, "Neither do I condemn thee." Thus I may enter the word "forgiveness" as a mental attitude that I want to hold toward self with respect to this aspect of my life.

Now notice under the "Physical" column that we are not concerned with conditions, but "what has brought, what does bring into manifestation the spiritual and mental ideals." Here we are concerned with what kind of activity or behavior can we take to manifest what we hold as an ideal mental attitude. If I consider the attitude toward self as a brother of Christ, what can I *do* that will bring this into manifestation? I must hold this attitude toward every one I meet. I can begin to think about people with whom I am having either a positive or negative relationship; and I can work toward the mental attitude that that person also is a brother of Christ. I must begin acting toward that person as if he were just that—a brother of the Master.

Or, with respect to my attitude toward sex, if the attitude at the mental level is one of seeking forgiveness, then what may I actually *do* or *apply* to bring that forgiveness into manifestation? Because I have been self-condemning, I may have refrained from engaging in some activities, such as healing or prayer, that would permit me to be of greater service in my relationships with others. Or, I may study my life and see where I have allowed self-condemnation to interfere with creative expression. Then I may begin, having now a new sense of forgiveness, to act more creatively in those endeavors and consequently enhance my attunement with the spirit.

The Ideal Sexual Life

Having considered how we set and work with ideals, let us study carefully a discourse on the proper expression of sex. Notice the priorities given in these instructions: "... [the] sexual life should be the outcome—not the purpose of, but the outcome of the answering of soul to soul..." It was a 35-year-old woman who asked the following questions:

Q-6. How should love and the sexual life properly function?

A-6. This, to give even a summary dissertation, would require a great deal of time and space.

In a few words, as we have indicated, the material things (or those in a three-dimensional world) are the shadow or the reflection of those in the spiritual life. Then, as God or the Creative Influence is the source of all things, the second law in spiritual life, in mental life, in material life, is preservation of self and the continuation of likes, or propagation, in sexual intercourse or life.

Hence, in their very basic forces, the relations in sexual life should be the outcome—not the purpose of, but the outcome of the answering of soul to soul in their associations and relations. And the act, or the associations in this nature, should be the result.

Hence these questions should be often weighed well, remembering that God, or Love (for it is One), looketh on the heart rather than the outward appearances. And that there having been set laws, by associations and relations in the material life (which are again shadows of the associations for which man in a material form was brought into being, to become a companion of the Father), and that morality, virtue, understanding, truth, love, are those influences that make for judgments of those that view the activities of individuals in the material life and judge according to those rules that govern such relationships, then it behooves—and becomes necessary—that there be the adherence to such regulations, that thy good be not evil-spoken of.

For, in the understandings, know that Love and God are One; that relations in the sexual life are the manifestations in the mental attributes of each as to an expres-

sion of that that becomes manifested in the experience of each so concerned.

For, unless such associations become on such a basis, they become vile in the experience of those that join in such relations.

Q-7. There seems to be a standard of nature and one of man. Just how should they harmonize?

A-7. Not with man's, but rather with God's laws. One the outcome of the other. One the impulse of the other. Not the aggrandizing of the impulses that may be fired by material things, but that which is the outgrowth of the soul's expression in a material world, with the necessity of conforming to that which has been set by man as his judgment of his brother.

Q-9. How can I know about love?

A-9. As one knows God and His associations with man (and this means woman*), so may one feeding upon the fruits of the spirit come to know that which is love. [*Edgar Cayce pronounced this wo-man.] 272-7

Sex for Fun?

What about sexual expression that is not for the specific purpose of procreation? Clearly the readings see a place for sex in the life of someone on the spiritual path. However, once we admit that sex is permissible or desirable for purposes other than procreation, we have opened the door to a consideration of other forms of sexual expression that have no prospect of procreation, such as homosexuality or masturbation. From a strictly logical point of view, if heterosexual activity is all right purely for the purpose of pleasure, there is no reason for prohibiting other forms of sexual expressions for the same motive.

We should think about what effects sexual expression has on the energy patterns of the body, the inner coordination of the nervous systems and the subtler energy patterns of the human aura. We may wonder if such expressions work against raising the energies in meditation and prayer in a manner that is different from the way heterosexual expression does. The more important consideration is that we begin on the spiritual path exactly where we are now. It is not as though we have to go somewhere else before we start.

If we experience certain sexual habits or compulsions in our lives, all the more reason for us to establish consistent steps toward attunement. As we allow the spirit to flow through us, we transform those aspects of ourselves over which we seem to have less control. If sex is to be a part of our regular life style, then clearly it should be in the spirit of joy and openness, with a sense of fulfillment, rather than self-condemnation. This would, or course, include positive attitudes toward the inner life of fantasy which accompany the external expressions. We come to an acceptance of ourselves at this point.

Insofar as we are willing to release negative patterns, we can approach the spiritual path without anxiety. However, if we feel we must defend or justify our life styles, then we lose one of the key criteria for being on the path—the openness of a seeker. Working with the sexual motivations which we presently experience, we need to be willing to accept whatever change of life style may be consequent to our movement on the path.

If we feel that a certain pattern of ours is inconsistent with the spiritual path, we may polarize the problem in our heads. We say the path is right and the behavior wrong. Then, when we do the wrong thing, we become discouraged. We may disqualify ourselves from the path in self-condemnation. But greater progress may be had if we are willing to accept all of our present being with all of its shortcomings and put it all on the path. Sometimes we experience a surprising and anticipated release without any effort. Sometimes we hope and pray and struggle for years and find growth to have been a needed mellowing toward centered maturity.

In the closing chapter of The Revelation we are told, ". . . the time is at hand. He that is unjust, let him be unjust still: and he which is filthy, let him be filthy still: and he that is righteous, let him be righteous still; and he that is holy, let him be holy still." (Revelation 22:10-11)

We sometimes say to ourselves, "Oh, I can't be expected to grow spiritually because this thing in my life would have to be dealt with first, and I can't do that now." Could it be that The Revelation is saying simply that the time to start is at hand and that we can't go somewhere else to start? We must start with who we are, where we are, right here and now.

Your Spiritual Path

The setting of ideals, which the readings say is the most important experience for any entity, illustrates a starting point for us to set upon our own proper spiritual path. This path must be a course of growth that comes out of our own deep sense of spiritual destiny and personal sense of relationship to the Divine. At this point, we must be especially cautious of the "oughts" and "shoulds" that may be incorporated from expections which have grown out of our experiences with family, friends and the whole of society. It may not be anticipated that the spiritual path is easy. What is more important is that we sense that it is innately, properly, our very own and not imposed upon us by any external expectation or requirement.

In all of the lives of those whom we might most admire with respect to spiritual qualities, we may probably at no point find *anyone* who says of the spiritual path, or of his own spiritual path, that is was *easy*. What is important here, as we set out on the path, is that we understand we have required this only of ourselves and that any sense of rebellion must be recognized as our own and not be projected toward authority, tradition, mores, dogmas or other strawmen which may inspire rationalized resistance and become for us an excuse.

3

The Body Is the Temple

. . . thy body is the Temple of the Living God. Use it as such, and not as a place for the lowest of earth and low thinking. Rather treat it as the altar of God. Sacrifice therein thine own appetites and offering to Him those praises, those honors due for that He has given to thee. 3492-1

A clearly resisted insight of all spiritual teachings is the proper appreciation of the relationship between sexual energy and spiritual energy. Our separative and guilt-ridden ways of thinking have disinclined us from the study of the relationship between these energies and from the integration of them into our personal lives and application. There is something here that we wish *not* to understand fully. Why?

It has been our bent to compartmentalize many portions of our lives; we try to keep one area of endeavor separate from others. We hope to believe in our faith, to observe our ceremonies, to pay our dues, as it were, because we recognize at one level the importance and seriousness of religious things. However, we fail to make the full commitment required to integrate aspects of religious life into all other phases of life. The sexual impulse, specifically, periodically dominates our attention, leading us to avoid as deep an understanding as we may have. We are invited to:

Know, all the desires of the body have their place in thy experience. These are to be used and not abused. All

things are holy unto the Lord, that He has given to man as appetites or physical desires, yet these are to be used to the glory of God and not in that direction of selfishness alone. 3234-1

How can it be that spirituality and sexuality are so closely and deeply related? To understand this more fully, it will be worthwhile to review rather thoroughly that which we know about the body—physically, mentally and spiritually—and the special way in which the body may function as the temple of the living God.

In the Pattern of the Temple

We may understand ourselves more fully by considering ourselves in terms of the spiritual body, the mental body and the physical body. These structures have their individual associated qualities of consciousness. As indicated in the figure below, the physical body may be associated with conscious processes (the sensory system) and with the outer court of the temple. The mental body may be associated with the subconscious mental process (the autonomic nervous system) and with the inner court of the temple. The spiritual body may be associated with the spiritual centers (physiologically correlated to the seven endocrine glands) with the superconscious potential and with the temple's Holy of Holies.

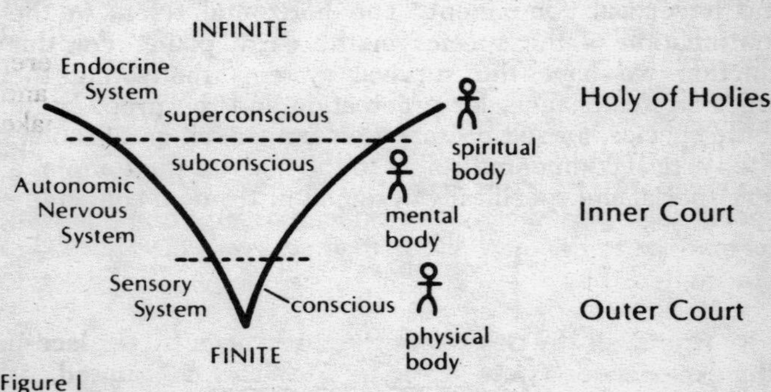

Figure I

Let us pursue further this analogy or parallel of *the body as the temple* with the construction of the Old Testament tabernacle. We may observe the relationship drawn in the Cayce readings between the lampstand with the seven lamps and the seven centers of light within ourselves represented physically by the endocrine system. To be sure, the endocrine glands are only physiological correlates, and even so do not include all of the processes which are understood to be involved respectively with the activities of these centers. For example, the third center of the endocrine glands is the adrenals; however, the readings point out that this spiritual center relates more accurately to the processes of the solar plexus. (This principle would be applicable to all of the centers.) Furthermore, as we speak of physiological correlates, we understand that the centers have their representation in the physical body, in the mental body, and in the spiritual body. The true spiritual center is in the spiritual body, and therefore it may become clearer why we speak of the endocrine glands as physiological correlates to the spiritual center.

The Twofold Purpose of the Body

As has been pointed out, the development of *Homo sapiens* as a physical manifestation in the earth was for a very specific purpose. Two major functions have been designated which may be visualized as having a horizontal and a vertical component. The horizontal refers to the continuation of the species in the earth plane. For this function we have the survival systems motivating the urges for sustenance, for procreation and the propagation of the species, for self-preservation and for self-gratification. The vertical component refers to the body as the temple, a very special and specifically designed instrument containing

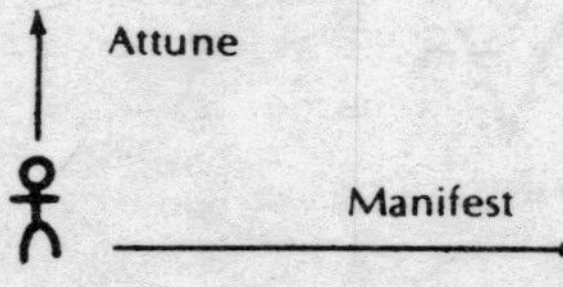

Seven Spiritual Centers & Symbolic Meanings Correlated*

A KEY TO THE REVELATION, ARCHETYPAL SYMBOLS AND REFERENTS IN THE HUMAN BODY

Seal	*Gland/ Motivation*	*Church*	*Faults & Virtues*	*Figure*	*Opening Vision*	*Element*	*Planet*	*Color*	*Lord's Prayer*
7	Pituitary/ Love	Laodicea	Neither cold nor hot	Father	Silence		Jupiter	Violet	Father/Glory
6	Pineal/ Light	Philadelphia	An open door	Christ Lamb	Earth-quake		Mercury	Indigo	Name/Power
5	Thyroid/ Life	Sardis	Repent/A few not defiled	Holy Spirit	Souls of faithful slain		Uranus	Blue	Thy Will/ Kingdom
4	Thymus/ Self-gratification	Thyatira	Fornication/ Charity, service, faith	Eagle	Pale (olive) horse	Air	Venus	Green	Evil
3	Adrenals/ Self-preservation	Pergamos	Stumbling block/ Faith	Lion	Red horse	Fire	Mars	Yellow	Debts
2	Cells of Leydig/ Propagation of species	Smyrna	Tribulation, poverty/ Insincerity	Man	Black horse	Water	Neptune	Orange	Temptation
1	Gonads/ Sustenance	Ephesus	Left first love/Labor and patience	Calf	White horse	Earth	Saturn	Red	Bread

***Compiled from readings in the 281 series**

all of the circuitry necessary for a full awareness of our Oneness with the Infinite. The sensory centers for this function are the spiritual centers.

If spirit is the life, it is the basic force that manifests both in the physical life in the earth and in the spiritual life in other planes of consciousness. For this reason, we have in the construction of the body a very interesting arrangement. *The very centers which are responsible for the most basic integration and motivation of the physical hierarachy of drives in the earth plane are also those very centers involved in attunement to other planes.* In other words, because there is only one force, then the basic motivational centers of the physical drives serve also as the spiritual centers for raising spiritual awareness and channeling of spiritual energy.

The following chart lists these centers and their respective physiological, motivational and cosmic relationships as well as the symbolic representation given in the Cayce interpretation of The Revelation of John.

The Centers as Senses

The spiritual centers serve several functions, one being as sensitive centers or sensory receptors. As depicted in the Old Testament, there was a stone with seven eyes. (Zechariah 3:9) The stone represents the physical body; the seven eyes, the seven senses of the spiritual body. The Revelation describes a lamb and other beasts full of eyes. (Revelation 4:6, 5:6) Evidently the *eye* is symbolic of a spiritual sensory receptor, and thus the lamb with seven eyes and the rock with seven eyes represent the pattern of the Christ with seven spiritual senses.

Just as the eye is sensitive to light and the ear is sensitive to sound, so there are sensory organs for our awareness of subtler realities and other dimensions. In other words, we are able to become aware of and to have experiences in other dimensons because built into us are sensory systems which enable us to have those awarenesses. Each of the seven centers is sensitive to vibrations and energy from seven respective planes and spheres. Through this system, the psychic or sensitive attunes to thoughts generated by other entities working from one of the levels of those respective dimensions (whether or not the entity is in the *physical* plane or working from some *other* plane).

The Centers as Transducers

A second function of the spiritual centers is as a transducer of energy. A transducer is an instrument for changing one kind of energy into another. One well-known example is that of a telephone which changes electrical energy into acoustical energy. Each of the seven centers channels the energy of its respective vibratory level into manifestation in the physical body. Likewise, as transducers, the centers may project thoughts from the physical level into other levels. Depending upon a person's motivation, a particular center is selected as the channel for projection. For example, a telepathic communication from one person to another may be motivated by sex (gonads) and anger (adrenals) or higher motivations. (We give an example of this on page 84.)

As Above—So Below

A third function of these centers is to manifest in three dimensions the kinds of energies and awarenesses that come from other dimensions. Every time spiritual energy manifests in the earth plane it bears some form. Relatively *universal forms*, which Carl Jung called *archetypes*, may be related specifically to each of the seven centers. When energy from another plane impacts on a person and is picked up by the center related to that plane, it may be given formal representation, as in a vision or a dream, through the archetypal image associated with that center. For example, in The Revelation, John has a vision of four beasts: a calf, a man, a lion and an eagle. These are the appropriate forms or archetypal symbols which are respectively related to the flow of energies through the four lower centers. For example, the lion or any cat is the appropriate archetypal symbol related to the activity of the adrenal or solar plexus center.

Because these centers are sensitive to the various planes or dimensions of reality, then the special emphasis of one of these centers and its accompanying imagery may be experienced as being of a religious nature.

In Zechariah 6 we are told of a vision of four horses, the same as those envisoned by John in Revelation 6:1-8. These horses are "the four spirits of the heavens, which go forth from standing before the Lord of all the earth." (Zechariah 6:5) As different peoples, cultures and sects have mobilized one center more than the others, then those people many experience a certain common imagery accompanying their religious practices. Consequently, that archetypal imagery may be elevated to the status as a god, because it is the form through which the Divine Force is experienced and manifested in the consciousness not only of the individual but also of the group. Thus we encounter the worship of the serpent or the bull or the lion or other archetypal images.

In the functioning of this system of seven centers, it should be understood that all seven are usually involved; therefore, it is a matter of the *relative dominance* of one or two centers over the activities of the others.

The Nature of Creative Energy

Energy flows through us in polarities, just as it does in a battery. We may therefore speak of two poles within the body which focalize the flow of these forces, as depicted in the Star of David. The triangle with its apex upward represents the Force rising from within. The triangle with the apex pointed downward represents the Divine Force entering from without.

The centers for raising the spiritual energies within us are the same as those related to sexual drives and motivations. The gonads and the cells of Leydig (the latter located structurally within the former) are the quickening and generative centers. They can be used to awaken and raise spiritual awareness or sexual activity. These are the same centers which the yogic literature describes as the coiled, sleeping serpent *Kundalini*, which, when awakened and raised in deep meditation, rises upward along those natural channels and flows from the first center through the seventh. This physiological, albeit esoteric, understanding of the nature of man is the basis for understanding the special relationship between the energy that may be raised within us to bring about spiritual awakening and that energy that may be given expression in our sexual activities. The energy is the same. Only the use of it varies.

As we come to a deeper understanding of meditation, we see that the physiology of the attunement process directly involves the sexual energies of the gonads and the cells of Leydig. For attunement to take place in deep meditation, these energies must be raised up through the other centers until there is an integration of the whole system. Furthermore, the lower four centers must be subservient to the direction and integration of the higher centers. The higher motives must be awakened and given expression in the life of growth in the spirit. The readings, of course, recognize this to be a growth process and invite a balanced expression according to the "complexities" of the flow of life.

The abstinence of or from relationships with the opposite sex is well when the creative force is put to creative activity in the mental, but when these are at variance with other conditions these may become just as harmful to the imaginative system or to the central nervous system, from breaking of activities with the sympathetic and the cerebrospinal, and thus become harmful. 5162-1

Sigmund Freud, the founder of psychoanalysis, has been much maligned because of his theory that the life force, which he called libido, was basically sexual. He theorized that the sex drive was the source of all creative and religious expressions. In light of our studies of Eastern yoga and the Cayce readings, Freud's speculations were not without basis. We must confront our own resistance to looking at and understanding sexual energy in relationship to other forms of expression. We must consider that the spiritual centers involved in spiritual awakening are the same centers which are involved in sexual motivation and expression.

We may be especially concerned about this relationship as we address the question of creativity. We as spiritual beings are made to be co-creators with God. That form of physical expression that is most clearly creative in and of itself is the act of procreation and propagation of the species. Yet *all* creative activity is related to these same energy centers.

Let us study carefully the way in which the readings express the interrelationships between the qualities of sexual and creative expression:

As sex is that channel through which creation in the material world brings forth that which is of creating itself, so are the organs of same—the centers through which all creative energies—whether mental or spiritual—find their inception in a material world for an expression. As has been given, when this force in sex is raised, or rated, in its inception through the mental forces of the body, this finds expression in that of giving the love influence in the life or lives of the individual, as well as that which may be brought into being as a gratification of a physical desire.

Hence this portion, this incompatibility that is between the two individuals as given here, is that which makes for the inability for any *creative* forces to become compatible between the individuals; for there is no soul but what the sex life becomes the greater influence in the life. Not as always in gratification in the physical act, but rather that that finds expression in the creative forces and creative abilities of the body itself. 911-2

Q-18. So much has been written about sexual relation-ships between husband and wife. Is it the correct understanding that this activity should be used only and

when companions seek to build a body for an incoming entity?

A-18. Not necessarily. These depend, of course, to be sure, on the individual concept of relationships and their activities. To be sure, if the activities are used in creative, spiritual form, there is the less desire for carnal relationship; or, if there is the lack of use of constructive energies, then there is the desire for more of the carnal, physical reaction. 2072-16

Are we prepared to use the energy constructively in "creative, spiritual form" and to diminish "the desire for more of the carnal, physical reactions"?

In Tune or Off Key?

The seven centers may be considered to be like a seven-piece band. Several of the pieces play in the background, while one or two play a solo or a duet. The combinations of motivational and emotional expressions form the rich textures of our lives. To illustrate with an extreme example: The negative motivations of the gonads combined with the adrenals (the solor plexus center) may combine the forces of sex and aggression in acts of sexual violence. This illustrates a mixture of emotions which may grow out of mobilizing different motivational potentials.

Hence it may be given in passing, to the entity, that the love of and for a pure body is the most sacred experience in an entity's earthly sojourn; yet these conditions soured, these conditions turned into vitriol, may become the torments of an exemplary body, and one well-meaning, and make for loss of purposes. 436-2

One of the criteria for the spiritual path was given by the Master, "If . . . thine eye be single, thy whole body shall be full of light." (Matthew 6:22) The eye may symbolize the master gland, the highest of the spiritual centers, the pituitary. The *Search for God* readings indicate that if one emphasized pituitary functions in his life for a period of seven years, he might become a light unto the world. The integration of the system is most enhanced by singleness of purpose. When our purposes toward our love partner are single, then whether in sex or any other activity, the body may be filled wih ecstatic light that is truly spiritual. When the purposes are not single, then mixed motivations may bring about internal physiological imbalances and external behavioral patterns that are undesirable; we become a house divided against itself.

Let us analyze the nature of our attraction to specific individuals. For example, the thymus gland is related to the heart. As the heart center, it is accompanied in its activity by the emotions of jealousy, pity, worry, self-concern and self-gratification. Our feelings of attraction toward a certain person may include motives based primarily on pity or empathy. Or for another person, jealousy may be part of the emotional, and therefore motivational, attraction. Yet when these basic attitudes toward the person are energized by the awakening and flow of the sexual drive, specific activities may develop without sex in its purest form as the only motivation seeking expression. Clearly, rape or other crimes of sexual violence are motivated primarily by aggression and only secondarily by the sexual drive. These examples can be used to understand subtler types of relationships.

It is clear that some seductions may be based more on the motivations of jealousy, pity, compassion or self-aggrandizement than directly on the basis of the sex drive alone. Failing to discern the mixed contribution of each of the motivational centers to such activities, we become confused by the overt manifestation of behavioral patterns which seem incomprehensible. When the motivations are mixed at the unconscious level, an individual may feel compelled to act in a certain way and yet consciously realize the lack of logic and even the lack of desire to act in such a manner.

As we study more deeply the unconscious interaction of our various motivational potentials, such as sex, and yet mobilize in its service one of the other motivational potentials, such as anger, we can begin to gain insight into the array of sexual impulses and activities that otherwise, with a simpler notion of sex, would be beyond comprehension.

The Centers as Storehouses

Now we may introduce a further function of these seven centers as storehouses of reactive patterns or karmic memories. We have now to deal with the concept of reincarnation, involving patterns of relationships and consequent sexual attractions we may have developed with other people. Considering this concept, we may come to realize how our reactions toward specific individuals can be so complex and unique. We may understand how our present feelings may be colored and compelled by past life patterns *in the motivational centers called to the fore in the present relationship*.

In the following case, a 32-year-old woman with specific gonadal problems asked about the spiritual source of her problem. (The expression, "The experiences before this," indicate the past-life behavioral origin of a present-life physiological problem.)

Q-4. What is the spiritual source of the glandular condition manifested in my physical body, and just how should it be met?

A-4. The experiences before this with the turmoils wrought by the questionings, as to associations and activities, brought about what now manifests as the glandular disturbance with the relationships having to do with the activities of the creative forces in the body. 4046-1

The centers become the physical instruments on which the tunes composed in a previous lifetime are given expression. The appropriateness of the particular instrument (the center) to the specific musical quality (the memory) may sometimes be in question. Two people may find themselves in a particular situation in which a sexual relation might seem appropriate—yet with a previous life relationship to the contrary. For example, in one reading a married woman who had a gentle husband feared sexual intercourse with him due to an experience at the time of the Crusades in which she was left in a chastity belt.

The circuitry through which the energy flows may lead to sexual attraction or temptation, yet the feelings may contain the mixture of another quality from a previous life relationship. When these mixtures are given physiological expression in the present hormonal and endocrine activity, the results may be either incompatibility or a burst of sunlight.

Meditation and Sex

The heart of the spiritual path is found in the great commandment—to love God with all our heart and our neighbor as ourselves. Two words, capturing the essence of these two aspects of the great commandment, are *attunement* and *application*. The expression of the love of God is given the most active day-to-day manifestation in seeking attunement with God through the process of meditation. The expression of the second part of the commandment, the love of neighbor, is given manifestation most fully in our daily lives in doing what we know to do to help the other fellow. In *attunement* and *application* we have the essence of our spiritual lives.

Let us consider attunement as sought specifically in meditation. As stated earlier, the energy that is involved and effective in meditation is the awakened and raised energy from the gonads and the cells of Leydig. These are also the centers motivating sexual expression. Whereas our spiritual path does not require us to put aside or give up sexual activity, it does require us to put sex into proper perspective in relationship to the higher motivations of love of God and fellow man. In order to understand how this may work in practice, let us suggest again a comparison with the worship procedures of ancient Israel. We have postulated that the body represents the temple; and the tabernacle in the wilderness, an external model of the true pattern within. In the tabernacle worship, the ceremony began with the priest sacrificing an animal on the altar in the outer court. He then took some of the blood from the sacrifice to the inner court and into the Holy of Holies. This practice, which might seem repugnant to us, may be most instructive when it is considered to be symbolic and indeed archetypal of true worship and therefore of meditation.

The instructions were that the animal to be sacrificed must be of the first fruits or the first-born and must be without blemish. Let us consider the sacrifice of a young bullock and reflect upon the parallel symbology of the calf as the archetypal imagery symbolizing the first center, the gonads. The instructions for external worship become applicable to the internal process of meditation. The interpretation then would be: Of those energies represented by the calf, the sexual energies, the first fruits of the first center must be offered up in purity (without blemish) in sacrifice. The blood, the life energy itself, must be carried upward into the Holy of Holies. That is the energy which is to be raised up into the highest centers within ourselves in meditation.

Now we have a principle that is immediately helpful in seeing the proper relationship between our use of these potentials in meditation and worship and our use of them in sexual expression. As we begin to work with this principle, we may introduce an extremely helpful and profound insight from the teachings of the Master which instructs us to "resist not evil." (Matthew 5:39) In application, this means rather than an attempt to *stop* doing wrong, we are to *start* doing something right; that is, instead of resisting some problem that appears to be sexual, we should dedicate ourselves to a regular practice of meditation. If we set that as the item of first priority in our daily lives, then we may begin to use the first fruits of that energy (that otherwise would be sexual) in enabling us to make attunement and to build a foundation for spiritual growth.

In the Old Testament, God did not ask the Israelites to sacrifice all of their products—only the best. We are not suggesting that He asks us to give up sex. Sex has its natural place in His creation. The point is, if we use the first of that energy in meditation, every aspect of the rest of our lives will be better. As meditation becomes the higher priority than the use of that energy in sexual expression, sexual problems will fall more and more into place in a well-balanced life and sex will assume its proper role in the hierarchy of our drives and needs. The direct relationship between meditation and sexual desire is made very clear in the following:

Q-6. Through my meditation, has the kundalini fire risen to the head or top of spine at base of skull? If so, was it because of sex abstinence and discipline that this happened?

A-6. It has risen at *times*, but has not remained; else there would *not* be those periods of confusion. For, when this has arisen—and is disseminated properly through the seven centers of the body, it has purified the body from all desire of sex relationships. For, *this is* an outlet through which one may attain to celibacy—through this activity. That it has *not remained* indicates changes.

2329-1

In this answer the reference to celibacy seems to suggest that meditation and raising the kundalini forces may purify the body from sexual desire, with celibacy as a possible natural consequence. This order is quite the reverse from some approaches which seek the vows to be taken first before the bodily forces are raised to make such appropriate.

Sex and Sustenance

In other references we have suggested a relationship between the function of the gonads and the basic drive for sustenance. The energy which we call sexual may be raised from the gonads; it is the life force itself; the source of energy for procreation. However, we have not fully studied nor understood its relationship to creation or creativity itself. As the source of the life energy from within, it is related to the basic animal drive for sustenance, represented in the Lord's Prayer by "Give us this day our daily *bread*."

Let us relate the symbol of bread symbolically and psychologically to an understanding of some other Biblical passages. We may remember from the story of the Israelites in the wilderness that God had provided for their sustenance a bread from heaven, manna. The Israelites tired of this and wanted to return to Egypt. Once they built for themselves a golden calf, using an archetypal symbol for the activities of the gonad center as it relates to fertility and reproduction. (The bull was a sacred Egyptian symbol for the god of fertility.) The symbolic effect of this act was to say no to God's plan of providing sustenance from heaven. They did not want to raise that energy so that a bread from heaven might be made available through it—rather they wanted to return to the expression of that energy more at the level of the earth-earthy, as they had in Egypt. The basic fear being expressed by the children of Israel at that time was the fear of lack of supply. They tried to mobilize within *themselves* an attempt to fulfill that needed supply rather than to depend in faith upon God. There was generated within them a motivational expression, which is man's physiological answer to supply; that is, sexual activity which leads to procreation and reproduction. The desire for supply was thus given expression in a physical mode of creative expression; but that same energy could be raised and the unlimited forces of the Divine could become the source of supply.

This story from the ancient days of the Old Testament, when interpreted symbolically, may have wide applicability in our understanding of many questions of present-day concerns regarding supply and our earthly attempts to meet those concerns. Thus we may understand how it is that in certain countries where food is in shortest supply there may be the highest birth rate. Following this psychological interpretation, we may understand that when man finds himself in need and tries to supply that from within himself, sexual activity with its subsequent expression in reproduction of the species is the logical and biological result.

Problems on the Path

In the Revelation of John, chapter 12, a great portent is seen in heaven. A woman is about to give birth to a child. A great red dragon with seven heads and ten horns appears and is about to devour the child. The Archangel Michael battles with the dragon and casts him down from heaven. Then it is said, "Rejoice, ye heavens . . . Woe to the inhabitors of the earth and of the sea!" (Revelation 12:12) Then as the dragon goes into the earth, it spawns two other beasts, one rising up from the sea and one from the earth. The one rising from the earth is the false prophet who has the ability to do wonders and miracles and to deceive.

Now this sequence of imagery in The Revelation relates, according to the Cayce readings, to a process that may take place within each of us as we take certain steps on the spiritual path. The new-born child represents the new Ideal of the Christ which is established when we set ourselves upon the spiritual path. The woman, the mother of the child, represents all of those experiences in the earth that have led us to this moment of giving birth to this, the highest ideal. Immediately upon the setting of the Christ as the Ideal and thus making the Christ the regnant pattern within, the spirit of rebellion, symbolized by the red dragon, rises to devour the child. The Archangel Michael, the guardian of the Christ Ideal within us, casts the spirit of rebellion down from heaven into the earth. That is, symbolically the spirit of rebellion is removed from the higher three centers, but it still may cause difficulty in the earth, the lower four centers. This spirit of rebellion stirs a response out of the earth, the gonads, thus quickening the psychic potentials of the cells of Leydig. The subsequent psychic awakening is referred to as the false prophet. The false prophet is not an external person or being, but rather an internal process that may take place in each of us as a natural step in the growth of the inner life.

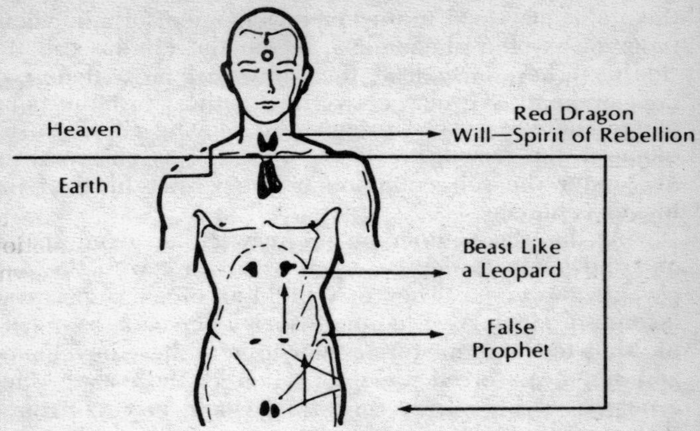

The Physiology of the False Prophet Stage on the Spiritual Path

It has been said that where you find the psychic, you find the sexual. Wherever there is heightened psychic activity or psychic phenomena, you may find an increased sexual impulse. The reason for this is simply that the awakening of the psychic abilities is related to the raising of the energy from those sexual centers. In its earliest stage of development in the individual, some of this quickening may be more in response to the dethroning of the spirit of rebellion rather than in the full and integrated direction of the Christ as King within. One of the most tricky aspects of this stage of development, which we may call the false prophet stage, is that the psychic phenomena accompanying it may indeed be valid in a certain sense. The phenomena may be accurate, helpful and healing.

A special problem may arise in this stage of development. The individual in question, with newly developing psychic ability, may assume too much about the stage of spiritual development to which he has arrived. He may think that he has *indeed* arrived rather than realize that the ability is in its infant stages. Getting off the track at this point may lead to further development of miraculous types of psychic phenomena, which the Hindus call the siddhis. These may lead the individual on a detour of development. We may get off the path at just the point where there is special promise for moving ahead to full bloom in the growth process to bring the psychic awakening under the full dominion of the Christ Ideal of the higher centers.

At this stage, other people may gather about such a one and begin to depend upon or to work with the new psychic awareness. They may build an organization or an income-producing work around such a person and contribute thus to the premature exploitation of these developing abilities. A preferred course of action for those about such a person who are truly concerned would be to surround that person with increased encouragement, prayer support and protection to help the individual work with this developing ability and work through this critical stage of the infancy of the Christ pattern ruling the individual. Such an individual needs the most constructive, helpful and protective support to grow through those initial vulnerable phases of psychic development to full maturity. However, because this early stage especially involves the first and second centers, then there may be the accompanying problems related to sex, which would naturally follow from the utilization of such energies without raising them fully through the whole system of the spiritual centers.

Sex and the Psychic

For one on the spiritual path meditation is the basic and requisite practice for attunement. It is well known that the practice of meditation involves the raising of that known as the kundalini from the lower spiritual centers, specifically the gonads and the lyden, upward to the pineal and overflowing into the pituitary. Meditation involves:

. . . allowing the influence of the generative force through the glandular system to be raised to the various

centers; first for the purifying of self, then for the obtaining of that necessary—through symbol, sign or vision—to be accomplished for individuals seeking. 2329-3, F.42

To understand meditation we must understand the physical forces of the body.

. . . there are centers, areas, conditions in which there evidently must be that contact between the physical, the mental and the spiritual.

The spiritual contact is through the glandular forces of creative energies; not encased only within the lyden gland of reproduction . . . 263-13, F.29

Since the practice of meditation involves the flow of forces through the endocrine system, especially involving and beginning at the sexual centers, it is necessary to prepare oneself to raise the energies that may be given expression in meditation or psychic activities. One seeker asked:

Q-1. Is there at present any danger to any particular body-function, such as sex; or to general health?

A-1. As we have indicated, without preparation, desires of *every* nature may become so accentuated as to destroy—or to overexercise as to bring detrimental forces; unless the desire and purpose is acknowledged and set *in* the influence of self as to its direction—when loosened by the kundaline activities through the body. 2475-1, M.44

Thus, in presenting instructions for meditation, the readings say:

. . . to *all* there may be given:

***Find* that which is to *yourself* the more certain way to your consciousness of *purifying* body and mind, before ye attempt to enter into the meditation as to raise the image of that through which ye are seeking to know the will or the activity of the Creative Forces; for ye are *raising* in meditation actual *creation* taking place within the inner self!**

When one has found that which to self cleanses the body, whether from the keeping away from certain foods or from certain associations (either man or woman), or from those thoughts and activities that would hinder that which is to be raised from *finding* its full measure of expression in the *inner* man (*inner* man, or inner individual, man or woman, meaning in this sense those radial senses from which, or centers from which all the physical organs, the mental organs, receive their stimuli for activity), we readily see how, then, *in* meditation (when one has so purified self) that *healing* of *every* kind and nature may be disseminated on the wings of thought . . .

Now, when one has cleansed self, in whatever manner it may be, there may be no fear that it will become so overpowering that it will cause any physical or mental disorder. It is *without* the cleansing that entering into such finds *any* type or any form of disaster, or of pain, or of any dis-ease of any nature. 281-13

The above information was given in a general reading on instructions for meditation. The same theme is found in an individual reading given to one with special psychic abilities:

First, this shows that there is innate in each physical individual that channel through which the psychic or the spiritual forces, that are manifest in material world, *may* function. They are known as glands, and affect the organs of the system.

In the activity, then, there is shown that an activity is evident in the creative forces of the body itself in *producing* or bringing about such phenomena in the material plane, so that the use of same may make for the more spiritual-minded individual or in the abuse of same one becomes more debased or bestial in their activity in the material plane. 294-141, M.55

In his instructions for himself and others, the Cayce source give additional information, stressing the role of using and misusing the reproductive glands in psychic activity.

Such analysis, then, is well for such students.

As illustrations from that as given, as is seen from such information:

The glands of reproduction in a body give up something that creation may be reached, or tuned into, when such an one—a psychic—attunes self to the infinite; and such used for abuses of the privileges as are material individuals' lives in such, what *must* be the lives of such individuals when attuned or awakened, or shown in a carnal or material world? *Think* on these things, Man—*think!* that the essence of Life *itself* is given in giving to another that as may bring the consciousness to another of an awakening in their own beings! Wist ye not that it was said by Him, "Who touched Me? for virtue has gone out!" Virtue is a lesson before some. What meaneth this, then, that such will be tampered with for only secular things, for the knowledge of whether this or that abuse has been made of those freedoms of self in associations with others? What *must* it bring? 294-140, M.55

The statement that where you find the *psychic* you find *sex* indicates that psychic abilities are related to raising the energies of the sexual organs, as in meditation, in order to bring about a greater attunement within the whole system of spiritual centers. When these centers are raised, unless purified, there may be the stimulation or even exaggeration of sexual motivation and desire. It is only in the maintenance of the spiritual ideal, of a constructive mental diet and of constructive physical activities that some of the dangers of these manifestations may be avoided. Thus one on the spiritual path, who is meditating and manifesting psychic abilities, must all the more be in attunement with his own inner guidance regarding sexual expressions physically and mentally.

The Body as the Temple

The body, as it has been so specially prepared, constitutes an extraordinary and very special opportunity for soul growth for every one of us. As a temple, it is not only a *place* where we may meet God face to face, but it is also a specially constructed *instrument*, containing the possibilities for attunement and awareness of the at-onement of our souls as spiritual beings with God.

From the beginning days of man's involvement in the earth plane, the encasement in the flesh was a consequence of an expression of carnality that bespoke more of the mind than of the needs of the physical body. The development of the body, then, as *Homo sapiens* became an opportunity for all of us as souls to give expression to that biological urge. But for us as souls, this was a desire of the mind before it became a physiological imperative.

With these bodies, we now have an opportunity to give expression to that desire of the mind, yet in a context that may be either creative or destructive. On the creative side it may be used not only in the act of procreation, but also as an expression of those attributes of love which characterize the fruits of the spirit. But, as a channel for expressing the lower self or self-aggrandizement, it may give vent to all forms of man's emotions which are destructive. Then that which makes the sexual activities spiritual (as is the case with any of man's activities) is the *purpose* for which these potentials are mobilized.

These may be divided into two categories: (1) those which bring forth life and express love in relationship with others and (2) those which bring forth death and express only self-gratification and self-aggrandizement. The element of pleasure may accompany either of these utilizations of expression. As a component of this activity it must not be confused with the deeper qualities of motivation of the individuals involved.

The more basic drive may derive from life itself, in which case its expression is indeed Divine, or it may derive from the lower self and the motives of self-exaltation and self-aggrandizement, thus being in fact demonic. It is not a question of sexual expression versus spiritual expression. It is rather a question of supremacy of the spiritual ideal (in which the sexual expression will be accompanied by the qualities of the spirit) or of the strength of the spirit of rebellion (in which the sexual expression will be accompanied by destructive influences).

What an amazing and beautiful opportunity it is to have these bodies as temples containing the potential to make attunement with the Infinite! Furthermore, how promising it is to have within ourselves a reservoir of energy which may activate this potential and enable us to move in consciousness to an awareness of being one with the Whole. What a simple request: dedicate a few minutes of each day specifically to raising that energy within to express our love of God and our desire to be one with Him, who indeed is our first love and the object of the soul's sincere desire!

4

Mind Is the Builder

. . . the key should be making, compelling, inducing, having the mind one with that which is the ideal. 262-84

The young man showing us around Lexington Hospital, the national hospital for drug rehabilitation, said he was 26 years old and that he had been a heroin addict for 20 years of his life. As he went from one room to the next, showing us the facilities for the patients, he described some of the events and problems of his life. Finally, regarding drug addiction, he said in summary that some people think addiction is of the body and therefore speak always of the physical addiction. However, he had become convinced from his own personal experience and the experiences of others that the addiction was not in the body at all but rather in a state or quality of the mind. For example, he said, a man may be in prison for 30 years or more without any opportunity for taking drugs. However, on the first day that he is "back in the streets," such a person may immediately seek them out and become involved in the whole pattern again. What mattered, he said, was not the body's physiological need, but what was happening in the person's mind which would lead him to pick up on the old destructive pattern of behavior upon being released.

This insight may be instructive for us in many aspects of our own lives and in understanding the behavior of others. However, for the present, we may find this hypothesis helpful in trying to gain a better understanding of the nature of sex and sexual desire. It is true that we are in physical bodies and physical bodies have certain capabilities and certain motivational demands. However, we need to differentiate the real needs of the body from desires that are generated exclusively by the mind.

The Nature of the Mind

Understanding the mind of man, as given in the Cayce readings, is one of the most challenging, complete, beautiful—and even surprising—portrayals of the nature of man that may be found in any source of information. From the point of view of these readings, we live in a three-dimensional plane of consciousness. Therefore, we work with triune concepts to help us understand the manifest world about us and even the nature of the Divine.

We are told that we are made in the image of God. Considering the nature of God as triune—Father, Son and Holy Spirit—we may ask whether we, as His children, have a triune quality about ourselves that corresponds to the triune nature of God. We are miniature replicas of the universe, microcosmic patterns of the macrocosmic Whole. Thus, a specific and surprising parallel is given in the readings between the attributes of God and those of man. Just as we are spiritual, mental and physical, so these may be related to the triune God; Holy Spirit, Son and Father. Spirit is the life, the readings say. The Spirit of the Divine is the same as the Spirit within us. It relates to the soul, its purposes and desires. The mind is the builder; the builder aspect of God is the Christ, the Logos, that One through whom everything that was made was made. *The Christ within us is the mind*. As mind is the builder, so that within us which corresponds to the *creative* aspect of the Divine is our own mind. The aspect of the Divine which is the Father (the Whole) is represented in the earth plane by the body, which contains both mind and soul.

Just as the macrocosmic Christ is the Way, so the Christ, represented within us as the mind, is the way.

Within ourselves, the mind becomes the way because it is the mediator between the physical and the spiritual; it partakes of the temporal and of eternity. That upon which it dwells becomes that which we meet, both in the physical body and in physical experiences and also in the spiritual body and in the realms of consciousness in which the soul will sojourn after it leaves the physical plane. In other words, that upon which the mind dwells, that on which it feeds, it builds into the body and into the soul. Let us study carefully and reflect upon several ways in which the readings present this principle:

As we would give, an entity body-mind was first a soul before it entered into material consciousness. Individual entities become aware in a material world of the earth as a three-dimensional consciousness, having its concept or its analysis of good or of Creative Forces or God in a three-dimensional concept, God, the Father, the Son; the Christ the mind, the soul the first cause of an individual entity as it may become aware or conscious in a three-dimensional or material world . . .

For as you look at or analyze yourself, you find that you have a body-physical with all its attributes. It is in itself combined of flesh, and bone, nerve tissue. Yet the motivative forces through same are the connections in the central nervous system to which the organs of the central body respond. The central nerve and blood supply are in general heart, liver, lungs and kidneys and then there is the general sympathetic nervous system. These control the activities of the organs of the central nerves only in conjunction with or coordinating with the activities of the central nervous system or cerebrospinal system. Then there are those activities in the three-dimensional experience of the senses themselves, through which this sympathetic system receives its impressions. Again we have the three-dimensional idea or pattern. All of these in the body are dependent one upon another and the variations that cause the characteristics or the personality or indi-

viduality of each entity to vary according to the reaction that is brought into play in the mind. For remember, mind is ever the builder. Mind is represented in the Godhead as the Christ, the Son, the Way. The Father is represented in the earth as the body. The soul is all of those attributes that manifest in the body. 4083-1

Cultivate them. For know, though thy body, thy mind, thy soul be as the triune, they are one; with each endowed, by the Maker, with each attribute of the various phases of the experience.

The body-physical with the emotions of same is physical and spiritual; the body-mental with its desires is both carnal and very spiritual. The *spirit* is willing. The spirit desires, the spirit seeks the greater understanding, the greater knowledge of thy relationships to the Creative Forces or God.

Then cultivate—in thy mind, in thy body—those attributes which are endowed with that seeking for the knowledge of the true relationship of every soul with its Maker.

For as in the Godhead there is the Father, the Son, the Holy Ghost—so then each may be termed, the Body as the First Cause, the Mind as the Son (which is the Way, which is the Manner, which is the Builder in thy consciousness of the manifestations which are thy daily experience). 1754-1

In the Godhead there is found still the three-dimensional concept—God the Father, God the Son, and God the Holy Spirit.

Hence—if this is acceptable to the entity in its conception of that which has been, which is, which may be—these are still founded in that summed up in "The Lord thy God is One" . . .

As is understood then—Father-God is as the body, or the whole. Mind is as the Christ, which is the Way. The Holy Spirit is as the soul, or—in material interpretation—purposes, hopes, desires. 1747-5

And as He hath given, we are brethren one of another. We are indeed the offspring of that Creative Force, and thus may become heirs and joint heirs with Him; in that the Lord hath chosen, hath given each the abilities to do.

Thus seeking Him first is the whole duty of an entity. For one finds self with and in a three-dimensional world, with a three-dimensional body—yes, a three-dimensional mind—but that may be universal in its scope.

Hence we find Father, Son, Holy Spirit as the three-dimensional mind's concept of the Godhead. We find self with body, mind and soul. *These* each have their counterpart in that Godhead.

Then as the Son is the Way, so is the Mind the Builder—that makes for both at-onement with Him and a condition of being at variance with Him. 2549-1

What is the purpose then, we ask, for our entering into this vale, or experience, or awareness, where disappointments, fears, trials of body and of mind appear to mount above all of the glories that we may see?

In the beginning, when there was the creating, or the calling of individual entities into being, we were made to be the companions with the Father-God.

Now flesh and blood may not inherit eternal life; only the spirit, only the purpose, only the desire may inherit same.

Then that error in individual activity—not of another but of ourselves, individually—separated us from that awareness.

Hence God prepared the way through flesh whereby all phases of spirit, mind and body might express.

The earth then is a three-dimensional, a three-phase or three-manner expression. Just as the Father, the Son, the Holy Spirit are one. So are our body, mind and soul one—in Him.

Now we have seen, we have heard, we know that the Son represents or signifies the Mind.

He, the Son, was in the earth-earthy even as we—and yet is of the Godhead.

Hence the mind is both material and spiritual, and taketh hold on that which is its environ, its want, in our experiences.

Then Mind, as He, was the Word—and dwelt among men; and we beheld Him as the face of the Father.

So is our mind made, so does our mind conceive—even as He; and *is* the Builder.

Then that our mind dwells upon, that our mind feeds upon, that do we supply to our body—yes, to our soul!

Hence we find all of these are the background, as it were, for the interpreting of our experience, of our sojourns in the earth. 1567-2

Mind and Motivation

Most of us think of ourselves as having rather fixed or set kinds of motivations. If we have studied the teachings of dynamic psychology, we may even have come to consider that we have unconscious motivations. We may be able to some measure to entertain the idea that some of our behavior may be motivated by forces of which we are consciously unaware. Nevertheless, we tend to think of these as drives that are rather set and to which we are in some relative bondage. It would be far more accurate and helpful for us to understand that we have motivational *potentials*.

We have already discussed the way in which the endocrine system constitutes the physiological basis of our motivational potentials. The secretions of the endocrine glands, the hormones, are the biochemical messengers which instruct the body in ways that we experience as drives or motives. We may think that these work in some rather fixed biological pattern; however, much of our behavior clearly demonstrates that we have a considerable measure of control over the activity of these centers.

Let us imagine, then, that our seven centers are like a kitchen range with seven burners. We may turn these "on" or "off"; we may leave them on "simmer" or on "high." This measure of control comes more from the food

that we feed our minds than by the fixed nature of the biological requirements. For example, one who constantly dwells upon anger or resentment is continually triggering the activity of the adrenal glands, secreting those hormones into the body which prepare it to flee or to fight.

With our thoughts, we may dwell upon resentment, but the body experiences itself as being instructed to prepare for a fight. Then the hormonal messengers go out to all the cells of the body, each organ responding according to its assigned contribution in an emergency situation. Some of us so continually dwell upon anger or resentment that our bodies are more or less always in a state of preparing for an emergency. This state works against rest, relaxation, and thus healing and regeneraton. The long-term consequence is the breakdown of some of the systems, leading to certain types of physical disease.

It is by the mind and that upon which the mind dwells that the selection is made as to which of the motivational centers will be activated. The mind, of course, has a great ability to roam, but once it begins to dwell upon a certain subject, especially investing its imaginative and visualizational forces, the imagery of the mental body awakens and builds that being held into the physical body. Just as the mind, by dwelling upon anger, can trigger the response of the adrenals and prepare the body to fight, so may the mind, by dwelling upon sexual thoughts, trigger responses in the body that prepare it for sexual activity. With the awakening of the physiological response, there is a new dimension of drive or urgency for expression and we then have a new state of affairs with which to deal. At this point, we call these biological needs. However, it is important for us to understand that most of our sexual needs are derived from the mind. Desire patterns, thought forms and imagery on which the mind dwells lead to the biological response which we interpret as a biological imperative.

The Mind and Meditation

We may, for a wider scope, define meditation as "motivated mentation." This definition then includes negative as well as positive forms of meditation, and gives us a fuller understanding of its true meaning and effect and of the mind's potentials. By motivated mentation, we mean that upon which the mind dwells combined with the involvement of the desire system on one hand and the physiological-response system on the other.

If mind is the builder, then meditation may be understood to be dwelling upon that which we are to become. If we set a high ideal and dwell upon that, we grow in attunement and conformity to that ideal. If we allow the mind to dwell upon and build a response of probabilities related to other desires, then we enhance the likelihood of those being given expression in our bodies and in our behaviors. If we set a spiritual ideal and dwell upon it, the energy may be raised through the motivational system (that is, through the endocrine glands) to the centers which deal with the motivational qualities of that ideal. If we dwell upon *Oneness* or the highest form of *love*, then the energy awakened and raised may go through the whole system and rally at the seventh and highest center.

On the other hand, as we dwell upon sexual thoughts, then the same energy is awakened as it is awakened in any other form of meditation, but it is raised only to that level of motivation and physiological expression to which the imagery is appropriate. As we dwell upon sexual thoughts—and we may truly consider this to be a form of meditation—we prepare our bodies and subsequently our behavioral expressions to manifest that which we have been building with the mind. For example, if a man has been meditating on the love of the Christ and afterwards a woman smiles at him, he may interpret this as a response of the Christ within that person. However, if he has been dwelling upon sexual thoughts and the same woman were to smile at him in the same way, he might interpret that as being a sexual overture on her part. Just as our perception of experiences is interpreted in terms of the dominant physiological process, so are our subsequent responses to those perceptions. With this example, we can see that what we dwell on prepares the selectivity and interpretation of our perceptions and inclines us to certain types of responses.

Another way of thinking about the working of the mind is that of memorizing content and response probabilities with respect to subject matter. As we memorize a poem, for example, we are subsequently more able to verbalize that poem. As we dwell upon a certain type of behavior, it becomes more probable that it will be manifested in our overt actions. A further step involves the activity known as planning. As our minds dwell upon something, we subsequently seek out opportunities for experiencing or expressing that. Dwelling upon constitutes "planning," whether we consciously call it that or not. When a person studies travel magazines and is attracted by a certain place as a likely spot for a pleasant vacation, he sets about arranging the opportunity to visit such a place. He begins making vacation plans, saving money and collecting information about the place, and thus makes the visit more and more possible. As we dwell upon a mode of sexual experience or expression, we are in essence laying plans which set in motion behavior sequences which, in turn, begin to bring this about sooner or later.

Although this is quite obvious and commonplace with respect to some of our everyday experiences, we may not appreciate the far-reaching implications of such a principle. We may also be setting up experiences to be met years or even incarnations later. These patterns built by the mind may be called memories, programming or karma. Some of these patterns may best be termed "thought forms." Certain systematically constructed patterns may come eventually to have an autonomous or independent quality. Although they are part of ourselves, to be sure, they may seem to act and express themselves independently of the conscious mind.

The Thought Form Lover

On many occasions people have come face to face with their own thought forms. These experiences are sometimes dismaying and distressing, to say the least. One such case is of a woman who for many years would have nothing to do with psychical research, but her daughter had been a serious student of this field for years. However, on one occasion the woman saw a book belonging to her daughter, picked it up out of curiosity and discovered that it described how to do automatic handwriting. She decided to give it a try. Immediately, on her first attempt, there seemed to be a force or being that wanted to write through her. Her handwriting was rapid and distinct and the information seemed to be coming from a discarnate entity. She asked, "Do you come from the Christ?" The reply was "Yes!" By this sign, she came to feel there could be no danger and she pursued the writing for a period of time.

As is frequently the case, at first the messages were beautiful and encouraging, then they began to tell her that she was being prepared for a special spiritual work. Next, again as is the case with many of these instances, the source of the information told her that she was being tested. She was asked to do unusual things to meet this test. Then, a turn in the quality of the writing signaled the beginning of a series of experiences that became truly a nightmare. At night, even when in bed with her husband, she would experience a presence that was almost physically tangible. It would make an indentation in the mattress as it sat upon the bed by her side. Subsequently, a sexual approach was made, accompanied, again as is frequent in such cases, by a specific feeling of energy being drawn from the sexual organs themselves. This became extremely distressing, and the woman seemed to have no control over the expression of these forces.

As she pursued the automatic writing and answers were sought concerning these experiences, the nature of the source of the writing was revealed. It represented itself finally as being *her own thought form—a thought form lover* that she had created in a lifetime of day dreaming and fantasy in a previous incarnation during the 15th century. Apparently she had led a lonely life at that time and had day dreamed an imaginary lover, and she had given this fantasy such form and richness of expression that it became a thought form with a quality of autonomy in her own psyche. When given an opportunity for expression through the opening of her unconscious in the mechanism of automatic writing, the thought form burst out full-blown with no diminution of power from centuries elapsed. It was of such a quality that it not only acted in an autonomous way but indeed came almost to possess her. This story may be interpreted at many levels, of course. It may be taken at face value for what it said it was; or we may dismiss it with the remark, "It is all psychological." Whatever the interpretation, the seriousness is the same.

With our minds we can build into ourselves thought patterns that may indeed possess us. It behooves us to use these extraordinary potentials of the mind to build only that which we would make an enduring part of ourselves, that which we are willing to own, guide or direct as experiences in consciousness.

We have suggested that most of our sexual impulses are more a product of the mind than of the body. Of course, the mind participates in and is the seeker and experiencer of *all* that we do, including sex. Of course, it is also the mind that seeks the more specific form of gratification. We do not mean that this is wrong or that it should be otherwise, but rather we must understand the role of the mind not only as the *experiencer* but also as the *builder.*

A Place Prepared

Jesus said, "I go to prepare a place for you." (John 14:2) The mind is the mediator between the temporal and the eternal, between the physical and the spiritual; it builds or prepares the place of our experiences, not only for the rest of this incarnation but also in the dimensions in which we may sojourn after the death of the flesh body. The readings say that the place which is prepared for us is that of our own construction by virtue of the fact that the Christ within us is the mind.

In our solar system there are eight dimensions, each represented by one of the planets. (For example, the earth is related to the third dimension.) Between incarnations in the earth, we may have one or a series of sojourns in another dimension associated with the planets. The planetary sojourns relate especially to *mental* experiences, whereas the earthly sojourns relate more to emotional experiences. The quality of an individual's mentality derives particularly from planetary sojourns.

The planet Venus represents the fourth dimension, that plane of consciousness or that dimension of awareness related especially to the complex of concerns regarding love and sex. The language of the readings regarding the specific nature of sojourns in Venus and the qualities of experience associated with that dimension are examined below. (The expression, "the love influence" when referring to Venus, indicates what would be only a constructive influence for the individual; however, the readings point out, love has its "extremes.")

In Venus the body-form is near to that in the three-dimensional plane. For it is what may be said to be rather *all*-inclusive! For it is that ye would call love—which, to be sure, may be licentious, selfish; which also may be so large, so inclusive as to take on the less of self and more of the ideal, more of that which is *giving*.

What is love? Then what is Venus? It is beauty, love, hope, charity—yet all of these have their extremes. But these extremes are not in the expressive nature or manner as may be found in that tone or attunement of Uranus; for they (in Venus) are more in the order that they blend as one with another. 5755-1

The above information was given for an individual who, following a Venusian sojourn, had an incarnation in France in which he "abused" his experience from Venus through love of self.

So the entity passed through that experience, and on entering into materiality abused same; as the wastrel who sought those expressions of same in the loveliness for self alone, without giving—giving of self in return for same.

Hence we find the influences wielded in the sojourn of the entity from the astrological aspects or emotions of

the mental nature are the ruling, yet must be governed by a standard.

And when self is the standard, it becomes very distorted in materiality. 5755-1

In Venus is found love of home, companions, friends and close relations. Those with a Venus influence make friends easily, yet one person was warned not to let "entanglements of the heart, of the fleshly desires" mar her abilities (2682-5) Another was told:

In Venus we find the lovely becoming the expressions in activities in which there is the beauty seen in love, in companionship, in association, in music, in art, in *all* the things that bespeak of the *loveliness* even of nature and the material things, rather than the expression of same in the earthy form or manner. 949-13

Mr. [2416] was told that he was able to see beauty because of the Venus influence, but was cautioned that it was both an adverse and benevolent influence, depending upon his application.

In Venus we find that the beauty, the joy, the very natures of things become expressive. When they are applied in relationships to others *as* creative influences, they grow beautiful. When they are applied as emotions that satisfy only *bodily* desires, they become stumbling blocks sooner or later. 2416-1

A talented and successful costume designer in the present lifetime, Mr. [2416] had this same talent during an incarnation in France in the court of the Louises. His position of authority enabled him to influence the fashions in a way that would either "inflame the desire for body" or would "blend with the characteristics of the individual." He was warned about this for his present work:

Thus the entity gained and lost, gained and lost. For, that of any creation of the mind which is to appeal to the

animal rather than the spiritual natures, or mental-mindedness, is sin. That which is created within the mind that may present such measures as to laud the virtues, minimize the vices in the experience of human relationships, is good.

Think of these, as ye apply thyself in the applications of thy abilities, in the designs for those in *whatever* walk of life or of depicting the activities of individuals.

The body-beautiful—there is little or nothing more holy, but *that* exposed or covered in such manners as to arouse *only* the desire for *possession* is evil! 2416-1

Influences from planetary sojourns are experienced primarily as urges. As we study the kind of influences about which some people were warned, we may better analyze the source of some of our innate qualities.

Then, both in the inner self and in the material urge, the Venus influence has brought at times those things that were as confusions in the experience of the entity in the present. For, while love is of God and is God, it—the impelling force in same—can be made into the forms that wreck the souls of men and women, if not born of Him. If born of those things that partake only of the body-physical, it becomes a stumbling stone to the weary feet; yea, it becomes a rolling stone to those that in their own selves have seen a vision or find strength in their own purpose. 585-2

A young male homosexual was told:

From Venus we find both conflicting influences and those of friendships and associations that will bring closer relationships. But these, too, may become as stumbling blocks to the understanding lest they be made not for self-glorification, for self-indulgence, for self-exaltation, but rather used in the manner that He gave; that the glory of God may be manifested in and *through* those relationships, those friendships. 1089-3

Finally, let us study the answer given to [272] who had been told that her Venus influence was afflicted. A careful study of this information may be most instructive regarding the nature of the experience in Venus.

Q-4. Does the part in my life reading concerning Venus deal with the question I am struggling with now [whether or not to separate from her husband]?

A-4. Yes; deals with the question the body is struggling with now.

For, as we have given in part, where the experience in the earth has been such as for the choice or will of the soul to manifest in the environ of Venus, that there might be the consummation in act per se of those influences in the material affairs of individuals, when reduced to that activity where all influences are of a conglomerate or heterogeneous mass in the mental and impulse and influence in flesh force, each must meet, each must understand, that experience!

Hence, in some thoughts, this has been called karma.

272-7

Rapport, Telepathy and Prayer

All subconscious minds are in contact one with another. This contact seems to be more a potential than an active, ongoing, direct exchange of mental experiences. However, it is certainly true that the closer the relationship or rapport between people, the more likely that specific, telepathic exchanges occur. Parapsychological research has demonstrated that schoolteachers who have a good rapport with their pupils are significantly more effective as agents in telepathy experiments than teachers who are not as favored by their students.

One of the books most highly recommended by the readings, *Hudson's Law of Psychic Phenomena*, indicates that during hypnosis the subjective mind of one individual telepathically contacts the subjective mind of the other. Russian researchers have demonstrated hypnosis at a distance by telepathy and have records of the hypnotist having kept the subject under this kind of influence for as long as 30 to 40 years. We may begin to entertain the likelihood that all deep hypnosis is telepathic in the sense of the rapport between the individuals' subconscious minds. For this reason, the Cayce readings, which occasionally recommended hypnosis, were concerned with the quality of the mind of the hypnotist; not because the hypnotist might take physical advantage of the subject or try to influence him or her mentally in some undesirable manner, but because the rapport between the two subconscious minds made the recipient more telepathically vulnerable to the general quality of the hypnotist's psyche.

What about the kind of link which may be established between the subconscious mind of one who prays and the recipient of that prayer? A group of people who had gathered around Edgar Cayce to begin a great healing work through meditation and prayer for others, asked what connection must be established with those they were trying to help. The answer included the statement that "the imaginings of thine self become *materialized* in others' actions." (281-2)

This sobering yet beautiful promise of the power of prayer should put us on special notice regarding the highly energized thoughts we direct toward others. As pilgrims on the spiritual path, we have a great responsibility toward our fellow man.

Let us use those insights as a perspective for examining the impact not only on our own lives but especially on the lives of others that our thoughts and our fantasies may make. All "the imaginings [which may even] become *materialized* in others' actions." With implications of this potential in mind, let us examine a story with more specific detail as to how the sexual motive may establish rapport.

A team of sleep and dream researchers conducted laboratory experiments which demonstrated conclusively that a "sender," by concentrating on a target picture while a subject is asleep in a distant room, can influence the content of the subject's dreams. One subject who was most consistent in receiving telepathic impressions has described publicly on more than one occasion how he was so successful. He reported that, upon arriving at the laboratory, he would try to locate a member of the research staff, some young woman to whom he was sexually attracted. He would develop a flirtation of sorts with her and then ask her to be the sender in the experiment. As he fell asleep, he would think about his talking with her.

This episode illustrates the manner in which any one of the seven spiritual centers (in this case, the sexual center) may be mobilized as a psychic or spiritual center. By arousing motivations associated with that center's function as transmitter and receiver, a telepathic rapport may be established at that level of vibration.

A woman of prayer who was especially concerned about her brother spent a few minutes every day in prayer for him. One night a voice in her dream said, "Thou shalt not both bless and curse." Upon awakening, she immediately realized that she had been spending a great deal more of her time in projecting her unhappiness with him and in complaining than in constructive praying. We may use this example to consider the potential of fantasy or sexual thoughts in relationship to other concerns (such as prayer concerns), which we may project to others.

The readings say often, "Why worry when you can pray?" As we consider the telepathic potential of thought, we may paraphrase that to "Why send worry thoughts to the subconscious when you can send healing thoughts?" Taking this one step further, we may now evaluate the desirability of the sexual thoughts that we send to another with respect to the kind of thoughts that we personally and ideally would prefer that that other person receive.

Normal Fantasy

It is very important, of course, for us to understand and properly evaluate the role of fantasy in the normal sexual life. Sexual expression is not just physical; optimally, it involves the mental and spiritual as well. What is the normal role for mental activity in relation to sexual expression?

A young woman who came to a psychiatric hospital was given a diagnosis of reactive depression. At the time she was admitted, she was very disturbed. She had been engaged to a young man whom she loved who was killed in an automobile accident. Later she married another man; but, in the course of making love with her husband, found herself fantasizing about the previous lover. This was the essential content of her depression. Upon discovering the psychiatric staff's open acceptance of the nature of her fantasy, she was greatly reassured and almost immediately restored to a consistent and normal mood and spirit. She was assured that it was perfectly normal, even in the act of making love, to fantasize being with someone other than the present lover. She was very quickly discharged from the hospital with an immediate and apparently permanent recovery from a depression that had disabled her for months previously.

More recent research has provided a statistical basis for the normal nature of the fantasy experiences for this patient. As is the case with many considerations, the problem may not be so much "where we are" as "where we are going."

Anyone for whom we care enough to spend any considerable time in fantasy probably needs and deserves our prayers more than other imaginings. But if "the imaginings of thine self become *materialized* in others' actions," what kinds of impetus to action are we projecting upon those whom we love?

A serious consideration of fantasy includes a range of questions from what may be "normal" to that experienced by the individual as "necessary." There are extreme patterns of overt sexual behavior and of the inner life as well. For some individuals a certain thought pattern or fantasy is not only the most exciting to the individual but becomes necessary for sexual response. In its more serious forms a compulsive quality requires the individual through unconscious pressures to enact repetitively a pattern which may even be repulsive to the conscious mind.

As we seek an understanding of the role that sexual expression can play in a well-balanced life, we must confront the role of fantasy. What is the extent to which such thought patterns are to be encouraged, enabling us to be normal, spontaneous and free? To what extent are they to be eliminated because otherwise they enslave us?

Part of the answer may lie in the quality of the experience. Exploring the boundaries of the inner life, even sharing these with a loved one, may broaden one's acceptance of self and others. Such inner experiences may enable us to meet and deal effectively with the mind's deeper memories without our meeting or enacting them in outer expression. However, as we suppress or repress the mental imagery which arises from the unconscious, it may later be given less desirable expression in unconsciously motivated overt acts. For example, if a normally heterosexual person has an exciting homosexual fantasy, a measure of acceptance and exploration of this may lead to enhanced integration and self-understanding and intercept a series of events which might lead to an unnecessary physical enactment of the fantasy.

Part of the answer to this probably lies in understanding or appreciating the more pervasive motives and ideals that characterize the overall nature of the relationship. Where there is love and trust, mutual respect and consideration, the boundaries of normal expression may be deepened. On the other hand, where the mode of expression is compulsive, required and restrictive, then undesirable developments may ensue.

Sometimes, because we are souls with experiences of previous earth lives, we come into this life experience with a ready-made inner life that seems to compel us toward certain modes of thought and expression. Sometimes we seem to be the unwilling prisoners of such forms and, try as we may, we are unable to free ourselves from these inherent compulsions. To get on your own spiritual path is just what is needed. It is imperative for an individual with such problems not to allow his own unaccepting or self-condemning attitude to keep him from feeling that he can properly begin to move and progress on his own spiritual path. Let us remind ourselves again that we are taught to "resist not evil." (Matthew 5:39) We are to supplant and supersede less desirable patterns with more desirable ones. This is done by nurturing the good rather than attacking the bad.

As we begin to put more things right in our lives, then the more difficult problems which otherwise would not seem to budge come under the transforming power of the spirit flowing through us. Patterns heretofore seen as stumbling blocks become, much to our surprise, stepping-stones which enable us to be of greater service, rather than disqualifying us from progress on the path. This is ever the problem: how to change a stumbling block into a stepping-stone. The answer is to begin to do all we can to bring about attunement to the flow of the spirit within. As the love and grace of the spirit flows through our lives in meditation and service toward others, that same power transforms within us even the most recalcitrant and incorrigible patterns.

Numerous forms of thought and behavior may be evaluated for their relative contribution to add to or detract from progress on the spiritual path. Included would be the use of literature or photographs, certain types of music or certain types of dress for either exciting or tempering the sexual response. Rather than list these and try to evaluate their respective acceptability, let us work with these attitudes:

(1) We will start where we are;

(2) We will designate spiritual activities and practices that we feel are requisite to our spiritual growth; and

(3) We will endeavor more and more to be true and faithful in our practice and application of them, knowing that as we raise the energy in meditation, we will be given new strength of will, a new hierarchy of motivations and a growing sense of closeness to and guidance by the Divine.

In this context we may be most assured that that which we may have worried about or condemned in ourselves may be healed, diminished or put into its proper, constructive perspective. When we question or doubt, we should turn to the Lord, who will give us the desire and the power to do and be that which He would have us be. These are matters of choice, and we need to be consistent and persistent with these choices. However, there are also psychological concerns about utilizing certain mechanisms (repression, rationalization or denial) which have serious detrimental effects, psychologically and spiritually. We need not pretend to be something that we are not; strength of resolution is not necessarily a sign of healing or of attunement. The spirit of confession, on the other hand, or the prayer, "Lord, be merciful to me," reiterated frequently in the sincerity and desire to change, assures an answer from Him with the love and power that is the only true source of transformation.

The Nature of That Called Desire

If we are to understand sex, we must understand the nature of desire, since without a doubt the initiator of sexual expression is desire. We should not be surprised that the readings contain some very challenging information on this subject. Let us study some of these references in detail. First, considering the origin of desire:

Q-2. Where does desire originate?
A-2. Will. **262-62**

Desire, as will, is a portion then of the spiritual self. It is a continuous thing. Then gratifying of self, or the gratification for itself alone, may oft turn and rend they that would indulge in same without standards, ideals, or the showing forth of a purposefulness in the experience or activity. **1597-1**

. . . the desires are of a threefold nature. Spiritual, physical, and material. Two are the gratifications of self. The other is the keeping of that Divine Force that is within. The mental is the builder, for thoughts are deeds—they may become crimes or they may become miracles,

whether guided by the spirit of truth, or as to the gratification of self's own interests. 451-1

Desire may be godly or ungodly, dependent upon the purpose, the aim, the emotions aroused.

Does it bring, then, self-abstinence? or does it bring self-desire?

Does it bring love? Does it bring long-suffering? Is it gentle? Is it kind?

Then, these be the judgments upon which the entity uses those influences upon the lives of others.

Does it relieve suffering, as the abilities of the entity grow? Does it relieve the mental anguish, the mental disturbances which arise? Does it bring also healing—of body, of mind, to the individual? Is it healed for constructive force, or for that as will bring pain, sorrow, hate and fear into the experience of others?

These be the judgments upon which the entity makes its choices, as it guides, directs or gives counsel to those who are seeking—seeking—What? That Light—which has become, which is, which ever was the light of the world! 1947-3

Know, all the desires of the body have their place in thy experience. These are to be used and not abused. All things are holy unto the Lord, that He has given to man as appetites or physical desires, yet these are to be used to the glory of God and not in that direction of selfishness alone. 3234-1

As may be well gained by many, habit and desires are akin. Habit, however, is a physical reaction to the senses of the body, while desire is both mental, physical *and* spiritual, and when *inordinate* desire has been created by the use of those forces that make for the activities in all the sensory forces of the body, it becomes as the possession of those forces from without and from within that create, without the cleansing influence of the spiritual entering in from without, that which is hard to cope with. 486-1

. . . *for thoughts are deeds*, and are children of the relation reached between the mental and the soul, and has its relation to spirit and soul's plane of existence, as they do in the physical or earth plane. What one thinks continually, they become; what one cherishes in their heart and mind they make a part of the pulsation of their heart, through their own blood cells, and build in their own physical, that which its spirit and soul must feed upon, and that with which it will be possessed, when it passes into the realm for which the other experiences of what it has gained here in the physical plane, must be used. 3744-4

One of the more advanced discourses on desire is given in the Study Group readings related to the lesson on desire in *A Search for God*, Book II. In this reading the specific relationships of the mind and will are developed more fully:

As given in the Scripture, there was breathed into man the soul. Biologically, man makes himself as an animal of the physical; with the desires that are as the instinct in animal for the preservation of life, for the development of species, and for food. These three are those forces that are instinct in the animal and in man. If by that force of will man uses these within self for the aggrandizement of such elements in his nature, these then become the material desires—or are the basis of carnal influences, and belittle the spiritual or soul body of such an individual.

So, the basis of physical desire is adding to, contributing to, or gathering together in forces that which makes for the abilities for such a soul, such an individual, to reveal in those forces that are of the animal nature of that individual. Hence he becomes, through carnal or physical desire, one who has no recourse through other than spirit; though he is given the soul that it may be everlasting, that it may be a companion with the Creator, that it may be aware of itself yet one with those influences that make for the spiritualizing of that force which is

creative in itself—that makes for god-likeness in the individual soul or activity.

Then, what is the basis of mental desire? The mental as an attribute is also of the animal, yet in man—with his intellect—the ability to make comparisons, to reason, to have the reactions through the senses; that are raised to the forces of activity such that they create for man the environs about him and make for change in hereditary influences in the experience of such a soul. These are the gifts with that free-will agent, or attributes of same; or mind is a development of the application of will respecting desire that has become—in its essence—used as a grace, the gift to give praise for that which it has applied in its experience.

Then, the mental desire that is to laud self, to appraise self above its fellows, or to use that gift in its application to the various activities in the experiences of self or others, makes for that channel through which the carnal desires only become the stumbling blocks in the experiences of those who dwell on same.

For, as has been given as one of the immutable laws, that which the mind of a *soul*—a SOUL—dwells upon it becomes; for mind is the builder. And if the mind is in attune with the law of the force that brought the soul into being, it becomes spiritualized in its activity. If the mind is dwelling upon or directed in that desire towards the activities of the carnal influences, then it becomes destructive in such a force.

Hence, as it has been given, "Let Thy will, O God, be my desire! Let the desire of my heart, my body, my mind, be Thy will, O Father, in the experiences that I may have in the earth!" 262-63

From this perspective we may ask, as did the members in the original group:

Q-8. Is it necessary to give up physical desires for spiritual development?

A-8. Rather spiritualize the physical desires as He did in the garden. What there is shown thee as to how the

physical, the spiritual, fought—as it were—one with another? "Father, let this cup pass from me." This is as every experience in the physical man when there is the fear of the loss in this or that direction. There is the constant, "Father, save me from this—from this." Yet, even as He, if there has been builded in thine experience as was in His experience—offering Himself for the world—then thou must pass through same, in making the physical desire and the will of the Father as one, that there may be the cleansing in the soul of those things that may bring the consciousness of the Oneness with the Father in whatever realm. 262-64

This advice stressed spiritualizing the desire. How may we accomplish this?

***Thus* may you spiritualize desire, whether for those things that bring the comforts or the necessities or the activities in thine experience in the earth. What is spiritualizing desire? Desire that the Lord may use thee as a channel of blessings to all whom ye may contact day by day; that there may come in thine experience whatever is necessary that thou be cleansed every whit. For, when the soul shines forth in thine daily walks, in thine conversation, in thine thoughts, in thine meditation, and it is in that realm where the spirit of truth and life may commune it same day by day, *then* indeed do ye spiritualize desire in the earth. 262-65**

Finally, if we are truly seeking, we are assured of some *very* special aid:

Q-9. What should we hold in mind when we hold the affirmation in the present lesson, "Let thy desire be my desire," etc.?

A-9. What to hold in mind? Hold the Christ before thee, ever. For, He has promised to take His own self and to take thy burden upon Himself, as He bore same. Rather would thy prayer be, "*I cannot bear this alone, my Savior, my Christ. I seek Thy aid.*" And such a cry has

never, no never, been denied—the believing and *acting* heart. 262-65

As a concluding perspective on mind and desire, the following reading is given as a study, offering the full context for this supreme challenge: The most important experience for anyone is to know what is the ideal spiritually.

In giving an interpretation of the physical, mental and spiritual well-being of a body, in terms of a mental and spiritual reading—as we have so oft indicated, Mind is the Builder.

The mind uses its spiritual ideals to build upon. And the mind also uses the material desires as the destructive channels, or it is the interference by the material desires that prevents a body and a mind from keeping in perfect accord with its ideal.

Thus, these continue ever in the material plane to be as warriors one *with another.* Physical emergencies or physical conditions may oft be used as excuses, or as justifications for the body choosing to do this or that.

Ought these *things so to be, according* to thy ideal?

Then, the more important, the most important experience of this or any individual entity is to first know what *is* the ideal—spiritually.

Who and what is thy pattern?

Throughout the experience of man in the material world, at various seasons and periods, teachers or "would be" teachers have come; setting up certain forms or certain theories as to manners in which an individual shall control the appetites of the body or of the mind, so as to attain to some particular phase of development.

There has also come a teacher who was bold enough to declare himself as the son of the living God. He set no rules of appetite. He set no rules of ethics, other than "As ye would that men should do to you, do ye even so to them," and to know "Inasmuch as ye do it unto the least of these, thy brethren, ye do it unto thy Maker." He declared that the kingdom of heaven is within each individual entity's consciousness, to be attained, to be

aware of—through meditating upon the fact that God is the Father of every soul.

Jesus, the Christ, is the mediator. And in Him, and in the study of His examples in the earth, is *life*—and that ye may have it more abundantly. He came to demonstrate, to manifest, to give life and light to all.

Here, then, ye find a friend, a brother, a companion. As He gave, "I call ye not servants, but brethren." For, as many as believe, to them He gives power to become the children of God, the Father; joint heirs with this Jesus, the Christ, in the knowledge and in the awareness of this presence abiding ever with those who set this ideal before them.

What, then, is this as an ideal?

As concerning thy fellow man, He gave, "As ye would that others do to you, do ye even so to them," take no thought, worry not, be not overanxious about the body. For He knoweth what ye have need of. In the place thou art, in the consciousness in which ye find yourself, is that which is *today, now,* needed for thy greater, thy better, thy more wonderful unfoldment.

But today *hear* His voice, "Come unto me, all that are weak or that are heavyladen, and I will give you rest from those worries, peace from those anxieties." For the Lord loveth those who put their trust *wholly* in Him.

This, then, is that attitude of mind that puts away hates, malice, anxiety, jealousy. And it creates in their stead, in that Mind is the Builder, the fruits of the spirit—love, patience, mercy, long-suffering, kindness, gentleness. And these—against such there is no law. They break down barriers, they bring peace and harmony, they bring the outlook upon life of not finding fault because someone "forgot," someone's judgment was bad, someone was selfish today. These ye can overlook, for so did He.

In His own experience with those that He had chosen out of the world, if He had held disappointment in their leaving Him to the mercies of an indignant high priest, a determined lawyer and an unjust steward, what would have been *thy* hope, thy promise today?

For He, though with the ability to destroy, thought not of such but rather gave Himself; that the Creative Forces, God, might be reconciled to that pronouncement, that judgment. And thus mercy, through the shedding of blood, came into man's experience. 357-13

5

Sex and the Individual

When we think of sex, sexual expressions and sexual problems, we are likely to think too quickly of the quality of relationship that exist between two individuals. This viewpoint may mislead us to address only the relationship itself and thus obscure the fact that each individual in the relationship is a sexual being. Each has a vast background of factors which make him or her unique and which, if more fully understood, would aid in a truer understanding of what may transpire in relationship with another. As we consider the individual, specifically with reference to the sexual life, we know that numerous factors have combined and interacted to bring him to the point at which he presently finds himself. Several categories of influences may be defined.

First is the hereditary contribution. The extent of this influence on behavior has been greatly underestimated by Western man. We know that there are great individual differences of sexual sensitivity and sexual motivation, and the hereditary factor may be a strong component of these differences. No doubt, the activities of the endocrine glands and the balance of the endocrine system make major contributions to the individual's sensitivity, excitation and level of drive. But these endocrine activities have themselves a hereditary basis.

A second factor is the contribution of the individual's environmental, learning or training experiences. Freud drew our attention to the importance of these, but with the waning of his influence on modern psychology, there may be a tendency again to underestimate the role of childhood experiences in forming adult attitudes toward self and sex, including inhibitions and preferred forms of expression. Many times childhood memories are far more emotionally charged and powerful influences of sexual attitudes than current adult involvement.

To these two major sources of determining influences, which present-day behavioral scientists recognize, we may add from our study of the Cayce readings two additional factors; namely, the *emotional experiences* from numerous incarnations in the earth and the *mental experiences* from planetary sojourns between incarnations.

These are the four major sources of determinants in our lives: heredity, environment, previous incarnations in the earth and planetary sojourns. Of course, the essential nature of our being is spiritual: We are made in the image of God and are children of the Most High. With our free wills we may, at any moment, mobilize all that we have been previously into a number of different postures and orientations, and with our choices we can place ourselves quickly in a different stance or attitude.

In addition to these, there are, of course, outside factors that influence us to a greater or lesser degree as we permit them. These include the attitudes of those about us and the extent to which we allow our family, our peers, our friends, our partners to influence us about sex, its frequency or form of expression. Society makes a complex contribution in terms of psychological and religious attitudes and of role expectations, culturally defining expected behavior for people who are in love. In addition, we may be influenced by other consciousnesses. The readings indicate that all subconscious minds are in contact, one with another, and thus we may experience a contribution from the combined thought of mankind. Futhermore, we may open ourselves to influences from other planes, such as those of angelic forces and discarnate entities.

All of these factors contribute to the dynamic and ongoing process of the individual, his attitudes and motivations regarding sex and the quality of his relationships with others. Such an array of influences may seem potentially confusing, if not overwhelming; indeed it may become so unless we each are very clear about which forces we are going to allow to influence our own lives.

Then, when these are weighed, choose thou. For, as has ever been, there is no influence that may supersede the will of man; for such are the gifts unto the sons of men that they may make their souls such as to be the companionship with the All-Wise, All-Creative Forces, or separate from them. For, there is no impelling force other than that, "If ye will be my people, I will be your God." It is always thus. And when faults arise, and when temptations come, these are from contemplating on or visioning from those things that would satisfy some activity in the carnal force of an individual. 440-16

What Is Normal?

Since sex is and has been such an individual and private concern, most people have wondered about the normalcy of their own feelings and experiences. This problem, or question, has been intensified by the extremity of some of the sexual prohibitions promulgated by dogmatic religious teachings and, in turn, incorporated even into the law of the land. Laws enacted hundreds of years ago made illegal an array of forms of sexual expression which, in today's society, are considered "normal."

We have tried to define and delineate criteria for the spiritual path; one of these has been to move away from self-condemnation toward acceptance of ourselves *where* and *as* we are. The statistical studies of human sexuality may aid us in self-acceptance. Beginning with the work of Kinsey and continuing to this day with some of the carefully conducted objective research, there has been a considerable positive contribution, enabling many people to become more accepting of themselves, their feelings and their experiences.

Nevertheless, as we contemplate the magnitude of the implications of reincarnation, we realize that most of us have been incarnate in the earth plane scores of times. We still carry minutely and thoroughly detailed records of these experiences in our present being. Therefore, we may see that, contrary to what we had previously thought, each individual may be far more complex and unique in the richness and detail of his sexual experiences in life's various phases. Thus our qualities, specifically sexual qualities, may not at all be properly understood or appreciated if we measure ourselves simply from the perspective of a statistical study. Our very uniqueness may make us feel too different and thus cut off in some way from others or embarrassed about our true feelings and experiences. We may remain guilt-ridden and self-condemning in the face of our understanding of the expectations of our religion or society or our own spiritual aspirations.

The question of what is normal may become a burden. The real need is to know that we are *what* and *where* we are for reasons, the principles of which, if not the details, may be understood. The need is to *normalize* in the direction of our own spiritual path, to dwell upon ideals rather than idiosyncrasies.

Attitudes

Even though there are the influences of all that we have been, all that we are and all of the forces that are impinging upon us at any certain time, we still have *free will* with which to choose, both with respect to attitudes and, subsequently, with respect to courses of action. The first step, the formulation of attitudes as the most immediate and orienting activity, is of the greatest importance. A change of attitude does not change everything else; but, as it changes the way in which we look at things, it becomes the first step in directing ourselves to a new course of activity. We actually have a choice as to how we view ourselves and as to how we feel about ourselves, about our circumstances and about those with whom we have to deal.

One of the most effective ways of working with attitude is to become more aware and more positive regarding what we *say* to ourselves *about* ourselves. Many times major changes in our lives can be made simply by beginning to say something different about ourselves. For example, a person may for years say to himself, "I cannot fly in airplanes." However, at some point, he may simply say, "I *can* fly in an airplane." He tries it; it is not a problem at all, and now a whole new opportunity for national and world travel opens up that otherwise would have remained closed to him. Because of childhood experiences, concepts of ourselves, religious or family attitudes, or previous experiences, we may have begun in our sexual lives to say and reiterate certain things to ourselves that limit, disable or impoverish our attitudes toward ourselves and others. What we *say* to ourselves we build. Present attitudes may not be a reality in and of themselves; nevertheless, they contribute to the kind of reality which we will experience in the future.

We would do well to be very specific in examining our attitudes respecting what we *actually* say about ourselves and what we would *prefer* to say about ourselves. For example, do we say, "I'm the one who is always imposed upon," or "I'm the one who's always expected to take the initiative," or, "I'm the one who's always abused or mistreated," or "I'm the one who always has to make the special effort"? Then we can begin to replace these with another consciousness such as, "I'm the one whom God has forgiven and specially blessed to be in this opportunity for service," or, "I'm the one who can bring light and love into this situation and this relationship," or, "I'm the one who can truly forgive and forget and start afresh and live life in a joyous and creative manner." No matter what our earlier circumstances may have been, these affirmations may be truer of ourselves in terms of the reality of our present being and purpose.

Thus, as we become conscious of what we say about ourselves and affirm a greater reality in which we move in our new relationship with others, we may develop an entirely different and more promising expression of our lives. Here is an example of an attitude-changing affirmation:

Q-14. Will the Forces please tell me what I should think and work towards for the reconstructions of my life?

A-14. Find first that which is the *ideal;* not physically, but spiritually. What *is* thy ideal? What *thinkest* thou of life? Why life at all? What is the purpose of life? Then *look* at self in relationship to that which is the ideal. Let's illustrate:

There is some knowledge and understanding of what is the ideal moral relationship with individuals in their various walks of life, and as to what is the conception of the Creator as respecting the consideration of Its (the Creator's) creation. Follow it? See?

Then, as these are the ideal relationships, make for self that thought that "*This body, this mind, is becoming more and more normal, and capable of meeting and dealing with all manners of relationships, that will be as near in keeping with that I have set as my ideal as circumstances, surroundings, conditions at the moment permit; and I will not only think and say I will act that way but I will do it!*" 911-4, F.24

If we sincerely desire and affirm, "This body, this mind is becoming more and more normal," we will most surely become "capable of meeting and dealing with all manners of relationships" with respect to sexual concerns of every kind.

Categories of Expression

In dealing with the overall picture of sexual expression, two major categories are of concern to us. These deal with *what* (that is, what form of expression) and *with whom* (that is, who is to be my partner). The *what* is a question of type of sex (for example, intercourse, oral sex, masturbation or homosexual expression). Some forms may be considered pathological, such as sadomasochism or some of the fetishes. Questons of *what* also involve the consideration of whether it is more right or more in accord with the spiritual path to express or gratify oneself sexually by one method rather than another.

The question of *with whom* has to deal with selection of a partner, ongoing interaction with only one partner or experiences with several partners. These decisions involve questions of trust, faithfulness and fidelity and the expectations of the responsibilities for others.

The deep-seated preferences which we hold for a certain partner and a specific form of expression have been developed through experiences of the present life, especially the experiences of childhood, of previous lives and of sojourns in other planes. During all of these experiences the attitudes held and the accompanying mental processes are more formative than the experiences themselves. Thus we come as souls into this specific incarnation with strong predisposing patterns toward the selection of a certain type of person or a certain individual as a partner. We bring strong predisposing patterns which incline us to be drawn toward or especially excited by certain forms of expression in preference to other forms.

Some people seem to have settled for themselves the question of *what* but struggle with the question of *with whom*. They may insist that the only permissible sex is heterosexual intercourse. Yet for some such individuals there remain strong problems and decisions to be made respecting the choice of a partner. There may be problems of fidelity or even promiscuity. Other people seem to have settled the question of *with whom* but still struggle with the problem of *what*. They may have strong notions about fidelity to one partner—perhaps even establishing a lifetime relationship. Yet for these people there may remain a problem of form of expression, having such a demanding or even compulsive quality that the individual remains with a sense of beong unfulfilled except in the sexual expression of such a form. Many times the form preferred by one is offensive to the partner. An example of this problem is seen in the desire of some men to dress in women's clothing—as a sexual expression. Such an individual, though married to the wife of his preference, may yet have such a compulsion. Some of these patterns seriously complicate the individual's overall life, making it extremely difficult, if not impossible, to have a satisfactory sexual life in term of the form's demands and still interact successfully with society.

It is not that the *form* is necessarily bad, but the power we give it may enable it to rule our lives. Therefore, we may say that any form is undesirable if its compulsive requirements make the individual a prisoner to it. The more restrictive and demanding it is on the individual, the less desirable it may be with respect to the person's overall integration. If the continuation of this form impedes the soul's pilgrimage on the path or his effectiveness in serving others, and if progress is not made in his lifetime to free himself from such a compulsive form, then in subsequent lives the individual may be even more of a prisoner to this pattern. The ideal is to be free.

The major problem with choices of *with whom* involves the impact on the lives of others. There is a recent and increasing advocacy of a standard that says, "Anything is acceptable if it occurs between consenting adults." A relationship may be entered with both consenting, but one of these "consenting" adults may be very vulnerable to being hurt by disappointment or guilt or may be working with other problems, such as a jealous spouse, that may make a sexual encounter (though freely entered into) more burdensome than helpful. The spiritual path invites us to the challenge that we are our brother's keeper in a spiritual sense. We have a responsibility to others, even for what they feel within themselves in response to our actions. They who would be our partners have responsibilities, in turn, to many others.

These considerations of *what* and *with whom* define the two major areas, as it were, within which most of our decisions about sex must be made. We have suggested a major consideration with respect to each. Regarding *what*, an initial standard should include the ideal to become *free*. Regarding *with whom*, an initial standard should include a consideration of responsibility *to* others and the responsibilities *of* others. The present chater will deal now with questions of form, and the next chapter with relationships. A working understanding of both of these areas of concern requires a clear understanding of karma and how it functions in the present.

Understanding Karma

The concept of reincarnation and its law of karma have not only been greatly substantiated but also may be the only way in which we can make sense and meaning of man's experience in the earth plane. Even so, many people have a great deal of difficulty in being comfortable with these principles. Others have an immediate response of acceptance; reincarnation rings true to them the first time they hear of it. However, the immediate acceptance of these principles as being logical and equitable does not mean that the student has a clear understanding of how the law truly works in the individual's relationships to himself, to others and to the universe.

The law of karma is frequently thought of as the law of cause and effect. This terminology implies a beginning and an end, whereas the whole principle of reincarnation—and thus karma—implies a continuity of life and experience. A truer picture of karma is given in the expression "like begets like." This understanding demonstrates the flow of life without the limitation of event-and-judgment or debt-and-payment implications in the other understandings of karma. Sometimes karma is thought of as an opportunity to repay the debts we have incurred in previous lives. There is no way in which a repayment is either possible or required. It is true that we must set in order some things in our lives. Sometimes we go off in an undesirable direction, and this must be put aright. Such corrections can be made even in subsequent lifetimes. But meeting self does not mean paying debts. It means that if we are off the path, there may be some pain and effort involved in getting back on it.

Sometimes the word *retribution* is applied to the concept of karma. This again is in error because it connotes an independent judge, weighing all circumstances and handing down a sentence involving a punishment appropriate to the nature of the crime. We may not truly say that the law of God is retributive. It is rather that we meet ourselves. As co-creators with God, we build patterns which have continuity through subsequent lifetimes; these patterns affect or modify our relationship to ourselves, to others and to God. Since they are of our own creation, they are a part of us, and thus have to be met as we seek to put the whole of our being in attunement with God.

Carnal desires and their subsequent sexual expressions play a major role in our continuing incarnations in the earth. Much of that with which we have to deal, which may be called karmic in nature, has to do specifically with sex. Therefore, if we are to understand problems related to sex, we need to understand the nature of karma.

Let us imagine a silkworm which spins a cocoon about itself in such a way that it is completely encased and shut off from the outside world. It such a way karma is a "thought form" pattern of our own making, standing between us and our perceptions of ourselves and of the forces about us, including God and others; it is not just a record of an action. What we have thought and done becomes a part of ourselves in such a manner as to influence and color our perceptions. If in a past life we have been "untrue," we may tend to see or fear in others a tendency to be untrue. If we have left a relationship in preference for the religious life, we may now be fearful that our spiritually oriented partner will place a higher priority on spiritual things than on the present relationship.

One of the problems in our attitudes toward karma is considering it a record of something done a long time ago, arbitrarily opened at any time, at which point payment is required. An analogy suggested by the Cayce readings has the law of karma acting much in the same manner as food which is ingested and assimilated thoughout the whole body. This analogy of assimilation shows us how our karmic experiences are a continuing part of the fullness of our beings and are as contemporary as this present moment. A commonplace put-down of the study of reincarnation is the statement, "Why dwell on the past? What I'm concerned about is the present!" We are what we are right now because the fullness of all of our experiences is *present* with us now. It is not so much that we have to pay for what we were, but rather that what we did in the past is assimilated into and at this moment is a part of our present being. In other words, if we are to understand the present, we must take cognizance of previous life influences.

It is true that there is the element of time; certain past patterns may merge into our present lives in specific events and sequences. For one on the spiritual path these karmic patterns may be met "in due season"; that is, at the appropriate and optimum time for our learning from them and for utilizing them as stepping-stones instead of stumbling blocks. However, as we get off the path onto detours because of misguided choices, we may confront these patterns under more painful and less optimal circumstances. Nevertheless, we are assured by God's promise that He will not allow us to be tempted above that we are able to bear, but will make for us a way of escape. (I Corinthians 10:13)

Karmic Scenarios

In working with the concepts of reincarnations and karma, it is not at all necessary for us to have an unquestionably accurate psychic reading giving us the precise details of previous lives. Knowing these will not necessarily even be helpful, because that with which we have to work is more a matter of changing attitudes through understanding than of knowing the specifics of historical events. As we study reincarnation and karma in more general terms, we may become acquainted with an array of types of past lifetimes which constitute modes for our personal reflection regarding our specific present life problems.

Those who are students of the Cayce readings and open to other literature in this field have a greater opportunity for general understanding than some of the people who actually received personal Cayce readings. These people did not have access to the full body of this information plus the subsequent publications from this and other sources available to us today. From a study of these readings, we may imagine a number of karmic scenarios that may become working hypotheses for us in our own lives.

One of the surest of these karmic patterns is the likelihood that many of us who today are on the spiritual path have lived in past experiences in monasteries, convents, lamasaries, ashrams and the like. These life styles tended to have in common the vows of celibacy, chastity and poverty. Remember, we were warned 2,000 years ago not to make vows, but rather to let our yeas be yea and our nays be nay. (Matthew 5:37) If we make promises before God and others, we may build into ourselves patterns which may later cause inner turmoil and confusion when we find ourselves in a situation which is contrary to an earlier vow. Such was the circumstance for a woman who was told:

The entity then lives within self that it would have others feel about self, and that it feels deep within self because of its experiences and associations with individuals of the opposite sex, that very oft become repulsive to the entity, especially in sexual relationships. These are builded urges latent and manifested in the experience of the entity.

For as the entity took those vows of chastity, purity and devotion to celibacy, *these have become innately displeasing at times. Never satisfying or never gratifying desires for self or for others.*

***These will become and are stumbling blocks to the entity.* Yet these are not necessarily those things that should make for disagreements with others, for there are those abilities within self to meet the needs of those relationships in those directions when there is the choice. But as should be from every individual, there should be agreement between those individuals in such relation-**

ships and only when there is such should there be the relationships. For the lack of such agreement brings more discordant notes between individuals than any portion of relationships with the opposite sex. The disagreements may be very slight at times, but they grow. For these relationships are the channels for the activity of creative forces and not by mere chance. [Author's italics]
4082-1

As we try to utilize such scenarios, we must not always stop with the simplest form but rather inquire more deeply into some of the possible ramifications of such vows and life styles. For example, a monastic life style might create other problems than those deriving only from the vow of celibacy. Close relationships between the same sex might for one person subsequently predispose him toward homosexual attraction and heterosexual aversion. Another in the monastic life sytle may have gained control over the expressions of the body but not over the mind. He may have built an inner life of fantasy and desire so seriously inflated as to make the problems in the present life more serious than if he had a previous life with greater overt sexual expression. Over many years in monastery life, another might have a repetitive sexual fantasy and build a thought form or desire pattern to be stored in the unconscious, which may present itself in a later incarnation as an irrational impulse or compulsive desire.

Let us consider another scenario which may have some applicability. When one vows consciously to lead a life of chastity and yet has not resolved all of the unconscious components of the sexual life, there may develop compromise fantasies, such as the fantasy of rape. A woman may not allow herself, even in her fantasies, to enjoy romantic and straightforward sexual experiences because it is not permissible to think of herself as a person with "that kind of desire." However, she may be able to permit herself the fantasy of being an unwilling and resisting victim of sexual assault. Since mind is the builder, this fantasy may set the karmic stage for meeting just such a situation.

We may not be able to recall our previous lives or to obtain readings of unquestionable accuracy. We *can* work with "karmic scenarios" of our own construction to enable us to have a better understanding of how we came to be the way we are and to enable us to maintain a better attitude and stronger resolution about working with our present situation. As we construct a hypothetical situation for the purpose of deriving an applicable insight, we may put the concept of reincarnation to work for us in gaining a deeper understanding of the present than is otherwise attainable.

The concept of reincarnation is the great leveler of all human conditions. Because there may be a change of sex from one incarnation to another, great care should be taken in guarding one's attitudes so as not to join the battle of the sexes, especially in seeing the opposite sex as the enemy.

A very interesting and karmically rich phase of history was the period of the Crusades. The readings characterize it as a time of serving an idea without respect to the ideal. Many of the people who received readings which placed them in this period were told that they had been "Christians" who had experienced and learned love from the care given them by their "infidel" enemies. Some of the men who went off to battle left wives in chastity belts; they incarnated again in this life as men with sexual problems, such as impotence. Others, however, having previously been men, returned in the present incarnation as women with a different set of sexual problems.

Before that the entity was in the French land, during those periods known as the Holy Wars.

The entity then was among those who chose to go to war, for the entity then was in the opposite sex and chose—as did many—to make the surety in the relationships with the companion in its activity and experience.

Thus in the present the entity is meeting itself, in that it chose rather to make such a hardship upon its companion that it brought material separations in the experience; and in that activity the entity learned much

that will be met in the present. There is a way that seemeth right unto a man, but the end thereof is death, disillusionment, separation. That ye have learned—that ye must apply in thy present experience. 2281-1, F.32

If, in the present incarnation, we identify ourselves as of a certain sex over and against the opposite sex instead of as souls with continuing experiences in the earth plane with other souls, then the lessons to be learned from such a sequence of incarnations may be seriously obscured. Therefore, some men and women who are presently experiencing themselves as being victimized by the opposite sex are more truly meeting themselves. They are no doubt in such circumstances because in a previous life, incarnate in the opposite sex, they had established a pattern, the fruit of which they are now meeting. As we consider the human condition, we should always think in the inclusive term of "we" instead of "we and they"; as has been jokingly expressed, "We have met the enemy and they are us!" This is true not only of differences in sex but also in religion, race, nationality and other such categories.

Reincarnation Unnecessary

Another consideration regarding sex and the spiritual path is the relationship of sexual expression to graduation from the earth plane. The readings do not contain direct information on this subject; however, there is some interesting marital status information.

In her book, *Reincarnation Unnecessary*, Violet Shelley reports on 18 individuals who received readings in which they were told, were they to continue as they were going, it would not be necessary for them to incarnate again in the earth plane. What were the qualities of the persons given such information? Violet Shelley summed it up this way:

"A variety of patterns emerges from the life readings of these 18 people who were told that they might have the choice of not returning to the earth. Were they all saints? By no means. Their readings show them to be struggling with an assortment of problems. Frequently mentioned were lessons of patience, tolerance, and occasonally self-pity still to be mastered. Had all of these people's past lives been consistently on the plus side? Not at all. The readings indicate that in certain incarnations they had gained and in others they had lost.

"The planets influencing the individual's mental nature in almost every case included Venus, Mercury and Jupiter. Very simply, the combination describes a loving person with a broad universal outlook. Of the 18 readings, in one case astrological urges were not given. In 16 instances Jupiter was mentioned, Venus in 15 and Mercury in 13.

"Although these people are outwardly quite different from each other in their present lives, they have in common a willingness to put selfish interest aside for service to their fellow man."

Of the 18, four were males, three were married at the time of their reading and the fourth later married. Of the 14 females, eight were listed as Miss; however, one of these was married for one night; another was secretly married for a time; another was advised not to marry until after age 29. We do not know whether she did or not. Six were listed as Mrs., of whom one was divorced because of another woman. Another had been married and divorced twice and was questioning whether there would be a third husband.

Here are some examples of the information given to these people:

Miss [569] was the housekeeper for her widowed stepmother. She passed up an opportunity to marry because her stepmother did not approve of the young man. She was told, "keep in that same way as has been set in self, in purpose and in manner, for through the own efforts in self there need not be the necessity in returning to earth's plane . . ." The astrological aspects were "in the influence of love's forces, ever," and she was "always giving, giving, more than ever receiving." (569-6)

Miss [444] was promised, "if the entity will apply self

in those forces that make for the creating within self and those whom the entity may contact day by day, ideals that are of the standards making for creative influences in the mind, the soul and the physical influences, through same may the entity gain and develop in this experience to those influences where only through the desire may it be necessary for the entity to enter earth's environs again." (444-1)

Mrs. [1472] who was married was commended, "For keeping inviolate that thou knowest gives assurance not only in self but in the promises that He will bear thee *up!* If there is kept that purpose in self, there is little need for a return; save as one that may lead the way to those that are still in darkness." (1472-1)

Mr. [322] was married. Of him it was said: "Quite an enviable position, may it be said, that the entity occupies; in the matter of truth, veracity, clean *living*, that the entity has made in this experience! and there will be little need, unless desired, for a return to this earth's experience." (322-2)

Mr. [256] was unmarried at the time of the reading. He asked about marriage and was told that it would develop later. It did and he was married. He was told, "apply will's influence, by keeping an *ideal*—not an idea—an *ideal*—before self, will build for self that which will carry the entity to where few, if any, appearances would be necessary again in this mundane sphere." (256-1)

From these statements we may readily see that these who have almost "made it" with respect to the earth plane are people who are making choices based on ideals and who are living lives of integrity and service to others. Marital status did not seem to be a consideration, as such!

Oedipus Rex

Freud has been much maligned because of his theory of the Oedipus complex, which hypothesizes that a male child may desire his mother sexually. However, working with the concept of reincarnation, we may understand how such a situation might be far more deeply involved than even Freud might have thought. The play *Oedipus Rex* was written thousands of years before Freud. Its enduring classic qualities suggest that the pattern is universally instructive, though it may not be directly applicable in every case.

The story goes that at the time of Oedipus's birth a prophecy was made by an oracle (we would say a psychic reading) that he would kill his father and marry his mother. The parents were so concerned about this that they arranged for the baby to be cared for by others in a far distant place so that there would be no possibility for the prophecy to be fulfilled. However, on reaching adulthood Oedipus went on a journey, encountered an old man with whom difficulties arose, and slew him. The story proceeds with a series of events that lead to his marriage to an older woman. When the full truth is unveiled, it is learned that the man whom he killed was, indeed, his father and the woman whom he married was, in fact, his mother.

This play is very instructive with respect to the complex ways the laws of karma and attraction work behind the scenes, beyond our conscious minds. On the other hand, it is clear in the story's development that there are occasions in which Oedipus makes choices which were not for the better, but which put him in line for the fulfillment of the prophecy. Had he, at those moments when a clear choice was presented, chosen the better course, then the undesirable but predicted outcome would have been avoided.

Could he have chosen otherwise? The approach of the readings is that karma is nothing more than giving way to impulse. By his giving way to impulse, Oedipus enacted the karmic pattern and, thus, the prediction was fulfilled. The inclinations were story, but the outcome was not fixed.

We may hypothesize that Oedipus, at some conscious or unconscious level, desired the prophecy to be fulfilled. Otherwise he could have determined within himself to make clearer choices that would have prevented this sequence of events from occurring. However, we tend to be puppets just as he, in the working of the law, unless we evoke intervention of a power and wisdom higher than ou conscious selves.

Let us examine the more general implications of thi story. In a succession of incarnations in which the sam entities are drawn together again and again, the respectiv relationships may be the same or they may vary. The *Oedipus Rex* story suggests a situation in which a man an woman are lovers in one incarnation and, in a subsequen incarnation, the woman is the mother of the child wh formerly was her lover. This is only one of many ways i which previous life relationships between two individual or several members of a family may vary.

In the following example a 30-year-old woman asked

Q-1. In what incarnations was I associated, and i what relation, to my present mother?

A-1. The mother then, in the previous incarnation was the wife of self. As to the relationships with th mother, much may be said as respecting same in th previous incarnation. For how oft, even since the appear ance in the associations in the present, has the mothe sought counsel from the self; much more than self ha sought counsel from the mother! 897-1, F.3

In this case the present daughter was formerly th husband of the present mother. The reading indicates th the relationship between the two reflected some of th dependency of wife upon husband with the mother no depending on the daughter, rather than the reverse as on would expect.

In other cases in the readings entities who had bee man and wife or lovers in one incarnation returned int the same family as brother and sister. These cases a potentially very instructive in helping us understand th nature of our family relationships and, more importantl in instructing us about the implications of building deep within our minds patterns of anticipated sexual interactio with another entity. The *desire* held may bring the entiti together again in a subsequent incarnation, but they may come together under different family circumstances, such as sister and brother instead of wife and husband. A very frustrating and confusing incarnation may result. Thus the readings warn us to cling to that love which is unsexed.

The pattern of relationships in previous lives may be very complex. As a couple experience each other in various relationships in successive incarnations, there may develop a very strong basis for a good marriage. Considering this from the overview of several incarnations, we may see that each specific incarnation is a constructive step toward an eventually more constructive and creative relationship. One life as father and daughter, another as mother and son—experiences which may be frustrating at the time—may lead eventually to an especially promising relationship. In the following case a couple was told that they had been together many times and out of these experiences came the present very special opportunity:

For, as in the relationships ye have borne in the earth as husband and wife, that which is the ideal as set by the Maker Himself is in those means in which there would be two manifesting as one in their hopes, in their fears, in their desires, in their aspirations.

This do, and as ye have lived as father and daughter, as mother and son, as companions, as friends, as acquaintances, with differences, each with their own axe to grind, be patient, be tolerant one with another, as ye would desire a father to be patient with a daughter, a mother to be patient with a son, as companions with the hopes of their desire bringing into existence into a material manifestation a channel, a body for the manifestation of a soul recently from God. God's presence in the earth, God's manifestation to man, life, *life* as may be created by the union of bodies in body-manifestation, these are the ideals. These have been the purposes here for a manifestation in thy selves in such ways, and in such measures that all of these, and yet more, may be manifested in the earth. For, as ye seek to so live in thine own lives

as to manifest these, as the blessings, as the hopes, as the beauty of living in a material world that thy Maker has given ye, help thy fellow man.

Then go forward with the knowledge that as ye so live thine own life together, as ye associate with thy fellow man, as ye do unto them ye are doing to thy Lord, thy God; for it is the appreciation of thy fellow man also, as self, being a child of the most high God. When individuals, when a couple so blessed, recognize in themselves this opportunity, how gracious, how beautiful, how lovely is life itself! Ye have this opportunity, don't muff it!

2072-15, F.3

We should examine our relationships with family and loved ones, keeping in mind some of these karmic scenarios. They can be very instructive regarding the nature of present relationships and of our attitudes and feelings toward specific individuals. However, we must, more and more, look upon one another not as male and female or parent and child, but rather as soul to soul. As we generate these attitudes that the true and deepest nature of the relationship is soul to soul, then we will begin more surely to deal in a truly fair, considerate and loving manner one with another.

Homosexuality

One of the forms of sexual expression receiving extensive and emotionally charged attention today is homosexuality. For those concerned with this subject it may be instructive to examine carefully what is said in the Cayce readings. We should notice not only the content of the readings, but also the spirit in which the information and advice are given. It is the case here, as was frequently so with the Cayce readings, that no one asked the direct question of what the source thought of homosexuality, whether it was approved or not. Individuals came to Edgar Cayce seeking help and he responded, as was always the case, by trying to give that which was helpful and hopeful.

In the readings there are eight case histories which deal directly and indirectly with homosexuality. In one case 3685, a young woman who was not homosexual asked a question regarding this subject, and the answer given is especially interesting in the light of the emphasis placed upon the mental.

Q-9. Is there an element of homosexuality about me as someone suggested?

A-9. No, only as ye have retained such does it become a part of thy consciousness. Apply self in kindness, gentleness. But such is not a part of thee.

3685-1, F.29

In another case we are told, "the entity is through material surroundings allowing same to become builded in the system through the suggestive forces . . ." (1089-6) With this in mind we may further reflect upon the question and answer in 3685-1.

Of the other cases, 111-1 is more clearly a physical reading and does not appear to be directly instructive regarding general questions about homosexuality. Case 3545 was a man who admitted to a sexual deviation and later borrowed the collected information on homosexuality. However, it is not clear that his own problem, as he experienced it, was homosexuality. He reports that he was married at the age of 39 and later, in his correspondence, reports having a son of age 13. Therefore, this case does not appear to be instructive. The remaining five cases which are of special interest to our present study indicate a vast difference of basic problems and orientations. Thus we must understand that cases involving homosexuality do not come from one homogeneous group, but rather from varied previous-life influences and present-life physical, mental and spiritual conditions. Case 3364 is of a 42-year-old man who was told that his condition was physical, psychological and karmic. The reading begins as follows:

In analyzing the disturbances with this body, here we find not only the pathological conditions to be considered

but the psychological. For, these are the effects of karmic influences, thus having to do with something being met in self in the present experience.

Here, the complete analysis of an entity's being might be proof of those tenets (to those who would study such) that life is a continuous experience. And where one has met self in those activities having to do with the psychological (that is, the soul-self), as in this body, and also the physiological—or the physical body and its relationships to the spiritual or psychic body, as in this condition here, there is brought a homosexual disturbance that is to the body a mental and a physical condition to be met.

These, then, are the conditions to be met.

For, with the relationships in mind, in body of such, as to open the cells in the Leydigian (lyden) forces, there is the flow of the kundalini in and through the body which finds expression in the organs of the sensory system; not merely to the disgust but to the shame of the body in itself—and yet these become a part of the whole body-mind and being. Thus there is brought not merely a physical or purely pathological condition but a physiological and psychological disturbance to the body.

3364-1, M.42

He was given several suggestions for physical treatment and applications and, in closing, was told:

Do these, and we should have no further trouble.

Live and keep normal activities. Begin with the study of self—not anatomically but spiritually. And the greater spiritual lesson you may gain is in the 5th chapter of Matthew. Learn this by heart, then read the 14th chapter of John and the 12th chapter of Romans. Then live them! Live them in thy daily relationships to others. Know that these words are spoken to thee. Apply these with thy application of the mechanical and material things for the body. **3364-1, M.42**

It is interesting to note that only after receiving the reading in which the homosexual condition was specified did [3364] acknowledge that the main problem for which he sought the reading was homosexuality.

Another case, 4073, was of a 41-year-old man who stated in his background letter that he was born an ugly duckling and that this was emphasized to him by family and school associates for as long as he could remember. This he believed to be "the foundation of certain unshakable inhibitions." At age 12 he developed urinary weakness which required him to use manipulation to completely drain the urinary tract. He added that, lacking opportunity for normal relations with girls as a youth because of his appearance and temperament, he had turned within himself and definite homosexual tendencies had developed. Contacts then and at the time of his reading emphasized these tendencies. He aspired to be a pianist but was "thwarted by unsympathetic parents." He became a teacher, but was discharged for his "bluntness and bitter tongue." He had considered suicide several times. In his physical reading he requested advice for urinary, bronchial and skin problems.

The reading began by stating that while the disturbing conditions were not particularly serious at present, they would gradually worsen unless measures were taken; even those indicated outwardly—as sexual activities that were disturbing to his body—because of emotional characters set up with those of his own sex. Unless these conditions were removed, the reading stated, the urinary disorder would worsen. He was told:

. . . there should be first the suggestive therapeutics, or the having of a good psychiatrist or hypnotist to give positive suggestions to the body in regard to refraining from such activities.

The reading continued by saying:

These inflammations may be activative by the low cellular forces of electricity, but had better be through suggestion. Find an honest hypnotist—there are some.

4073-1, M.41

In this case it appears that the advice regarding homosexual expression may deal with more than just sexual expression; it may relate, in this case, to physical complications and disturbances arising from urinary tract difficulties.

Another case concerned a 22-year-old male. In his reading it is interesting to see the association of music and sex throughout his incarnations and his present life.

In the Atlantean land he was "among those who were then 'thought projections,' and the physical being had the union of sex in the one body . . ." The reading states that "the entity sought to be both and wasn't very successful at either." (5056-1) In this particular incarnation he was a musician, playing on pipes and reed instruments.

During Solomon's reign he was chosen by David for physical, mental and spiritual training "through the activities in the preparations in the school as had been undertaken or begun by Elijah in Carmel." And "when the Queen of Sheba visited Solomon the entity was chosen as the one to make music for Solomon to make love by, to the Queen." (5056-1)

In his last incarnation he was a student under Saint Cecilia who was "able to interpret the music of the spheres." ". . . music was forgotten in the desire physically for the Saint and it eventually destroyed itself." (5056-1) No wonder he later wrote that he believed music and sex go hand in hand.

His reading suggested that he apply himself to attain a spiritual awakening, which might be accomplished through nature, "searching for an answer to the voices of the night, the rhapsody of the moon upon the water and the voice of a sunrise . . ." (5056-1) These and similar actions in nature would take him out of the realm of physical emotions.

He was told to make music his career (specifically the piano) and only the classical and operatic. While working a year, saving and spending every penny only for music and lessons, he was to make physical hardships for himself: sleep on a hard bed, eat no sweets, attend no movies, not eat too much, and often go for days only on bread and water. He was also told not to allow anyone to give him anything. His reading said that there is nothing impossible for him to attain in fame, fortune or spiritual unfoldment and "yet these will *not* be easy until the entity has conquered self." (5056-1)

The reading also gave the following advice:

> **Do not, then, make an early choice of companionship! For this would be thy undoing. Do not wed before the thirty-second year of age! Do not wed, then, until at least ye have conquered thyself in the full training of the body, the hand, the mind in thy music! Use the piano alone!** **5056-1, M.22**

Six years after his reading, when he would have been about 28 years old, he visited A.R.E. and was interviewed by a staff member. At that time he told her that he was seriously considering marrying a lesbian in order to be free from the approaches of women. He also told her he couldn't "bear the thought of the relationship of marriage" and was skeptical of marriage because of his observations especially in connection with his immediate family. Later, in 1972, in response to a questionnaire from A.R.E. which included the question, "Did you marry before your 32nd year?" he replied, "No. The reading quite underestimated my basic antipathy to marriage (a state referred to in psychology textbooks as 'horror feminae')."

One of the questions he submitted prior to his reading was, "Am I a homosexual?" The answer was, "Read what has been given."

The most extensive case history is that of [1089], who received eight readings. A 20-year-old male student when he sought help from Edgar Cayce, he wrote saying, "I have a mental disorder." It had disturbed him so much that he had gone to the university psychologist, but had not been helped. A physical reading was given, 1089-2. His first reading had been requested by his parents when he had tonsilitis at age 10. Cayce said the physical experiences the young man was having were the result of the psychic attempting to come through, and the reading recommended meditation. When the young man received his reading, he wrote Edgar Cayce and told him that the reading had described his experiences accurately. He said he was a homosexual and added that had been so disturbed by his thoughts, which he found "impossible," that he had sought out the university psychologist who had told him he was a homosexual. He had had a good idea he was one before the psychologist told him.

A month later a life reading was given, which cited both a Venusian influence and a French incarnation that related to his disturbance. He had been a cartoonist and had depicted some of the sexual activities of the French court in his work. Apparently the attitude he had held in the production of these cartoons carried over and was influencing his present attitudes toward sex. He was told:

In the application of that experience in the present, know that thou gainest little in the condemning of that in thine fellow man of which ye were *inwardly* guilty.

Condemn not, then, that ye be not condemned. For indeed with what measure ye mete it will be measured to thee again. And that thou condemnest in another (yea, every man, every woman), that thou becomest it thine self! 1089-3, M.20

However, [1089] was also given extraordinary promise of the contribution he could make to a spiritual awakening in his time. In a past incarnation he had known the Master and had been close to Him. Much of his present difficulty was related to the beginning of the movement of the psychic forces through him, such that he might be "made a *channel* of expression or manifestation of spiritual activities." (1089-2) The emphasis on meditation was very strong and he was told:

But if there is set a definite period or manner of meditation, as may be given in a very close study of that which has been manifested or expressed through these sources and compiled in the paper on Meditation, there may be had a balancing . . .

For, guided by those that are the Creative Forces in manifestation in a physical body, there may come not only

for self but for humanity, for individual, for groups, that which may be the *great* manifestation. 1089-2, M.20

He was told again to meditate often and given the suggestion that he separate himself "for a season from the cares of the world. Get close to nature . . ." (1089-3), and read John 14-17.

The following day another physical reading was given as he was bothered by cough and congestion. This physical reading began by reminding him that, "There has been indicated for this body, as we find, the mental attitudes that should be taken; and these would work with the general physical forces for an improvement that would go beyond that as may be seen from the outward activities in the present. We would do these." (1089-4) The reading went on to say that the conditions in the nasal passages and the irritations to the throat and bronchi are "an extenuation or an aftereffect of the rising of the emotions through the glands, the influences and forces as indicated that need to be made in the manner as to do something *with*, something *about*, the abilities that really lie within the grasp of the body-physical!" (1089-4) (This is especially interesting when compared with the statement in [3364]'s reading that the kundaline flow expressed itself "in the organs of the sensory system . . ."). The reading then prescribed a cough medicine and closed with:

But, for the mental balance, for the physical body, for the general physical conditions, be mindful of that given.

For if the suggestions are followed as indicated for the meditations, and the general activity of the body made so that there is the exercising through the physical flow, the general blood supply, these physical disturbances will disappear. 1089-4, M.20

A few days later another physical reading repeated the admonition to separate self—if "in manual labors, fine!" or in nature. "But *choose*." (1089-5)

In May, 1936, he again wrote that "people of my own

sex affect me almost to distraction. What must I do in order to make myself attracted to the opposite sex?" In June, reading 1089-6 repeated that he must *conquer* and *know* himself and his emotions. He was told clearly that his homosexual tendencies were as much a *mental* as a physical condition and could be removed by the mind.

Those conditions that present themselves as mental aberrations, of a psychopathic and psychological nature, the entity is through material surroundings allowing same to become builded in the system through the suggestive forces as those conditions that have set barriers.

That there may be unnatural affections, unnatural associations or relations, or desires, is as much a *mental* as a physical condition! Yet we may add those influences to the physical forces of the body that may in a mental, through the physical reaction remove much of those disturbances—if the body applies itself in the *mental* manner to make same a portion of the experience.

These arise from those conditions that have been intimated, that have been given as to the relationships of the body-physical through its experiences in the earth plane that have been allowed to become builded in the present through associations, through the associations of ideas and of mental conditions in the body, and thus builded up.

They may have an inception in a physical condition but the reaction is *purely* of a mental nature, of a mental comprehension, of the conditions. 1089-6, M.21

A saltpeter compound was prescribed, and he was told it would not be effective "unless the mental forces are carried *with* same and there is the application of self in its associations, in its relationships with individuals of the same sex, of the opposite sex and the like in *natural* forces and in natural ways and means." (1089-6)

In February, 1938, he received his last reading. He had written asking if marriage would help him, and the reading advised him to seek a companion and assume the obligations. "Thus the sex life as well as the imaginative and the duties that go with such a union, that to the entity carries and will carry the obligations of every nature, will be more in keeping it that which will build the better conditions in an economic, in a mental, in a spiritual manner in the experience." (1089-8) Follow-up information indicated he later joined the service but did not indicate whether he ever married.

The final case available for study from the readings is that of [479]. This case is potentially so very instructive regarding insights from the readings' source on this condition that we wish to examine its implications carefully and present the entire reading. [479], 21 years old, was given the reading at the request of his friend who had promised not to be specific about his problem.

[479] was never married, but for many years had the close companionship of a younger man. Apparently it did not make him an outcast, since he finished his education and became a college English teacher. He must have been a good teacher, since he remained with the school all those years until his death at the age of 60. Although the suggestion given Cayce was for a *physical* reading, the source replied that ". . . it would be rather the analyses of the conditions physical and mental that confront the body, or that must be met by the body." (479-1) He had written to Edgar Cayce and asked, "Must I live so that my conduct would, were it generally known, win general approbation, or may I safely conduct myself to my own moral satisfaction? I do not admit of low moral standards." This is the closest that he came to saying his concern was with homosexuality.

We cannot help but wonder if the Cayce source foresaw that this man was indeed going to live as a homosexual. When his question regarding moral standards is kept in mind, it is interesting that Cayce said:

And, as He said unto the woman, "Neither do I condemn thee, but sin no more." Neither did He set for her any moral law but that which was conscious within

her own soul as to the acts in the physical that would tend to separate or to turn the light into darkness in the life of that soul.
479-1, M.21

Let us keep in mind then that, just as the Master did not condemn, neither did the source of the readings. And let us remember that the spirit of the readings was to give that which would be helpful and hopeful.

It may be especially instructive for us to examine the response to this reading by a young man who found himself in exactly the same state of concern as [479]. Also of homosexual orientation, this man came to us indicating that the readings in general, and for [479] in particular, were especially helpful to him. We asked him to comment specifically on the nature of the helpfulness of this particular reading. The following is his response:

> "Reading 479 is the one that salvaged me . . .
>
> "The brunt of articles I've read by authors who draw from the readings is toward curing the homosexual from his homosexuality. Reading 479 for me has a different meaning—to save the homosexual from himself, his self-condemnation. I think you will agree with me that there are many degrees of sexuality. It is not black and white, homosexual and heterosexual. There are bisexuals, to move just one degree. I am open to the thought that some of these cases represent entities who are physically heterosexual but mentally homosexual. The obvious direction would be to get mind and body together, hence the supposed 'cure' from homosexuality to heterosexuality.
>
> "I appreciate [479] as one whose cure was not his homosexuality but his resistance to using it as a stepping-stone. He seems inclined to rather condemn himself than be responsible for being different and using his difference to express God's love in new ways. Homosexuality by its nature is different from heterosexuality in the

morals that evolve from same. Promiscuity may have to be reevaluated and not from the heterosexual viewpoint only. Promiscuity can teach; do we seek companionship for sex or sex for companionship? I feel companionship is ever the criterion, not sex. Sex seems to be the insistant force to urge seeking the companionship. I personally worked with this reading to understand which direction God intended for me. My answer came from a stranger's innocent interpretation of my dream which indicated (that) the ultimate goal is the same no matter which path was chosen. I chose to admit being gay and to learn all I could about my responsibility to God's plan for man and my serving my brothers as I am. My Guide was pushing me ever in the direction to start my journey. My 'cure' is to relate to all on any level of sexuality without condemnation.

"I may develop heterosexual urges if that is the ultimate destiny; it is not my goal, but I would not cast out the possibility I might evolve that way. I say this not to appease the 'straight world' but to emphasize that I am concerned with what I am now and being the best example of what I am now and how I evolve sexually is not an issue. Nor should it be the criterion for judging anyone—to accept their state of homosexuality if they indicate they will strive at some future date to go straight. That is like accepting someone's blackness if they will eventually act white!

"We are marvelous creatures; it does not surprise me that we could choose to be homosexual just for the experience, devoid of karmic effect. My companionship has taught me more about myself than I feel I could have learned any other way. I have a different appreciation for women that only evolved after I stopped condemning self and accepted my gayness. Homosexuality is or may be quite natural if one accepts God as the standard of morality and not society's standard.

"I feel that it is important to say somewhere that being gay or homosexual is not always a state that must be hastily converted to heterosexuality. It is a unique gift to teach the soul other facets of God's love. Perhaps it is not natural, having few counterparts in nature (there are some!). Yet are any of us? Having flesh bodies, serving self's will not God's—does it not make us all unnatural?"

Now let us study thoroughly and carefully [479]'s reading, keeping in mind the commentary and perspective on that which has just been given.

Mr. Cayce: Yes, we have the body and those conditions physical and mental that disturb the better manifestations of life and its meaning through the physical forces as manifested in this body.

Now, as we find, in giving the physical conditions that may be aided in bringing about for the body better manifestations, it would be rather the analyses of the conditions physical and mental that confront the body, or that must be met by the body.

That there are physical defects in the structural portion, or in apparent manifestations through the mental, that are prenatal in their basic forces is too often condemned by the entity—and if there is the proper understanding of that which is Life in a manifestation, and the spiritual force that prompts the activity of same, these may be *by all* better understood.

For, when there are those activities in a material world that bring about the forces or influences wherein there may be the action of a soul in its development, that which is often counted as sin or error is for the mercy to a soul from an All-Wise and beneficent Father that is directing, planning, giving the soul an opportunity for the use of that which may come into the experience *of* that soul in the material plane. And what the soul, through its body and mind and attributes of same, does about the

knowledge and consciousness of the indwelling of the spirit of life through the Christ in the earth is the opportunity for that soul to develop.

Hence in this particular body, rather than condemning, rather than closing self to the abilities in self—or the opportunities wherein there may be made manifest in self that there is no condemning, but rather that self may use the opportunity, the privilege, to manifest—under handicap or under those conditions that are existent within self—for the better manifesting of the love that is shed among men, through the activities in any one experience or environ.

For, when a soul, a body-mind, a consciousness *condemns*, it is but a selfish manifestation—and is the attempt, as of the first errors, to *blame* that self has to do upon another.

But if the soul will but know that the love of the Father (that has been manifested through His Son, who overcame sin, error, dis-ease, disease and even death itself in the material plane) has promised that through the consciousness of that life of the Christ awakening within us, as the consciousness of His indwelling presence, it may bring also healing in His wings, and that which had apparently been a hindrance may come to be the measure through which others may come to have the greater knowledge, the greater understanding of the Christ Consciousness, the Christ Life in the own experience, then all material problems will be understood and overcome.

And rather than shutting self away from associates or companionship, if the consciousness will but make for the fruits of the spirit of the Christ being manifest, there will be the seeking on the part of others to *be near*, to be in the light of that which may be shed abroad by such a soul, in such a body making manifest in this mundane sphere that love, that life, that graciousness of the Christ spirit in the life.

Hence, as we would find, if the body will thus find in self and in self's experience, there may come that *cleansing* within the physical forces of the body that will *make* the body-*soul* whole indeed!

Hence, *seek* to know *His* ways with thee. Not alone

by denying that sin or error exists. *True,* sin and error is not of *God*—save through His sons that *brought* error, through selfishness, into the experience of the souls of men, the body by which angels and archangels are separate from the fullness of the Father. For, in His mercy He has given to all that which is the desire of every heart in a material plane—to seek companionship in a manner that there may be the exchange of experiences in whatsoever sphere the body-soul may find self. And in so doing, if there is the manifestation of greed, avarice, hate, selfishness, unkindliness, ungodliness, it makes for the harkenings that bring their fruit—contention, strife, hate, avarice, and separation from the light. For, those that have turned their face *from* the light of God can only see shadow or darkness—and that light is only for those far away. Yet, if the soul will but turn to the Father of love as manifested in the earth through the Christ, in this life also may there be seen the light and the glory of a *new* birth.

That all have been conceived in sin is only a partial truth; hence often makes a whole lie to those that in the body find their own physical selves may find that which to their own consciousness they can condemn in another. But to condemn—even as the Master taught when the moral laws, or when the physical laws or spiritual laws were being broken and were presented to Him as example whereunto they would question Him, He always answered: "Thou hast no power over me save it be given thee from the Father, who has not left His children alone but ever seeks that they should know that the Redeemer liveth." And His light, His life, His love, *cleanseth* every *whit!* And, as He said unto the woman, "Neither do I condemn thee, but sin no more." Neither did He set for her any moral law but that which was conscious within her own soul as to the acts in the physical that would tend to separate or to turn the light into darkness in the life of that soul. And as she came to be known among those that had sought the light, her life became that which led many to an understanding—and still will bring life, light and comprehension to many.

So in thine own self, know that *therein* lies the spirit of God—the *soul* of thine self. The spirit will quicken, if the soul will but acknowledge His power, His divine right *within* thee!

Then, let the acts of thine body, the temple of thine soul, be kept clean in thine own consciousness—even as the presence of the Master cleansed every body that sought aid from physical dis-ease or corruption and made for the manifesting of the fruits of the spirit, of truth in their lives. Not that it saved the *body* from the grave, not that it saved a body from its transition from one sphere to another—but *quickened* rather the soul and *its* mind to such a degree that it would ever cry as did the Master in His message of old to His peoples that had been led through the trials and tribulations, "Others may do as they may, but as for me *I*—my soul, my body, my mind—will serve the *living* God!" [Joshua 24:15]

Blessed is he whom the Lord chasteneth, for He loveth every one—and will quicken those that call on His name and act in accordance with the directions that are given every soul to know to do good and to do it not becomes sin, but to know that He—the Christ—will stand within thy stead and will cleanse the soul-body every whit, that it may stand before the throne of grace every whit *clean!*

Then, make thy prayers unto Him, giving glory, power and praise unto Him—and in this manner may that which has *seemed* to be to thee as a hindrance become a stepping-stone to the glory of thine own soul!

We are through. 479-1, M.21

Finally, if questions remain concerning our attitude toward this condition let us consider and keep in mind the following advice:

Q-2. When one is working out a karma, it it right to try to help that one?

A-2. This may be answered, even as was that "Who sinned, this man or his parents? That the works of God might be manifest before you!" When there are karmic

conditions in the experience of an individual, that as designates those that have the Christ-like spirit is not only in praying for them, holding meditation for them, but aiding, helping, in every manner that the works of God may be manifest in their lives, and *every* meditation or prayer: *Thy* will, O God, be done in *that* body as Thou seest best. Would that this cup might pass from me, not my will but Thine be done! 281-4

Care of Self

According to the readings, the greater study of individuals, groups and nations should be the study of self. The ultimate job of all souls is to fulfill the greater commandment of loving God with all one's heart, mind and soul, and one's neighbor as oneself. However, we cannot fulfill these commandments without growing in a better understand of ourselves. The Edgar Cayce readings encourage every one of us to grow in a better understanding of the functioning of our minds and bodies and of the effect of the food, mentally and physically, that we ingest.

. . . for what we think and what we eat—combined together—*make* what we *are*, physically and mentally. 288-38, F.2

The readings indicate that the love of and for a pure body is among the most sacred experiences in an entity's earthly sojourn. (436-2) The body is the temple and special care of this temple is needed. On one occasion Cayce asked an individual, "What have you dragged into this temple?" If we consider the body to be, indeed, the temple of the living God, then we should examine more carefully the mental and physical food that we drag into this holy place.

In the material conditions in life, consider first that as is necessary—that the mental and the spiritual may have a place of manifesting; for the body-physical is truly the temple of the soul, the dwelling place of the mind, o

the mental body, through this material plane, and needs same for physical manifestation. Care *first* and *foremost* for these, finding in this development in self that to which the body-mental, the body-physical, may even worship.
5615-1, F.29

With respect to care of the body, the readings offer an approach involving various procedures, applications and formulas for its finer attunement. Meditation helps in attuning the physical and mental to the spiritual, and thus the caution regarding certain odors, the kinds of music we listen to and our thoughts and motivations as we eat. Study the following reading regarding:

. . . the influence which has been had from the agricultural standpoint not only as it is understood in the present, but what it has meant and does mean for the peoples of all nations, all races even; as to how their diet may fire and does fire those portions within the body as to set the very influences that bring destructive conditions in the experience of the body.

In this vein and in this line may there be much given that will be of help, of hope; creating not an outline of a menu of this or that, not an outline showing that there should be only this or that! For as is generally known and seen, in each land there is that prepared—as it were—by nature or the creative forces—to make for the body-development of those within that particular environ. And in how many lands is *wheat?* It is the greater portion, and should be the greater portion of that which is to supply not only body-heat but body-development for an equal balance in the mental influences upon the physical forces of man in his activity; rather than the fleshpots or the brews that may be made by outside influences or combinations that destroy much! 826-5, M.34

Music plays a powerful role in affecting our emotions. The readings see music as the bridge between the infinite and the finite. Ours is a time in which this is far more important than in the period when the readings were being given because today we are surrounded by music through radio, television, recordings, in our homes, automobiles and places of business, as well as greater access to concerts and other live musical presentations. One individual, who was very emotional regarding sex and also very responsive to music, was instructed to utilize music to deal with emotional forces.

One that is very well versed in the abilities to attract those of both sexes.

One that has a great deal of latent talent in the high mental development towards things of a psychic or spiritual nature.

One that is very emotional in the sex life. Thus this may be abused or used. For it becomes a portion of the disturbing influence in the present, because of the inclination to turn more of those activities of the emotional self into expression in relationships to *material* activity. However, if such activities are turned into the channel more for spiritual insight, they may raise one to a high *mental* expression, as well as to a plane of judgment that may bring greater understanding and advancement.

One that is capable of bringing in to experience a great deal of that which may be either for confusion or a great deal of satisfaction in regard to the relationships with others as in those activities that would have to do with creative forces of *every* nature or character.

One that is well developed for giving expression in music, particularly as would pertain to the nature of the chant, or especially of any nature of a pastoral scene, or the like.

These—the emotions in the music—should be greatly manifested in this experience, to rid the system or body of those emotional forces that find expression in other directions.

2054-2, F.42

The body is not just the problem of the flesh because we are incarnate in the earth plane, but rather it constitutes a very special opportunity. The readings tell us that the destiny of the soul is with God, and the destiny of the body is with each of us as individuals. We are invited to the challenge to take back to God in our return a *glorified* body. We will return, because our soul's destiny is with God. But, with what kind of body we return is up to us. And so we need to commit ourselves to growth in the continuing attunement of the body-mental and the body-physical.

As we address questions of sex and the individual, one of the concerns of some people is that of the place of masturbation in their sexual lives. Answers to these questions may not be the same for society in general as they are for individuals on the spiritual path in particular.

Reflect upon the consequences for society's maintaining mores in child-rearing practices in which the parent is intolerant of the child touching himself in the genital area. These attitudes in child-rearing practices may lead the individual to a deep revulsion of a perfectly normal biological inclination. Because of the strength of impressions from this childhood training, the adult may feel such repugnance that masturbation becomes the less desirable alternative to illicit sexual encounters—a practice that might have dire and far-reaching consequences for the individual as well as for the culture.

From society's point of view, consider the millions of cases of unwanted pregnancies, venereal diseases and marriages troubled by the consequences of experiences outside the marriage contract. We may then wonder about the wisdom of such child-rearing practices and cultural attitudes. However, addressing again the question of the spiritual path and the processes involved in spiritual attunement, we, as individuals on the path, may have different considerations.

In the Cayce material at least seven readings either directly or indirectly address the question of masturbation. The following chart gives the individuals' ages, sexes and the section in the reading that reflects the source's attitude.

268-2	F. 44	glands "*impoverished* by such activity."

960-2	M. 13	". . . reproductive glands in the system, that in their *excessive action* have produced" physical problems.
1330-1	M. 23	". . . tendencies for or towards *self-abuse*. Turn these rather into constructive channels rather than sensual thoughts."
34-4	M. Adult	"These generative organs have been directly or indirectly responsible, through their *misuse*, for part of this trouble."
3700-1	M.28	". . . the result of karma as well as the *abuse of self* . . ."
5187-1	M.19	". . . mental disturbance, and *most* of this is self-condemnation which comes from *self-abuse*." [Author's italics]

The expression "self-abuse" is introduced and utilized by the source of the readings and not by those asking the questions. This term may be very appropriate and instructive, considering that it may not at all be a euphemism for masturbation, but rather a factual statement regarding the extent or frequency of this practice.

The six cases referred to in the chart have a variety of other symptomatic problems of physical, mental and spiritual origins, which may make these reports not directly relevant to the general population. However, the expression "self-abuse" does make one consideration very clear. It has become so commonplace in much of the present published literature on sex to indicate that this practice is not only normal but there are no deleterious effects from it no matter how frequently it is practiced. The readings make it very clear that there *can* be excessive stimulation of these potentials, leading perhaps to various detrimental conditions—physically, mentally and spiritually.

With the interpretation of self-abuse as "pertaining to excessive sexual activity which may have deleterious effects," the following reading, for a man told to act his age, is very clear:

As we find, considered all in all, there are very good conditions with this body. While there is not the best coordination between the impulses of the body and the central nervous system, we find that if the body would rather be itself and its age, it would—with minor changes—build back to greater strength and vitality.

There are those tendencies for a nervous digestion. Much of this in a manner is produced by the attempt to overenergize the creative forces or the nervous system of the genital system. This naturally brings excess energy to the solar plexus, to the base of brain, to the general activity of body, and thus depletes the heart's activity and in a minor manner depletes the blood pressure.

As we find, for regenerating the body, refrain from those excesses through the activities of the imaginative system and of the genital system, for periods of at least six to eight weeks. 3686-1, M.65

Now let us consider the one reading in which a direct question was asked about masturbation, remembering that even this reading may not be generally applicable because of the problem of pelvic lesions with which the patient was dealing. However, the answer given is clearly twofold:

Q-7a. Is masturbation or self-abuse injurious?

A-7a. Ever injurious, unless it is the activity that comes with the natural raising of the vibrations in system to meet the needs or the excess of those impulses in a body. 268-2, F.44

Examine the *unless* portion of the answer with respect to those actively on the spiritual path. We have before indicated that those energies raised in deep meditation are the same energies involved in sexual excitation. In some stages of meditation, these may be awakened with the direct awareness of sexual involvement. Could the *unless* portion of this answer refer to such circumstances?

Some people are discouraged from meditation because of the occasional sexual excitation which accompanies it; others seek meditation for this very reason. Within a balanced context and perspective and with an understanding that abuses could follow from this answer, nevertheless, the readings' response seems to suggest the appropriateness of such expressions as a natural event in the course of spiritual awakening and attunement.

What happens if "the needs or the excess of those impulses in a body" are not met? In the following reading note the "Unless these find expression . . ."

Q-3. Does sexual expression or repression cause this condition, or have any effect on same?

A-3. This was a part of the beginnings of it; for when the lyden (Leydig) glands are opened, which are in the gonads—or the centers through which the expression of generation begins, they act directly upon the centers through the body. Unless these find expression they disintegrate, or through thy association cause dis-association in impulse and the central or body-nerves. 3428-1, M.44

The words, "unless these find expression," seem to suggest "sexual expression" as an alternative, if not an optimum way of dealing with such conditions when they arise. (This interpretation is also strengthened by 268-2 above.)

Let us re-emphasize that that which is most responsible for awakening these centers and the consequent motivations is that upon which the mind feeds and dwells. This includes not only inner fantasies, but also that which we eat, that upon which we allow the eye to fall, that to which we are attentive by ear (especially in the selection of music), and that which we absorb in the selection of reading, television and movies.

It should also be observed that always when one is tired or more relaxed, there is a lowering of ego defenses. Many thoughts which would be unacceptable or unthinkable in the brightness of the morning sun become more congenial to the mind at midnight. As the barriers between the conscious and unconscious are relaxed, fantasies, inclinations and impulses are allowed to creep into the realm of the possible. Content, which may not be acceptable to the midday clarity of the mind's reasoning and morality, may be entertained and even acted upon in such a state of lowered defenses. The content of these thoughts and experiences, especially those preceding sleep, are of the utmost importance because they give direction to the mind's movement in the subconscious realms of sleep. The direction given determines the kinds of experiences the soul will seek through the night; and these, in turn, impact their influence on the subsequent day. The use of pre-sleep suggestion is one of the most powerful ways to align the unconscious forces to the consciously established ideals. An attitude of prayer and meditation before falling asleep, seeking those experiences which may enable one to learn or to serve during the night, is very important in spiritual growth.

There are some people, statistically perhaps many, who have developed a pattern such that it seems to be impossible to fall asleep without engaging in sexual activity, either intercourse or masturbation. In such cases we invite again a consideration of the replacement theory, emphasizing actively using the period just before sleep for inspirational reading, meditation and intensive intercessory prayer for others. As we offer these "first fruits" of our energy in such a service, we may anticipate that subsequent behavior patterns will more surely align themselves with a normalizing development.

To summarize our attitudes on masturbation: As we find ourselves on the spiritual path, it seems that *normalizing* our behavior keeps us more on the path than either overemphasizing or criticizing. There are clearly occasions in which engaging in this form of expression, along with maintaining a positive attitude toward self, is the more normalizing attitude than many alternatives. It is also clear that some of the basic needs which motivate us to seek sexual activity are not at all sexual in the physical sense. The desire for love, companionship, sharing, communication, affection, appreciation, tenderness, mental and spiritual stimulation are many of those qualities which we, as human beings in the earth, value most highly. These are clearly related to attributes of the spirit. However, because they may also accompany a good sexual relationship, there is the problem that the seeking of them may be associated too closely with seeking physical sex. Then, when the loved one is not present, the need felt may seem to be sexual. The more we are willing to reaffirm that our true need and love is closeness with God, the more we will release much of the loneliness that is misinterpreted as the need for sex.

6

Sex In Relationships

It is amazing how much of human behavior directly involves sex and sexual relationships but is not basically sexually motivated. Therefore, when we address the question of sex in relationships, we always have to deal with the complexity of human motivation and the dynamics of human interaction. These factors are complex enough in psychological theories that deal with only one life experience. But when we add the richness of those relationships carried over from previous lives, we have indeed a most complex study. Therefore, we are almost never dealing simply with a question of sex.

The readings say that the greatest study of mankind is the study of self. Setting out on the spiritual path, we are especially committed to growth in understanding ourselves and the nature of our relationships with others. For this purpose it may be helpful to try to develop a psychology of human relationships which will include many factors from the philosophy of the Cayce readings.

A Psychology of Interpersonal Relationships

A model for this psychology would deal not only with individuals and their subconscious, but also in a deeper sense with environmental factors that stand between the two and their relationships one to another.

The following diagram, not meant to be inclusive,

illustrates how two individuals become friends in a matrix of very complex influences.

The model is based on a dream of Edgar Cayce in which he indicated it would be helpful to individuals trying to understand this information. If we keep this model in mind as we try to comprehend and organize the many insights derived from our study of the readings, the integration of these insights may be considerably enhanced.

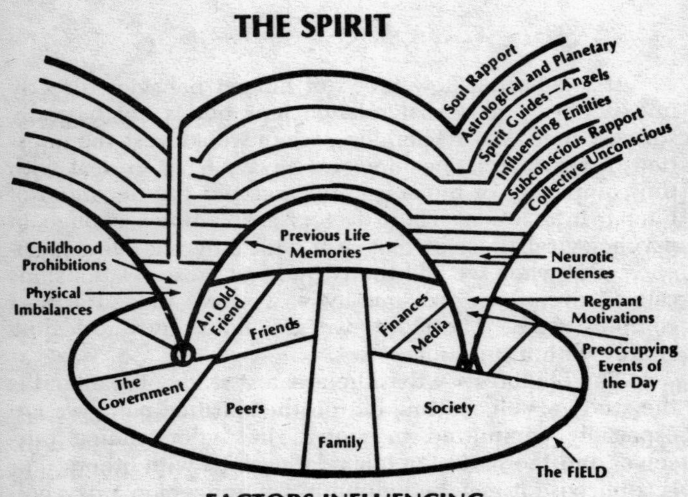

FACTORS INFLUENCING
INTERPERSONAL RELATIONSHIPS
How do O and M become ONE?

The two cones in the diagram represent two individuals; the points of the cone represent the focal points of immediate consciousness. The oval field beneath represents the environmental context, along with barriers created by it through which the two have to move or deal with as they relate to one another. Also included are internal factors from the conscious mind, the physical body, the personal unconscious and the patterns of the collective unconscious through which they view one another. There is also telepathic rapport, past life memories, influences from other beings (both discarnates and guardian forces), soul memory and spirit rapport. Where do these individuals have a chance of becoming one? Only in attuning to the spirit—the possibility of which is indicated by label "O" in the diagram. When this occurs, it enriches all other factors potential to the relationship, making them alive and applicable, and places them in proper perspective.

The Relationships of Souls

One of the most frequently asked questions about human relationships by students of reincarnation concerns "soul mates." Of course, many forms of this question and many possible answers exist because of the complexity of the nature of relationships between souls over thousands and millions of years. The readings do not deal with this question in a precise and definitive manner; however, enough is given to help us develop proper attitudes and make practical applications in our lives. A key sentence that is instructive for us is the following: "But know, the soul is rather the soul mate of the universal consciousness than of an individual entity." (2988-2)

Several problems arise from the teaching of soul mates, a concept implying that two people are destined to be together. Individuals become restless in a continuing quest and may feel not fully fulfilled unless the "true" soul mate is found. However, from the readings come several principles we shall consider.

First, in the soul's experience there will indeed be individuals—sometimes more than one—with whom, as souls, we have been closely and deeply related. These relationships should be recognized and cherished when the remembrance is authentic. Second, the readings indicated on occasion a present life situation involving parent and child, a case illustrating the impossibility of establishing a marriage relationship between the two even if they were soul mates. Third, we must meet our present life's responsibilities. When two souls meet and are drawn together on the basis of positive previous life relationships, they may see the possibilities of another beautiful relationship together. It seems, however, from the readings, that the Cayce source never encouraged the pursuit of such possibilities in preference to responsibilities already assumed and established in the present life.

Within the Marriage

The Edgar Cayce readings are very affirmative with respect to the importance of marriage.

> *Q-2. Is marriage as we have it necessary and advisable?*
> **A-2. It is!** **826-6, M.34**

The readings say that Jesus sanctioned marriage, indicating it was not only a desirable state of relationships but constituted a spiritual pattern as well. As a social structure, marriage was established—the readings say—in prehistoric Egypt under the leadership of the priest, Ra Ta. When this occurred, it was said that the angels of heaven rejoiced over the advance in opportunities for soul development promised by the new structure.

Choosing a Partner

The readings make some very strong and clear statements regarding the criteria by which one should choose a life partner. The following questions and answers illustrate these principles:

> *Q-5. With which of these would marriage be successful?*
> **A-5. This should be determined by the entity itself, in the studying, analyzing, of the purposes and ideals.**
> **For, in consideration of marriage—if it is to be a success—it must be considered not from merely the outward appearance, a physical attraction; for these soon fade. Rather it should be considered from the angle of spiritual ideals, mental aspirations, and physial agreements. These should be analyzed in the experience of the**

entity, as in the experience of the companion, in the choice of such relationships.

For, these relationships are representative of the purpose of propagation of specie[s], as well as those ideals that arise from spiritual and mental relationships—see? 1776-2, M.31

Q-3. Regarding the life companion, would . . . be this helpful companion?

A-3. As given, this must be the choice of self; not from here. Do their associations come in that category of not merely of mind, not merely of body attraction, but of the spirit answering to spirit, purpose answering to purpose? Have ye the same ideal? If you haven't, be careful! 361-16, M.24

Q-7. How may I best determine if I have chosen a mate intelligently?

A-7. As has been indicated, not as an axiom of Scripture but rather as an axiom of thine own study, "My Spirit bareth witness with thy spirit, saith the Jehovah, the God, the First Cause, the Creative Energy, the I AM."

Seek to know in self if there is the response, in not just the biological or *just* the emotions of a mental state! But are the thoughts, the activities, the desires, a complement one to another?

If not, not wisely chosen.

But when these become as the mortise is to the tenon, as the copper is to the nickel, as the light to the darkness, as the morning rays are to the dewdrop, *then* ye may know that such associations are chosen well. 440-20, M.25

Q-7. What type of person should I marry—that is, what characteristics—

A-7. [Interrupting] That should come from within self, for unless there is the proper answer from within as respecting such an individual—and relations with such—that would not be the proper person, see? Do not force an issue of such nature; for there should stand first and

foremost with *every* woman: Choose him thou would have as the father of thy children, and do not consider place, position, or other than that that must answer to the Creative Forces as are brought into unison through such conditions. See? 349-3, F.23

The following sequence of questions and answers illustrates just one of the many kinds of previous life relationships which might lead to present life difficulties in a marriage quest:

Q-1. Why am I* not *married? A companion and home has come to mean much to me. Will I ever have them in this life?

A-1. This depends upon self. Ye have rejected such heretofore. This has suddenly come to be a part of thine inner self from associations which have brought about this latent urge that has suddenly grown to mean much. This depends upon self, not upon suggestions from here.

Q-2. Is there a karmic link between myself and [5766], when and where did it take place, what was the relationship?

A-2. In the activities when the entity was queen [Esther], then this entity [5766] was as one who opened the doors, who was as the guard, who was as the one caring for the queen in those experiences.

Q-3. Did I once hurt him [5766] emotionally?

A-3. Not so much hurt as disregard of the affection shown. The difference in the position after the entity was made queen caused more of the hurt.

Q-4. Why has he had such an emotional effect upon me, stirring me to such depths. I find him almost distasteful at times after a short contact, yet a glimpse of him often leaves me deeply stirred, and extremely lonely, why? Was he ever a knight, or warrior? His carriage seems to bring haunting memories, and a sort of pride back to me, why?

A-4. Look at the conditions that must have existed then: being almost betrothed to the entity, then suddenly being made queen, causing the difference in the positions. Hence this is natural that the entity allows self to

become emotional over the variations in the positions at present.

Q-5. What is physically wrong with him, can he be cured and brought back to complete manhood?

A-5. We haven't him physically. 1298-3, F.50

A 57-year-old woman asked:

Q-7. Who and where is my real mate?

A-7. This may best be found by considering that as was the experience in those activities during the Palestine period, yea those full activities of the entity *as* Judy in that period with the Essenes. Study even that little which has been preserved of same. Ye will find him studying same also! 1472-1, F.57

The intimation of this answer is that if those seeking a proper mate would pursue and engage in their own proper activities, they would most likely place themselves in a position of meeting that one with whom they might develop a good relationship.

Being in a marriage that is well advised does not necessarily mean that all will go well! A 27-year-old woman, who had been told that she was Mary Magdalene and the one taken in adultery and forgiven by the Master, asked as follows:

Q-12. In regard to the entity's life reading, just what is it that is innate in the entity that would lead to unhappiness in marriage?

A-12. Mistrust of men!

Q-13. Does this mean the entity should never consider marriage in this life, but go through life never expecting to have a home of her own, for which she has yearned since a child?

A-13. Be well to choose, or to take that one [mentioned in question 16?]—if she so desires—and bear the consequences! Make her a bigger and a better woman! but those conditions as we have outlined are as we have seen them!

Q-14. How can the entity best overcome the lonelines that so often besets her?

A-14. Fill the life with the interests of others, an not so much of self—or belittle self, or condemn self fo the conditions. Fill the life in the interests of others.

295-2, F.2

Apparently from this answer the readings encouraged he to marry for her own growth; however, it did not seem t indicate that such would be easy for her.

We may wonder if in some destined way each of u has waiting for us "the one person" whom God would hav us marry. Only on rare occasions do the readings sugges that such might be the case. There can be no doubt tha souls, as individuals, do incarnate in certain times an places with the specific purpose of eventually meeting an engaging in some form of relationship with other specifi souls. However, the general philosophy of the reading seems to indicate that, for any one individual, there ma be several potential partners with whom an appropriat marriage could be entered into and meaningfully maintained

In our search for the proper or optimum partner, w can begin and end at no better place than in prayer. Th following has been suggested (and reports indicate it being very successful): "Lord, send me that one whom can love and help and who can love and help me." Th problem with our understanding of prayer is that it ma take some time for the forces to arrange for the optimur meeting to occur!

The approach to selecting a partner is the same as fo making any decision. There are two essential ingredient (1) We must make our decision on the basis of spiritu ideals and, (2) having decided, we must attune ourselve and ask within. The problem lies in insisting upon our ow present desires or willfulness rather than being confiden in our inner access to true guidance.

The readings state that anyone who wants to may b "successfully" married. Of course, there will be som work to do! To those who never married, the readings gav priority to a life of service. Such individuals were encour aged to find themselves in a genuinely rich and fulfilling relationship with the Christ. It "is only by choice that one remains out of relationships with the opposite sex in marriage . . ." (826-6, M.34)

The Beauty of Sex

Withing the context of a well-balanced life and the setting of proper ideals and purposes, the readings see the physical and mental body as an outlet for the beauty of sex.

Do not look upon sex as merely a *physical* expression! There is a physical expression that is beauty within itself, if it is considered from that angle; but when the mental and the spiritual are guiding, then the outlet for beauty becomes a *normal* expression of a *normal*, healthy body.
1436-1, F.27

Other affirmative statements from the readings indicate, "that the love of and for a pure body is the most sacred experience in an entity's earthly sojourn . . ." (436-2, M.28); that the "relationships in the sex are the exercising of the highest emotions in which a physical body may indulge" (826-6, M.34); and "the relationships that come from that which is of the highest vibrations that are experienced in the material world are those that may be found in such relations . . ." (911-5, F.24)

Another reading affirms:

This again is a matter of principle within the individual. The sex organs, the sex demands of every individual, must be gratified in *some* manner as a portion of the biological urge within the individual. These *begin* in the present with curiosity. For it is as natural for there to be sexual relations between man and woman, when drawn together in their regular relations or activities, as it is for the flowers to bloom in the spring, or for the snows to come in the winter, when the atmospheric conditions are conducive or inducive to such conditions. 826-6, M.34

It is clearly indicated in this information that these relationships may be properly entered into for purposes other than conception or procreation. Even so, he advises that there should be "the educating as to . . . that the force, the vitality, that goes for the gratifying of emotions may be centralized in creating . . . spiritual blessings" in the lives of others. (826-6, M.34) That the key lies in the purpose is indicated in the sexual expression. Notice that the main point, as indicated, is that "the relations in sexual life should be the outcome—not the purpose of, but the outcome of the answering of soul to soul in their associations and relations. And the act, or the associations in this nature, should be the result." (272-7, F.35)

Q-6. How should love and the sexual life properly function?

A-6. This, to give even a summary dissertation, would require a great deal of time and space.

In a few words, as we have indicated, the material things (or those in a three-dimensional world) are the shadow or the reflection of those in the spiritual life. Then, as God or the Creative Influence is the source of all things, the second law in spiritual life, in mental life, in material life, is preservation of self and the continuation of likes, or propagation, in sexual intercourse or life.

Hence, in their very basic forces, the relations in sexual life should be the outcome—not the purpose of, but the outcome of the answering of soul to soul in their associations and relations. And the act, or the associations in this nature, should be the result.

Hence these questions should be often weighed well, remembering that God, or Love (for it is One), looketh on the heart rather than the outward appearances. And that there having been set laws, by associations and relations in the material life (which are again shadows of the associations for which man in a material form was brought into being, to become a companion of the Father), and that morality, virtue, understanding, truth, love, are those influences that make for judgments of those that view the activities of individuals in the material

life and judge according to those rules that govern such relationships, then it behooves—and becomes necessary—that there be the adherence to such regulations, that thy good be not evil-spoken of.

For, in the understandings, know that Love and God are One; that relations in the sexual life and the manifestations in the mental attributes of each as to an expression of that that becomes manifested in the experience of each so concerned.

For, unless such associations become on such a basis, they become vile in the experience of those that join in such relations.

Q-7. There seems to be a standard of nature and one of man. Just how should they harmonize?

A-7. Not with man's, but rather with God's laws. One the outcome of the other. One the impulse of the other. Not the aggrandizing of the impulses that may be fired by material things, but that which is the outgrowth of the soul's expression in a material world, with the necessity of conforming to that which has been set by man as his judgment of his brother. 272-7, F.35

Agreement—The Keystone

A major ingredient of a good sexual relationship, indeed a keystone that holds it all together, is "agreement." Let us examine a statement from the readings regarding this.

The entity then lives within self that it would have others feel about self, and that it feels deep within self because of its experiences and associations with individuals of the opposite sex, that *very oft become repulsive to the entity*, especially in sexual relationships. These are builded urges latent and manifested in the experience of the entity.

For as the entity took those vows of chastity, purity and devotion to celibacy, these have become innately displeasing at times. Never satisfying or never gratifying desires for self or for others.

These will become and are stumbling-blocks to the

entity. Yet these are not necessarily those things that should make for disagreements with others, for there are those abilities within self to meet the needs of those relationships in those directions when there is the choice. But as should be from every individual, there should be agreement between those individuals in such relationships. For the lack of such agreement brings more discordant notes between individuals than any portion of relationships with the opposite sex. The disagreements may be very slight at times, but they grow. For these relationships are the channels for the activity of creative forces and not by mere chance. 4082-1, F.52

Another woman, aged 33, asked the following:

Q-9. In what way am I meeting myself in the experience that occurred some time ago that I found so distasteful, and how may I eliminate a reoccurrence?

A-9. There must be the unity on the part of the associations with such activity. Unanimity, then, is necessary; else it will grow to be more and more an obnoxious association to the body. 1523-15, F.33

Similar advice was given to a 58-year-old woman:

Q-4. When one partner in a marriage loses desire for sexual relation and to the other it is still necessary, how may this problem be met?

A-4. Only a united effort on the part of each to fill that which *is* the need of each. 2035-1, F.58

A 29-year-old woman asked how to make sex relations more pleasant and what attitude she should hold towards them. She was told: ". . . have a perfectly normal body—then such relationships and such attitudes towards same becomes the *natural* conditions and not a forced issue ever." (2175-2, F.29)

A woman with latent hate from an incarnation in which her Crusader (and present) husband left her in a chastity belt asked:

Q-1. I have a very gentle, patient, and understanding husband. Yet after almost eight years of marriage, I continue to have terrific fear of the sexual relationship. What causes this? How can this be overcome?

A-1. Knowing as to why and when, this must be overcome in the mind itself. As has been indicated, there are manners, there are means in which there may be aroused the desire for association, for companionship, for affection, for love. Choose such with thy companion.

Q-2. What was the relationship between myself and my husband?

A-2. As indicated, you were husband and wife then—in the French experience. 2762-1, F.32

Notice that this reading encouraged the woman to work out the problem in pursuit of a more satisfactory relationship.

It seems, then, that the first lesson is cooperation; on the one hand not a forced issue ever, and on the other "a united effort on the part of each to fill that which *is* the need of each." (2035-1) Abstinence from relationships was advised on occasion when the two agreed upon a special period of attunement; it was also recommended when bodily disorders made excitation of the physical or mental system inadvisable. A man with some physical disturbances was told:

The abstinence of or from relationships with the opposite sex is well when the creative force is put to creative activity in the mental, but when these are at variance with other conditions these may become just as harmful to the imaginative system or to the central nervous system, from breaking of activities with the sympathetic and the cerebrospinal, and thus become harmful.

There is an activity in the body that we know as coordination. When the mind and the body and various functionings of organs in the body are kept in better relationships one to another, we will find there will be bettered conditions in the body. 5162-1, M.45

Creativity and Conception

The readings indicate a direct and strong relationship between sex and the creative forces. The organs involved (the sexual centers) are also the centers through which all creative energies are given expression. As conception is a physical manifestation of this creative ability, so does creative expression flow through an individual in the same manner. Furthermore, when difficulties exist regarding these reactions, there may be corresponding difficulties in attempts at creative expression. The following reading makes this relationship clear:

Hence this portion, this incompatibility that is between the two individuals as given here, is that which makes for the inability for any *creative* forces to become compatible between the individuals; for there is no soul but what the sex life becomes the greater influence in the life. Not as always in gratification in the physical act, but rather that that finds expression in the creative forces and creative abilities of the body itself. 911-2, F.24

The next reading states that when there are creative spiritual activities, there will be less desire for carnal relationships:

Q-18. So much has been written about sexual relationships between husband and wife. It is the correct understanding that this activity should be used only and when companions seek to build a body for an incoming entity?

A-18. Not necessarily. These depend, of course, to be sure, on the individual concept of relationships and their activities. To be sure, if the activities are used in creative, spiritual form, there is the less desire for carnal relationship; or, if there is the lack of use of constructive energies, then there is the desire for more of the carnal, physical reaction. 2072-16, F.34

The first step on the spiritual path is to normalize, ıen spiritualize! To someone who asked, "What will I do ith the biological urge that arises?" the reading said:

> ***Purify* same in service to Him in expressions of love, ı expression of the fruits of the Spirit which are: gentle-ess, kindness, brotherly love, long-suffering. These are ıe fruits, and these as the urge of sex, are in the nature f the association of ideas, conditions or positions as elated to the various conditions about the body. They set ıe activity in motion and these become either that which ıkes hold on hell or that which builds to the kingdom ithin.** 5747-3

It is in this context that the readings challenge us to ıold rather than to anything else to that *love* which is n-sexed!" (5747-3)

Birth Control, Abortion, and Pregnancy

The intent of this book is the study of sexual expres-on itself in relationship to the seeker on the spiritual ath; thus, questions of birth control, abortion, and preg-ancy appropriately should be dealt with as separate top-s. There are a number of excellent publications on these sues from the viewpoint of the Cayce readings, one of hich is *There Will Your Heart Be Also* by Drs. Gladys ıd William McGarey. It may be said, however, that the eadings' viewpoint very strongly focuses on the major urpose of the sexual relationship: to become channels ırough which spiritually oriented souls may make an ppropriate entry into the earth plane. The fact that the eadings indicate that there may be occasions for sexual xpression *other* than for conception gives a basis for ssuming that utilization of birth control methods would gically follow.

There is only one specific reference to birth control in ıe readings. The question was asked, "Is the broadcasting of birth control information advantageous in improving th race?" Answer: "It is like shooting feathers at an eagle: *It' a move in the right direction,* but that's about as much a might be said." (826-6, M.34; author's italics) The expres sion, "It's a move in the right direction," suggests approva of the principle of birth control; however, in the sam context the Cayce source also questions the motives c those who promulgate such information.

Regarding birth control methods, it is our opinion tha only those which are strictly mechanical should be em ployed. The point is that many birth control techniques in volve the endocrine system and, since the endocrine systen involves the spiritual centers, we caution against any tam pering with the hormonal messages that are sent by thi system. The utilization of chemicals, as in the pill, obviousl has effects on the endocrine system; however, it may no be widely known that intrauterine devices, although seem ingly mechanical, may also send messages to the endocrin system as a part of the way in which they function.

There is at least one case in the readings of a mentall retarded child for whom sterilization was recommended The use of surgery, of course, is a serious consideration We again emphasize making decisions based on guidanc from the spirit within.

The question of abortion is not a sexual question a all, but one dealing with entirely different considerations It is obvious, of course, that as a means of birth control i is unthinkable. Once the pregnancy is established, the other considerations should be addressed regarding suc decisions. The readings do not deal directly with th question of abortion; however, we submit three conside ations. First, in the case of an unwed mother, the reading encouraged her to go through with the pregnancy. Sec ond, a tremendous reverence for life and for natur processes is found throughout the readings. Third, th readings are very clear, as in the remarks regarding proh bition of the sale of alcohol, that one cannot, through leg process, legislate goodness.

The readings give very strong, important instruction regarding intercourse during the period of pregnancy!

Q-40. Does intercourse while carrying child interfere with the physical or spiritual development of the child?
A-40. After three months, yes. 457-9, F.34

Building Relationships and Building the Home

In the readings the *home* represents the major, central and essential social structure for the growth of the soul. "For, the home represents—or is a shadow of—that eternal dwelling place with the Creative Forces." (2271-1) Marriage is the essential relationship for the maintenance of a home structure, and sexual expression is to be an outcome of, and not the purpose of, marriage. Building a solid marriage relationship and building a home, therefore, while constituting the essential purpose and context for sexual expression, are not questions of sex in and of themselves and should be dealt with in another context. There is a vast amount of information in the readings on home and marriage, on child training, on interpersonal relationships, and on attitudes and emotions and their importance in relationships with others. Therefore, we will endeavor to give only intimations of the readings' viewpoint on these questions, since they require another context.

The following excerpt illustrates the spirit of building a marriage relationship. Apparently the husband had been previously married and had a son; his new wife is asking about developing their relationship:

Q-1. Why are we so uncomfortable with one another?
A-1. They each have made up their mind that they don't care and they don't like to be together; yet if they will analyze—together—those problems of each that have existed, and try—*try*—to meet them on a common basis, the situation will be understood and the uncomfortableness will be erased. Pray over it. Don't—*don't*—attempt to do the analyzing without taking it to Him!
***Q-2. How can we feel more* married?**

A-2. By making the purposes of each as one.

Q-3. Why is it so hard for us to agree on anything?

A-3. Each looks for the differences, rather than that on which ye *can* agree!

Q-4. Should we plan some specific hobby or recreation together, periodically? If so, what?

A-4. This would be a very, *very* good start. Where the planning of recreation, of activity, of thought or study, or interest, is separate, ye grow apart. Where the interest may be together—whether in a hobby, in a recreation, in a study, in a visitation, in an association—ye grow in purpose as one.

The *law is, not* that ye may go one this way and the other that, and then your ideas and purposes be one; but where the treasure is, there may the heart be also, there may the activity be united.

Q-5. When [1467] spends his time off with his son, should [263] occasionally go with him?

A-5. This depends rather upon the son. While there should be interests alike, interests together—that there is a difference of opinions such, it may depend more upon what *has* been said by others. But this, too *can* be altered for good of all. It would be well to be undertaken, but once begun *don't* let it break the purposes!

Q-6. How should she conduct herself so as to produce harmony between the three?

A-6. In the same manner as ye ask, in the same manner ye desire that [1467] show toward thine own. These must be as a unison. Thy purposes, thy activities should be in the same accord as that deference, that judgment [1467] has shown, does show, toward thine own. This should be in keeping with the principles that have been set forth—seek *where ye may be of one purpose! Minimize the faults, magnify the virtues!*

263-18, F.31

Advice to study oneself and to follow the Golden Rule was given to hundreds of people, as indicated in the following for a 57-year-old man:

Q-8. How and in what manner can I . . . make my home life happier and my wife more pleased with my actions?

A-8. Study to show thyself approved unto thy Maker, a workman not ashamed, rightly dividing the words of truth and keeping self unspotted from the world. Do in thine own home as ye would have those in thy home do to thee. Not as a show, but with that feeling, that hope, that desire to show the appreciation of the love that is shown thee.

1965-1, M.57

Another reading emphasized the importance of the home to a 43-year-old woman:

. . . do seek another companion, as a husband, though, and there will come into the experience of the entity, in either instance, if those suggestions are adhered to as to tolerance and as to making selfless and less for gratifying and satisfying but as a unit of strength and purpose, the accomplishing of much for the home. This is the nearest representation of that to which each soul seeks to attain, to be one with the universal consciousness and yet aware of itself. This ye alone can attain, in making the ideal that as was manifested by Him, who is the way . . .

Q-1. What type of work am I best suited to do?

A-1. Home building is the best type. Any business, any activity, anything that is of routine: as running a machine, even mechanical devices or weaving machines, but *home* is best.

5106-1, F.43

Another woman, seeking special advice in strengthening her relationship with her husband, was told that the greatest career of any wife is creating, making, building a home.

Q-6. Can I help my husband more, and fulfill his ideal and dream of what he expects of his wife, by studying and going on with plans for achievement in a profession, or by going deeper into the career of a house-

wife? He has so far shown little interest in a home as such, but that may come—I want him to be happy.

A-6. The greatest career of any wife is creating, making, building a home that is of such a nature, so attractive that it becomes of any individual, which is permitted to the wife, is to build the home in such a way and manner as to make it a retreat, as a place where *all* of those activities are such that it fills the longing that is in the heart and soul of each and every individual who has taken a mate for such.

As to whether this can be combined with a career or not is dependent upon the application of self in the directions of its abilities; for it may be used as same. But *do not* let other associations or affiliations make it rather as a place to hang the hat or to rest. *Build* a home!

Q-7. Can I reach a true understanding of my husband's temperament, needs, and of marriage, so that our future together will be harmonious and happy?

A-7. If you study same in the light of that which has been indicated; that is: Analyze as to what are the purposes and desires. Analyze as to what the purposes and desires were that brought you and your husband together. If they were for a gratifying only of physical, or for the desire of a physical nature, that's all there will ever be then!

But these go deeper; and as we find, if there is the attempt, and the *real* attempt—and the analyzing of the purposes of each, they can be understood and each become as a strength, as a stay one for the other.

For that which prompted the very activity of being brought into the relationships was from the spiritual import; while having the physical, the mental as well as spiritual aspects. Build them in a creative, constructive and spiritual force. 1579-1, F.34

In the following case the individual had apparently been working on building a home since her Atlantean incarnation, through Egypt and Palestine, up to the present.

There we find the entity was in a state of turmoil because of the activities of the sons of Belial, and with those of the daughters of the children of One. For the entity had disputations—being physically in love with one of the sons of Belial, and yet giving in its service, giving in its activities with the children of the Law of One.

Hence disputations, and the giving away of fleshly desires arose.

Leave these far from thee in the present. For know, while they arise in thy experience in the present, there is the healing which comes in Him and the knowledge of His presence abiding with thee, that taketh away the *desire* even for those weaknesses of the flesh.

The name then was Asmen-n.

As to the abilities of the entity in the present, that to which it may attain, and how:

Study to show thyself approved unto God, a workman not ashamed, but rightly giving the pressure where it is needed; giving credence where it has proven the measure to the standard in Him, thy Ideal.

The *home* is the real adventure, the real purpose of the entity's expression in the earth. For as seen, in Atlantis the desire for same brought disturbance; in Egypt it brought the better understanding; in the time when the Master taught thee, there was the perfect home with His presence abiding there *after* the awakening; in the experience in the present land, it brought a helpful force.

Hence in the present, build thine own home upon the sure foundation. Thou hast met him—thou lovest him. He has disappointed thee, but bring that into thy heart and mind that—with the Christ-life and purpose—ye will bring into material experience a *channel* to be the blessings of the many. 1968-1, F.28

A 37-year-old woman, "indeed a woman," was encouraged in the care of the home—if not her own, then one for others.

This entity is one that is indeed a woman. For, little or no consciousness is in the manifestation of the entity as

to an entrance into material manifestation in the opposite sex.

Hence the entity is unusually attractive to the opposive sex. Yet the entity finds self rather questioning self as to its choice of a mate.

But know, the soul is rather the soul-mate of the universal consciousness than of an individual entity.

Thus may this entity be much, in a large measure, to many. And the greater hope, the greater influence the entity may make, the greater contribution the entity may give in the experience, is the care of a home; if not by its choice of its *own* home, then in *making* one for those who have not been so fortunate a to have one. 2988-2, F.37

The following instructions illustrate the central spirit and attitude of the readings in encouraging individuals to build their relationships one with another.

Q-5. Why do I get so little love, consideration and appreciation from those to whom I pour out the most service and devotion?

A-5. Study that which has been given thee relative to such, and ye will see that it is patience ye must learn, that ye must add to those virtues that have made thee ever the burden bearer for the many throughout those periods when the awakenings were coming.

Faint not because of thy loneliness, for who can be alone with His love, His promises abiding with thee!

These may make for a blooming into activity in thy experience, and *will*, if ye will give expression more and more to those promises that are thy very own.

For He, as He hath promised may bring to thy remembrance *all* things—from the foundations of the earth. Know the Lord is nigh; and that those who keep watch, who keep faith *with* thee, are even as those of old—when there are the hundreds, yea the thousands that have never bended the knee to Baal, but as thee—only need that light, that assurance that He *is* the guiding light! 1472-1, F.57

We would minimize the faults, we would magnify the virtues. For we have many of each. And the greater injunction may be: don't think more highly of yourself than you ought to think. To be sure, so live in thine own life that you can look all in the face and tell them where to go (that is very warm), but be sure ye know what has prompted those activities. For as indicated in thy abilities to attract the opposite sex—for what purpose is it? That ye may aid them or that they may contribute to your vanity? Think well on these things. 3640-1, F.27

Q-9. What approach should be made to my husband to clarify his understanding of spiritual and psychic truths?

A-9. Live it first in self, and let *that* be the answer rather than trying to bring the lesson home by word or other than just living it!

Q-10. Is there any way I can be of service to him in the direction of his life? Or is the apparent confusion in his mind something that I can help correct?

A-10. Not so much by talking, but *living* the truths—as indicated—is the only or *best* manner.

Q-11. Why is there a seeming barrier between us?

A-11. Those influences as brought thee together have made and do make for the *needs* of a closer spiritual understanding. 1833-1, F.53

Alternative Relationships

One of the major questions on sex of this century, perhaps of every century, regards the seeking of sexual relationships outside of marriage. Those who came to the source of the readings with such questions were, of course, of varied backgrounds and life circumstances. As is frequently the case in studying the readings, the exact wording of them is important and worthy of careful examination. Such is true in cases of their response to questions about such alternative relationships.

We may note the consistency with which the readings indicate that the choice is up to the individual, the consistency with which the individual is called to make that choice according to his own ideal, and the consistency with which the readings decline to condemn or even judge with respect to such a decision. Therefore, let us examine several questions related to this topic and look carefully at the wording with an attuned and seeking attitude.

Q-1. Is monogamy the best form of home relationship?

A-1. Let the teachings be rather toward the spiritual intent. Whether it's monogamy, polygamy, or whatnot, let it be the answering of the spiritual _within_ the individual!

But monogamy is the best, of couse, as indicated from the Scripture itself—_One—ONE!_ For the union of one should ever be _One_.

Q-2. Is marriage as we have it necessary and advisable?

A-2. It is!

Q-3. Should divorces be encouraged by making them easier to obtain?

A-3. This depends upon first the education of the body. Once united, once understood that the relationships are to be as one, less and less is there the necessity of such conditions. Man may learn a great deal from a study of the goose in this direction. Once it has mated, _never_ is there a mating with any other—either the male or female, no matter how soon the destruction of the mate may occur—unless _forced_ by _man's_ intervention.

This does not indicate that this is the _end_, and should _only_ remain as such. For, as we have indicated, _this_ is indicated by the name and the meaning of the name itself. For this is the extreme.

Q-10. Should men or women who do not have the opportunity to marry have sex relationships outside of marriage?

A-10. This again is a matter of principle within the individual. The sex organs, the sex demands of every individual, must be gratified in _some_ manner as a portion of the biological urge within the individual. These _begin_ in the present with curiosity. For it is as natural for there to be sexual relations between man and woman, when drawn together in their regular relations or activities, as

it is for the flowers to bloom in the spring, or for the snows to come in the winter, when the atmospheric conditions are conducive or inducive to such conditions.

When a man or woman has chosen (for it must be choice, and is only by choice that one remains out of relationships with the opposite sex in marriage)—if it has chosen to not be in such relationships, then be true to the choice; or else it is to self a sin! For that which one would pretend to be and isn't is indeed sin! 826-6, M.34

Q-1. Is sexual intercourse outside of marriage injurious morally and spiritually?

A-1. This must ever be answered from one's own inner self. Those attributes of procreation, of the pro-activity in individuals, are from the God-Force itself. The promptings of the inner man must ever be the guide; not from *any* source may there by given other than, "Study to show theyself approved unto the God that thou would worship." As ye would have men do to you, do ye even so to them. In the light of thine own understanding, keep thy body pure, as thou would have others keep their bodies pure. For thy body is the temple of the living God. Do not desecrate same in thine own consciousness.

826-2,M.33

For, the entity is one who may have had, or may have, many affairs in this experience; for it is attractive, one of those natures as to draw about self others of the opposite sex as well as of its own sex.

Thus the greater need for the entity to indicate and to stress in its associations and contracts with others the spiritual life; not using its goodness as a shield or as an outward show, but rather letting the impelling influence be from the ideals of the entity. 2835-1, F.56

Q-4. Is it desirable for this body to have sex relationships other than that obtainable through a marriage, if it has its inception in the spiritual mind?

A-4. The relationships that come from that which is of the highest vibrations that are experienced in the material world are those that may be found in such relations, and are the basis of that which is termed the original sin; and hence may be easily misunderstood, misconstrued, misinterpreted in the experience of *every* individual; but these should be known—that the control of such, rather than being controlled *by* such, gives that which makes for the awareness of *spiritual* intent and purpose. To overstep those conditions created by those environs in social relations and atmospheres that are brought about by such, however, is to take those leaves with self that may not be *easily* retained. Take not, give not, that that cannot be taken and given in the spirit of "*His* will, not mine, be done!" Each must judge such for themselves, in the light of *their* understanding. Each has the right to say I will, I will not.

Q-5. Need I fear loving any man, or *must I be calculating?*

A-5. When self has found self, such relationships are the *natural* inspiration of the spiritual. As has been given oft, know *in* what and *in* whom thous has believed. If such has its inception in constructive life, fear not! If such has its inception in the gratification of selfish interests, fear! for when fear entereth, doubt entereth; and he that doubteth is lost already! 911-5, F.24

Q-5. What are my obligations to the man who has recently returned in my life? and how should I conduct myself for our mutual development?

A-5. Keep self unspotted from the world. As to what the conduct should be, let it never be for only emotional satisfaction—but creative in its nature.

Q-6. Through my meditation, has the kundalini fire risen to the head or top of spine at base of skull? If so, was it because of sex abstinence and discipline that this happened?

A-6. It has risen at *times*, but has not remained; else there would *not* be those periods of confusion. For, when this has arisen—and is disseminated properly through the seven centers of the body, it has purified the body from all desire of sex relationships. For, *this is* an outlet

through which one may attain to celibacy—through this activity. That it has *not remained* indicates changes.

Q-7. Since my husband has been impotent these many years, would sexual relationships with some trusted friend (a bachelor) help me so I can function positively and rhythmically in carrying on the normal business of home life and work? Please advise me in regard to such.

A-7. Such questions as these can only be answered in what is thy ideal. Do not have an ideal and not attempt to reach same. There is no condemnation in those who *do* such for helpful forces, but if for personal, selfish gratification, it is sin. 2329-1, F.41

As a short study on "affairs," the following sequence of questions and answers offers an interesting perspective:

Q-1. Where and how was I associated in past incarnations with N . . . ?

A-1. He broke thy home in the experience before this. Will ye break his, or thine own, in the present?

Q-2. Are his intentions sincere toward me, or am I just another "affair" at the present time?

A-2. You are just another "affair." Will ye accept, will ye reject, the truth?

Q-3. How should I go about breaking off my relationship with him and re-establish myself so that I would be happy and forget him?

A-3. In doing something for someone else! Not in gratifying of self's own desires, nor in answering to the desires of the body. Make those relationships with one with whom ye have *almost* broken off. *There* ye will find help and strength, *if* ye *will* but take hold! Trust in the strength and the might of Him who hath given, "I do not condemn thee, but *sin no more!*" His power alone may now take you away from that unholy desire that consumes thee, in thy relationships just now.

Q-4. If E . . . came east and I broke up relationship with N . . . , could I ever re-establish my former friendship with E . . . . , and would this be advisable?

A-4. As just given, there is hope there. There is none in N. . .

Q-6. Where and how was I associated in past incarnations with my father . . and why is there so much animosity between us?

A-6. He was thy husband in the experience before this. And would not there be animosity, with the home broken? 2960-1, F.20

A special insight regarding attitudes to be held by those on the spiritual path may be seen in the following given for a 67-year-old woman. Although the question does not deal specifically with sexual relationships, the problem of the conflict between responsibility and freedom is the essence of many such questions.

Q-3. How may I solve the problem of a home and freedom to be myself?

A-3. Let thy acts day by day in all of thy associations be such that ye may continue to ever be at a Oneness with Him in thy relationships with thy fellow man. And know thou art His, God's—and leave it as this:

"My problems, my experiences, my conditions, I leave them—O God—in Thy hands! They are Thine, as I am Thine! Use me in those places, in those channels, in those ways where Thou seest I may be of the greater service."

And then ye may be very sure that these—if ye live them, if ye be them, if ye are them—are cared for in *His* way. And every soul should be even as the Son in the example gave, "Not my will but Thine be done in me, through me." 1299-1, F.67

Separation and Divorce

A number of people came to Edgar Cayce questioning the advisability of a separation. As usual, he advised the individuals involved to make the decision from their own ideals and inner guidance; however, on some occasions couples in an unpromising marriage were encouraged to stay together, and on other occasions the source indicated that it would be for the better, for both involved, to separate. The following information, although given regarding a broken engagement and not a separation in marriage, may contain the essence of the problem for those with this question.

It is a fact that, as we have given, there is the conviction in the heart of each that the *better* relationships for the good of each may come through their being joined together in their efforts in this present experience.

Yet, as given, to *crucify* self's ideals to the whims or fancies of any man is *not* development for the body!

316-1, F.25

The following information given to a 57-year-old woman contains the same principle in a more elaborated and instructive statement:

Q-1. What true relation does my husband [from whom I'm separated] bear to me, and why did he come into my life? Can I help him other than by good thoughts?

A-1. This question—in relationship to husband and others for this entity or any one soul—is well.

As has been indicated through these channels, there is never a chance meeting, or any association, that hasn't its meaning or purpose in the development of an individual entity or soul.

Then, as we have indicated, if any entity, any individual, takes a meeting, any association, with the purpose or the desire to use same for self-indulgence, self-aggrandizement, and no thought of the purposes of any activity through the development of the soul for its purpose as it enters, then it becomes that as may be or is called *karma*—or the individual becomes subject to *law*!

And, as has been pronounced, the letter of the law killeth, but the spirit of the law maketh alive.

Then the spirit of the law is exemplified in He that *is* the Law of Love, and Grace, and Mercy, and Truth.

And they that use such associations, such meetings as such, become helpmeets one to another—or stepping-stones for a greater development.

Then as indicated in the question sought here—as regarding individual association: While a greater or broader truth might be gained by comparison of what each of these as individual entities had done and have done and are doing respecting the soul developments through the planes, we find—as indicated by the association—there have been meetings before, of course as in the experiences before this—a very close association, though *not* as man and wife. *Rather* as brother and sister.

And their activities as one towards another were as variations to conditions, as to the purposes for which and the manner in which they each applied themselves towards creative influences and forces during the experience.

One—as we have indicated—applied self for an advancement, the other for retardment.

The natural associations were attractive one to another; but when there came to be questions as to that which was self-indulgence and that which was for glorifying of the spirit, the developments of the cross purposes showed themselves.

These as we find then in the present—under the present associations, it is well or better for each if there is rather the good intent and purpose through the *mental* self than the *physical or* mental associations. 1648-2, F.57

Thus we are given from the source of the readings that when *self-indulgence* is being sought by one and *glorifying of the Spirit* is sought by the other, then separation, at least in some circumstances, is recommended.

On a number of occasions when the readings advised separation, the decision was based partly on some physical condition of one of the partners which needed correction. The following information given to a 30-year-old woman continues to affirm the physical nature of the difficulty which she had clearly interpreted as a fault in the relationship:

Q-1. Is there anything I can do to make my husband fall in love with me again?

A-1. There needs to be rather those separations there—unless physical conditions with the husband, in his ideal *of* material relationships, are changed by surgery.

Q-2. Why do we seem to have so little in common, so little to talk about?

A-2. As indicated, these are the meeting of self from those experiences through the sojourn just previous to this—when the relationships were rather as father and daughter; yet *brought* relationships where it required the separate activities for the greater benefit of each.

And so it may become here, *unless* those activities of a material nature—and physical conditions—are changed.

Q-3. Why does he seem to have lost all physical love for me?

A-3. As indicated—it is a physical defect—a *physical* condition in that body—the husband.

Q-4. What has come between us?

A-4. As indicated, it is a physical defect—not a mental, not a purposeful one. But the entity must choose for itself, see?

Do, then, that as indicated. Study within self, first! What is thy ideal, spiritually—thy ideal home? Not as to what is the ideal thing that *others* should do, but the ideal manner that *ye* should do! And do that! 1872-1, F.30

A 24-year-old woman and her 35-year-old husband had been advised in earlier readings to separate; however, on one occasion, they asked specifically why a separation would be best for them. The somewhat complex answer may nevertheless be quite instructive as to the manner in which the readings perceived and advised on such questions.

Q-1. Is it not advisable that [912] and I should separate permanently? Explain why this is best for both of us.

A-1. As has been given, each individual has its own duties and responsibilities, not only to itself but to those

with whom it associates, as well as its relationship to that which is its ideal. As to what each individual here concerned has made its ideal, neither could very well define; neither could either tell just how much duty, obligation and hope may be found in their association or separation, until they have a standard by which such ideals of selves and selves' abilities, selves' duties, selves' obligations, may be measured; neither would or could there be given as to what *either* should do! That the conditions at the present are basically an error would be evidenced by the fact that neither have found themselves, nor their duty or obligation to each.

Then, as has been given, first each should find their selves; then they will be better able to know wherein they have failed and what their relationship should be. This *should* be decided by themselves *when* they found themselves—see? 911-5, F.24

Some who had been separated or widowed questioned the advisability of marrying again. They were usually told, as in the case of this 57-year-old woman, that they should set their purposes and begin to prepare themselves to be a better spouse.

Q-2. How can I marry again and make the best of the marriage for both of us?

A-2. This must yet be an experience. But the purposes or the aims, the hopes have not been set as yet. If ye do, it will be one abroad. Ye can make it a success. How? It's a fifty-fifty proposition, not a seventy-five-twenty-five.

Q-3. How can I best prepare for old age?

A-3. By preparing for the present. Let age only ripen thee. For one is ever just as young as the heart and the purpose. Keep sweet. Keep friendly. Keep loving, if ye would keep young. 3420-1, F.57

Sexy? For Seduction or for Service?

One type of experience, mentioned several times in the readings, was that of an individual who is sexually attractive to many people, yet without an accompanying character development that prepares him or her to deal with such responses. Those who came with these problems were encouraged in the strongest terms to utilize these powers of attraction, even of sexual attraction, for purposes of serving rather than seducing those who came their way. The following extracts give specific instructions for persons dealing with this particular kind of situation:

As the entity finds, it is attracted to and attracts many an individual of the opposite sex. This at times, unless the entity has set its own ideal or idea of metes and bounds, may bring disturbing conditions to the entity. These may be used and not abused, such that the entity may become a contributing factor to the betterment of all whom the entity may meet. If the ideals and purposes are turned to creative forces, to that way of being ever constructive in its relationships and activities with others, as to find that which is the better part, that which is creative or constructive in the mind and activity of an associate or companion, and these are stressed, then the entity may be helpful. When these are turned in that way of being possessive or destructive, these should be discarded by the entity without question. Without such the entity will find itself continually pulled between two ways. Remember there is a way that seemeth right to a man but the end thereof is death. Possessiveness, yes; selfishness, yes; anxieties in which there may be brought jealousy and hate—such activities bring destruction. Those that are creative bring the better forces. 3704-1, F.23

As we find in the personality and individuality, an influence in appearance may be very troublesome to the body and may appear to others as something undesirable, yet may be used the entity to accomplish more than is granted to most people in the position of the entity.

Here is an entity who, if it passed through a throng of men without speaking, all of them would follow if they were free to. Hence to the entity this becomes disturbing, yet if properly used may bring help to many an individual.

This, too, becomes disturbing to the body because apparently the entity is an "easy number"; that is, everyone is trying to sell something or to obtain something or to find favor with the entity, and from just what has been indicated you see why.

How to turn this into a helpful experience: By nature the entity is a teacher, as will be seen from the experiences in the earth. The entity is a natural magnet for the opposite sex, as well as a great influence among its own sex. Use these, then, as a means for telling of the love of Jesus. Let it become such an activity in self that everyone may come to know what would be the first words of the entity, and let them be this, though changed in form for the entity's own friends and experiences. Have you prayed to God today? Men won't follow you; men won't think you are an easy mark. Mean it, for in that manner ye may teach many a man with evil intents to know his place. For remember, no one, no one can stand in the presence of the Lord, the Christ, when words are thus spoken in earnest and in sincerity, no matter what their intent may be, and you will attract those with whom ye may administer much. But in thy activities ever be the teacher of the simplicity of the Christ-child, His birth, His education, His ministry and, as the climax the last acts for ministry with His disciples. "Who would be the greatest among you? He who is the servant of all." When you find individuals too good to do this, or that, for others, something is the matter with their theories, and the soul is shrinking, they are little. Remember what was said of him who was the greatest of men born of woman, that he was the least in the kingdom of heaven, for he forgot to be humble and meek.

As to the astrological aspects, these have meant little in the life of the entity and in the present mean less. These urges are indicated in the personality, not in the individuality, and thus the entity does at times much

more than is considered the proper thing to do, by those who are supposed to give rules for the activities in social circles, or according to Mrs. Post. These, then, mean little to the entity, for it is capable of making its own rules. And they who are the servants for the Christ's sake to others make their own rules in all the activities or associations with others.

Thus Jupiter, Mercury and Venus are all a part of the entity's experience. This is why some follow close to the entity physically and fall far away mentally and spiritually. But dare to do right according to the dictates of thy conscience, if thy conscience is not seared by worldly things. 5089-2, F.50

This is one entity who might take any man and wind him around her finger—by a look and by a wink, or by her own movements. Yet these have not only been eliminated by suppression but purposefully, though they may still be used to advantage if spiritualized, in aiding self as well as anyone else in whom the entity might interest itself. 3577-1, F.56

Sex and Society

For those of us seeking to be on the spiritual path and concerned about the nation and the world, there can be little doubt that many expressions today of a sexual nature are undesirable. Some of the behavioral forms most difficult for us to understand are the excesses of sex, such as in crimes of violence involving sexual abuse. The following excerpts invite us to a perspective of the nature of love in human experience, that may be extremely difficult and challenging for us to cope with, yet very instructive and worthy of our reflection:

Which is the more real, the love manifested in the Son, the Savior, for His brethren, or the essence of love that may be seen in the vilest of passion? They are one. But that they bring into being in a materialized form is

what elements of the one source have been combined to produce a materialization. Beautiful, isn't is?

How far, then, is ungodliness from godliness? Just under, that's all! 254-67

. . . until the beautiful or the beauty of a Creator may be seen in the vilest of the vile that is expressed in mortal body, there is little pure concept of the relationships of the souls of men with God, with the universe.

For as the earth is *only* a portion of a mighty array of forces and influences in our *own* little solar system, so man—though but a speck upon the earth and only as a grain in the universe—is a portion of that divinity that urges *on* and ON and *ON* and ON! that makes for that eternal hope, that spark of light, that thread of soul in infinity itself!

Words fail to come to give those experiences of the entity in that experience, as words would fail to give that as to how the entity besmeared itself with the vileness of men!

In the experience the entity gained and lost; lost in self-indulgence.

Learn the difference, then, between self-indulgence and tolerance. One may be tolerant and yet self-indulgent, even in tolerance—to the extent that one becomes lacking in those very forces that may make for holding to the image of Him that must be in every heart, soul, experience, if one is to keep in the Way. 1298-1, F.43

The essence of these instructions is that there is only One Force which is God; but we, using this force, may bring undesirable expressions of it into materialized form.

How may we, as individuals, groups, or an organization, begin to make a positive contribution to raising the world's consciousness? Two readings, which should be studied in full, 5747-3 and 826-6, cover an array of questions dealing with sexual expression. Especially they challenge us to a long-range commitment of doing a better job in training, by precept and example, our children—a work which must begin prior to conception and continue to involve education on the beauty of sex before the child reaches ten, eleven or twelve years.*

As a final consideration on sex in our society, we may study at length one of the World Affairs readings (3976-8), which summarizes a plan for the solution to all of our problems. This reading says essentially that all *must* have the same ideal: to love God with all our hearts, minds and souls, and our neighbor as ourselves. We may say, "This is impractical!" Though man's answer to everything has always been power, this has never been and will never be God's way. How can this ideal of the great commandment be made practical? By individuals making it applicable and working with the law that a little leaven leavens the whole lump. Our neighbor, the readings say, is anyone who is in need of help; we *are* our brother's keeper and we must answer for him. Finally, a special suggestion about the most constructive contribution we may make is given. Quoting from the Genesis story of Abram as he prayed for Lot, the Cayce source says that many a city, many a nation, has in fact been saved from destruction by the prayers of a few. If we will take to heart this simple question, "Why worry when you can pray?" and begin a committed program of prayer, meditation and the living of our ideal as we understand it, we can be assured that the response in the power of a loving God may indeed save a dying world.

Karmic Vignettes

Since the readings comprise literally thousands of individual cases, to get a true sense of their flavor in dealing with the human condition it is necessary to read many of these cases. Therefore, the following vignettes, reflecting primarily the karmic sources of sexual orientations, are given. Taken as a whole, these examples should give the student an authentic sense of the stance and spirit of the readings' source with respect to many aspects of the sexual question.

---

*These readings are given in their entirety in the Appendix.

One Who Knew to Do Well

In the one before this we find in that first representative sent to this land to represent France, in this as a land. In the name Rau de Claudia. In that experience the entity gained and lost in the application of that as was gained in the *mental* body, for the entity *knew* to do well but allowed the desires of the flesh and of the eye to overcome that as was best in the abilities of the entity. In the urge as is seen, the love of mystery, and of that not wholly understood—yet the innate doubt as goes with such lack of understanding. The reason, the lack of basic forces to set self on a firm basis with the correct criterion as the position in the development of self. 4145-2,M.26

One Too Easily Obtained

And as in thine abilities, in thine *innate* desire—*none* may be more beautiful in purpose, in the life, in the ability to *give* to others joy, peace, contentment—with all the attributes of the earthly things combined—passion, with all of its material loves, all of its material desires. These ye knew well; but unless these be tempered with thine ideal, thy *will* may lead thee in the paths that become troublesome, dark and disagreeable!

Know, then—He, thy Lord, thy God, thy Christ, is in that position—"If ye will be my child, I will be thy God."

Determine then whom ye will serve. That of thine own self that may bring discouragements, despairs? Or Him who hath promised, "My peace I give—not as the world giveth peace, but that which is love, and hope, and kindness, and godliness."

These are such as are creative in thy experience.

As to the appearances in the earth—these as we find have much more to do with the emotions and the materialization of same in the present experience—or that as from which ye may draw comparisons.

Before this we find the entity was in the land of the present sojourn.

It is not then by chance, or that as merely happened, that ye are in this environ in the present. For here before

ye found both the good and the bad—in that during that known as the American Revolution, in this environ ye made for those peoples both wonderment and helpfulness, as well as disappointments—in the name Carol Fanenshaw.

The entity was in the environs of what is now Jamestown, Yorktown, Williamsburg and the like. For the entity was among those whose hand, whose company, whose associations were sought by many—and at times, and during a portion of the experience, too easily obtained.

However, we find the entity in the experience gaining and losing, and gaining; according to that as was manifested in the experience in keeping with the ideal, or in the gratifying of the material and the desires of self without regard to the mind, the purpose, or what people would say.

In the application of self in the present ye will find disappointments in individuals; as ye caused disappointments in the minds, in the experience of others. For know, this is an immutable law—"As ye sow, so shall ye reap!" And it is not only others, but thy *self* and the sorrow and the disappointment ye have caused in others that ye meet *in others* in thy experience.

But, showing mercy, asking judgment, being patient, ye may overcome. For as He has given, "In mercy and patience possess ye your souls." 1754-1, F.62

A One-Woman Man

In the one before this we find in that land known as the Indian in the present, in that period when the peoples from the mount went into the valley, and many of the *men* were destroyed and the *women* were taken as prisoners for the building up of the land. In this period the entity led as a warrior, gaining much during a portion of the experience; losing in the latter portion, and from that experience of many women may the entity be called now a one-woman man, for the experiences were sad in the latter portion of that period. 5-2, M.36

The Letter of the Law

For in the experience before this the entity was in

the French land, where the entity was among that group of sisters who were with the Louis's.

The entity didn't like much the activities or the associations of the sisters, for the entity then was matter of fact, yes—but ruled rather by the principles being set by the church, and to the entity one must hew to the line, the letter of the law without too much spirit.

Thus condemnations came in a part of the entity's experience, condemnation even of those of its own associates. Such must be eliminated. For thy associations in the present will bring thee in the activities, as they have, with thy companion in the present—yea, some of thy associates that will be and that are in the immediate a part of thy associations. Ye condemned them for their activities, that to the self were in disobedience to the law. But one who is weak in the flesh is his or her error greater—or that one should know that condemning of others is already condemning self? Which is the greater sin? For as the Master gave, it is the greater sin to look on a woman or man to lust after such than to perform the act itself that may be forgiven, that may supply those experiences that will bring an outpouring of creation in mind, in body, from a spiritual purpose.

The entity then was known as Sister Celecia. The entity gained, the entity questioned, the entity finds itself confused in the present . . .

Q-4. What is the spiritual source of the glandular condition manifested in my physical body, and just how should it be met?

A-4. The experiences before this with the turmoils wrought by the questionings, as to associations and activities, brought about what now manifests as the glandular disturbance with the relationships having to do with the activities of the creative forces in the body. 4046-1, F.32

Taking Too Many

In the one before this we find in the days of the peoples coming from the waters in the submerged areas, of the Southern portion as is now Peru, when the earth was divided, and the people began to inhabit the earth again. The entity among those who succeeded in gaining the higher grounds, and then in the name of (which was changed afterwards) Omrui, and changed to Mosases, for the entity became the ruler and the guide, or the patriarch of that age and gave much assistance to the few as was gathered about the entity. Only failing in taking unto self too many of the opposite sex of the land, bringing then the enmity of many of the peoples in the later days. In the present we find this urge to keep and steer clear of intrigues of such natures that brings the difficulties in such relations, yet these conditions ever presenting themselves to the entity. One condition to combat. 470-2, M.34

One Who Took the Vows

Man may not live by bread alone. Man may not live by the gratifying of appetites in the material world. For man is not made for this world alone. There is a longing for those experiences which the soul, as an entity, has experienced. And without spirituality the earth is indeed a hell, an individual soul do what it will or may. Such longing may not be gratified from without or in the consciousness of, and the experiences that pertain to, the forces and influences without self. For the body is indeed the temple of the living God. Act like it! Keep it clean. Don't desecrate it ever, but keep it such that it may be the place where you would meet thine own better self, thine own God-self. As ye do this, there may be brought harmony, peace, joy. As in everything else, if ye would have joy ye must make others happy! Bring joy to others. If ye would have love, ye must show thyself lovely! If ye would have friends, show thyself friendly! If ye would know God, search for Him, for He is within thine own self! And as ye express Him in the fruits of spirit; love, grace, mercy, peace, long-suffering, patience, kindness, gentleness; ye will find such within thyself. For if ye would have life indeed (and life is the manifestation of God) ye must give it. For the manner in which ye treat thy fellow man is the manner in which ye treat thy

Maker. This is the source of life, the source of love, the source of peace, the source of harmony, and as ye give expression to same, it may come indeed to thee.

In the application, then, know thyself, thy ideals, thy purposes. Then study to show thyself approved unto God, condemning no one, for with what judgment ye mete, it is measured to thee. Ye cannot judge others harshly and not expect to be judged harshly. Ye cannot do evil that good may come. For each tree, each body, each life is known by the fruits it bears within itself...

Q-3. How did the entity's inferiority complex originate?

A-3. For the fear or dislike of men. You cannot be one who took the vows the kept them and then lightly turn around and try to gratify the appetites of those who are not easily satisfied. 4082-1, F.52

Another's Companion

Before this we find the entity was in the land of the present nativity, though of a different environ, in the early portions of the settlings of the land; in the pre-Revolutionary periods when there were the settlings and the dealings with other lands and other groups as they gathered.

We find the entity was a teacher—yea, of song; also of the abilities to draw and to weave things that made for conveniences through those periods of activity.

The entity gained in the greater portion, until the allowing of *selfishness* to fulfill the longings of the *bodily* forces and it partook of those things that were, even to self, unlawful—taking another's companion; bringing upon self the satisfaction for the moment but in the end remorse—that eateth as a canker, producing hate and jealousies that made for a manifestation which in the present brings those inclinations towards self-centeredness.

Beware of these in thy experience. Replace them rather with that beauty that is capable of being manifested through the very material activities as well as associations with others. 1828-1, F.20

An Easy Life

Ye became strong by that simple trust in Jesus and again ye may find thy strength of thy mind and thy body in His purposes alone.

Before that ye were among those in Atlantis who used the divine purposes among the sons and daughters of the law of One and the turmoils of the sons of Belial—yea, life is easy, and peace becomes at times such as to make sad the heart of those who look upon gratifying of the flesh. And ye partook!

These come to thee again in the warring of the body for the material things, and these must pass away. But the hopes, the desires, the purposes may change not. And the law is perfect—that ye sow, ye reap. If ye sow it to the flesh, in the flesh ye must reap. If ye sow it in the mind, to the mind it must be made straight. For it depends upon what spirit ye entertain. For it is only with the spirit of truth as manifested in that light, that knowledge of God deep within self, that ye may make thy paths straight. See, hear, know, act—and the world is thine. For He withholds no good thing from those who seek and love His coming.

Do that . . .

Q-1. Have I lost my opportunity to work for the Masters in this life?

A-1. When ye come to lose—only thyself may separate thee from the love of God. No power in heaven or hell may separate thee save thyself. 3660-1, F.53

Smiles and Wiles

In the one before this we find the English rule, when the peoples came in from the Norse country, and the entity then a Norse maiden, in the name Djhrldte, and the entity then brought much consternation to many of the young men of the day, especially in and among those of the ecclesiastical nature, for many were the suitors, and many took the hood, or the recluse life, from the rejection of those smiles of the entity, and the entity both developed and retarded, for little judgment was used in the wiles of the sex of the entity in that day, and the entity finds, in that inner urge, that desire to be very sure of self in *any* respect as regarding such relations at the present sojourn, and little of such nature enters into the personality, yet is deep-seated and latent in the entity's being, yet with the feeling that the real or right condition will present itself through the action of mentality, rather than sentiment. 2486-1, F.22

Too Oft Affairs

Before that the entity was in the English land during those periods of the Crusades, when many an individual—stirred by a zeal for an undertaking—forgot purposes and ideals; forgetting that each entity, each soul manifesting in the earth is here by the grace of God, and has its place. Then it is not by might nor by power—as the entity learned in those periods of material as well as physical suffering—that God makes manifest; but rather in the lowly things, the little things, the beauty, the joy, the love that creeps in through patience, kindness, gentleness. These grow. For they are as the manners in which ye cultivate the spirit of truth in the earth.

In that experience the entity gained in spirit, in mind; lost in body. For, as in the present experience, too oft affairs with the opposite sex may bring disturbing influences. Let not thy good be evil spoken of because of weaknesses of the flesh

The name then was Oran Carson. 3308-1, M.63

A Nation Loses

Hence as a counselor, as a statesman in the *inner* workings of same, may be a portion of the entity's experience; yet the beauties of nature are a part also. And if these are guided aright they may make for many a saving grace, a saving experience for the entity during this sojourn—if they are not weakened by the influence of the fair sex that becomes more of indulgences for the entity than for thoughts of the peoples of a state or nation as a whole. 1332-1, M.5 mos.

Sensuousness and Habits

So, be mindful—as He warned Thomas, Philip, Andrew and Peter, as well as showed to James and John, that these things are oft hard to be understood by those who may only know that which answers to the sensuousness-consciousness of an entity. Not the senses as the higher realm, but sensuousness that begets (and its children are!) lasciviousness and those forces that engorge or indulge in those things that gratify appetites, and those things that become a part of many who become self-indulgent in habit forming, habit creating.

For, the animal man is a creature of habit. But learn rather from such the lesson, and not become so much a part of same. For in nature and in the animal instincts we find only the expressions of a universal consciousness of hope, and never of fear—save created by man in his indulging in the gratification of material appetites. 2067-1, F.52

Keeper of an Inn

There we find the entity acted in those capacities that might to some in the present be called questionable. For the entity was a keeper of what would be called a hotel, or inn; and many of the characters of that period came to the entity at one time or another, under this or that circumstance, for counsel, for advice.

The name then was Maggie McGuirah. In the experience the entity *materially* had a great deal of dissension and turmoil, yet spiritually and mentally the entity gained throughout the sojourn.

Hence in the present many of those turmoils have arisen, not only in its marital relationships but in its friendships and its church affiliations, and associations, that have brought questionings. And yet, as ye know in *whom* ye have believed, know that He is able to keep that thou may commit unto Him against every experience that may be thine.

For, His promises are true; that ye abiding in Him, as He abides in the Father, ye may ask and receive—if ye *believe*, and *live* it!

Know that His commandments are not grievous; for

as He gave, "Take my yoke upon you and learn of me, for my yoke is easy, my burden is light, to those who love their fellow man."

Then, know that He *is* thy friend, thy Lord, thy Master; that there is none other name given under heaven whereby a soul may indeed find its way back to its Maker. For He is the way, the truth *and* the light!

2035-1, F.58

A Traveler Alone

In this experience the entity gained and lost. Gained through much as was given to the peoples through the associations of those that were about the priest and the keeper of the jewels, the moneys, the things as were contributed; yet when the entity stood *alone*—with the passing of these—in being sent *to* the other lands, the entity allowed those of the opposite sex in the lands to lead the entity astray, falling in that way that so easily beset those that have set self for a purpose. In *this* the entity lost. 2122-1, M.38

Unsought Attractions

Before that the entity was in the Roman land, among those peoples during the period when there was the attempt of those in authority to embrace the activities of the Grecians—and especially their spread of the acting, whether for the arena in [feats] of manhood or otherwise—and these later became—or took on—the greater expression of speechmaking, or declarations, or declamations and oratories.

Then the entity was in the opposite sex—being beautiful in body, and made those experiences when the ability for its attraction for the opposite sex brought periods of turmoil. And these may be met in the present experience by the inactivity that attracts when not meant to be.

The abilities as the speaker, writer, also arise from that activity, as Guilfuld. In that experience the entity gained, the entity lost.

And in the meeting of same in the present, keep thy judgments. 2655-1, F.29

Excesses of Emotions

Before that we find the entity was in the Grecian land, coming to the Arabian and Persian land; for the entity was among the Grecian maidens who came into the "city in the hills and the plains."

The entity was among those who were not convinced, for the entity held to that as a duty for which it had been sent—for the conniving for the destruction of those peoples in that environ.

Hence, with the great divisions as arose among the peoples, the entity sought to return rather to those channels through which there was the exaltation of the body-beautiful, and the excesses of appetites, of desires and emotions.

Thus we find the end of the entity's experience there was very revolting in self, as well as many of those who had been and were the companions of the entity.

Hence we find that those things of such natures—whether in the dance, the beauties in art, in literature, or all of the higher arts as may be termed in the present—become channels through which the entity may give the expression of the emotions that arise. Make such creative. For ye have known and been told and given what is creative. That which is *ever*lasting!

The name then was Ecleas. 1999-1, F.32

Loss of Self-Control

Before that we find the entity was in the Atlantean land, during those periods when the first of the upheavals were brought about, when the activities of the sons of Belial brought to the daughters of the children of the Law of One the abilities for enjoying the pleasures of excesses of *every* nature in human relationships, as well as those activities related to same.

These were the beginning of the excesses in the experience. For the entity, turning to its abilities for excesses of indulgence, lost the hold upon the self-determining.

Turn rather to the powers within, then. For only through that which answers to that within which is creative may helpful forces *ever* be brought to an individual, including this entity.

For each soul is self-willed.

What will ye present to thy Maker? 1999-1, F.32

From Broken Vows to the Crusades

Here, in the present environ, was the entity's appearance in the earth before this—one who had taken vows and found love of the material things caused the entity to break those vows of celibacy. This brought to the entity material joys, and yet the entity feared throughout the experience that these were for self rather than toward that purpose which had been determined by the entity.

Know, all the desires of the body have their place in thy experience. These are to be used and not abused. All things are holy unto the Lord, that He has given to man as appetites or physical desires, yet these are to be used to the glory of God and not in that direction of selfishness alone.

In that sojourn the entity suffered. And in the present some doubts and fears arise as to whether this or that experience is holy or whether it will hinder in making the material or spiritual success that is so desired.

Let this be rather the tenet of the mind, of the soul, of the body: Success must be to the glory of God rather than to the gratifying of any appetite, of any desire, of fame or fortune. Know that fame and fortune must be the result of thy seeking in His paths first, and then all will be lighted along the way.

The name then was Mary Anthony.

Before that the entity was in the French land during those periods when there were the activities known as the Crusades. And the entity, in the joy of its love of its companion, of its hopes for a home and for offspring, was suddenly brought to dispersion in that its mate was called for that which to him was a service. Being left alone, the entity —in doubt and in fear, in remorse—made itself miserable.

So may the entity in the present, not taking on the joys of the very present activities, not taking on even the hours of toil in practice, the hours of toil in just being patient, just being kind, will find that it will become sour—unless life is made a joyous thing. See the humorous side of every situation. Read humor that is of the nature to cause one to enjoy life; and we will find that those experiences there—as Renee Fecherr—will be eliminated from the consciousnesses that arise when certain characters of activity become a part of the daily experience in associations with others. 3234-1, F.24

She Has Been a Man More Than Once

What an unusual record, the entity having been a man more than once! Thus an individual entity who is in its characteristics and mental processes quite efficient and at times quite sufficient unto itself.

The entity finds self with the ability to love, yes—but rather not inclined to be affectionate in any way. These are tendencies or characteristics that are a part of the entity's experience because of the variation of the sex. We find that these contribute in many ways to the abilities of the entity yet in many of the emotions, as has been the experience of the entity, have been at times quite confusing; as the entity's emotion towards its own sex under certain conditions, we well as repulsion and attraction to the opposite sex . . .

The social life, the social experiences of individuals and groups as related to their relationships to others of the entity's own sex or the opposite sex are of the universal nature. These at times, brings wonderments and confusions to the entity. 4067-1, F. 42

You Were One

The entity was among that group, and thus a man, or in the opposite sex. Thus in the present, the peculiar feeling toward sex and men, and as how the entity can see through them and what they are thinking almost. It's because you were one, not because you're so wise! These are the urges. 5259-1, F.46

Deep Fears

. . . there were *fears* created in the body and mind through the associations and happenings in relationships to others of various characters and tribes, and the relationships to the opposite sex. And these have brought, with the present experience, some fears that are *deep* in the innate experiences of the entity. Not that these should be cast aside, yet if there will be builded in the material conditions of the body—through the types of suggestions—that strength which is so often sought, the abilities to find expressions in the activities of self in out-of-door games, in associations of various kinds where an athletic expression is sought—much of this will be overdone, and there may be the entering into such with such a way and manner as to overcome much of the *physical* fear that exists in the innate experience from that sojourn. 768-4, F.15

A Crusader's Wife

Before that the entity was in the French land, during those periods when there were definite activities called the Crusade periods.

There the entity was associated with, and the companion of, the present companion. Because of those manners in which there were the doubts, the fears as manifested by the companion, and the manner in which there were those precautions to prevent the relationships of the sexual nature with others, when the companion went to the Crusade activities, there are those doubts and fears arising from latent hate—created in that experience for the entity during that material sojourn.

The name then was Marcella Hershamonl. In the experience the entity found hardships of mind, hardships of purpose, owing to those conditions created or brought about—that are conditions to be met in the

present by an understanding. For, if ye would be forgiven ye must forgive. For, with what purpose, with what ideal ye sow, that ye must reap—as ye are doing in the present.

Thus those choices of ideals, of manners, of giving material expression in the hates, the innate hates, the innate jealousies, the innate activities. These must be met in self . . .

First, find and know thy ideal. 2762-1, F.32

These vignettes, samples from a number of individuals' life readings, should give us a clearer sense of the variety of previous life contributions to present sexual concerns with which the readings deal, and the spirit and attitude of the readings' source in responding to these individuals. No matter what the situation or condition had been, the individual was always encouraged to make of it a stepping-stone to a better understanding of his present life and to establish and begin to make choices in the present life in accord with a high ideal.

For, each soul enters not by mere chance but to fulfill as orderly a development as is manifested in all of nature's growth; and to fill that promise, that purpose from the Divine—He hath not willed that a soul should perish, but hath with every temptation provided a means of escape.

For, He has no pleasure in death, nor in sin, but loves those who repent and who use or apply themselves in the material associations with others as to be a helpful, constructive experience for themselves, and in the hopes, and aspirations of others. 2416-1, M.48

7

Decisions, Decisions, Decisions

"See, I have set before thee this day life and good, and death and evil . . . therefore choose life . . . " (Deuteronomy 30:15, 19)

That spiritual path is a path of decisions. The sexual life is a lifetime of decisions. We are souls with free wills, invited to choose. We think of choices as decisions about what is right or wrong. A deeper essence of each choice is: Does it, in the long run, enhance *life* or *death*? With each choice we may move toward attunement with good and an enhancement of life within ourselves—physically, mentally, spiritually—or we may move toward manifesting evil and a construction of patterns that eventually lead to death. We are invited to choose!

For, *will and desire are spiritual as well as carnal, as well as mental.* These are attributes both of the spiritual influences and of the carnal forces in every entity's activity.

As to what an entity does with or about knowledge or understanding gained in its activity is the entity's own, and not to be shoved into, persuaded, or even driven to such an activity.

These are, then, not merely sayings or trite quotations; rather what has the entity set in self, self's own consciousness, self's own mind, self's own body, as an ideal. For, if the ideal falls short of that as would be accomplished within self, then doubts and fears must continue—and must ever arise.

If the influences chosen or set in the experience of

self are capable of fulfilling the promises within self, then these may be attained by the following of those things that have been set by the ideal as to the better relationships with self, with its Maker, with its fellow man! Choose thou! For, there is this day set before thee life—and death; night and day. Choose thou! [Author's italics] 315-3, M.27

What constitutes a reasonable choice? If we have an issue in which there is one choice that is clearly right and another which is clearly wrong, what is reasonable to expect of ourselves? If it is reasonable to make the right choice, had we a hundred or a thousand choices, would it not be reasonable to make each in accord with that we know to be right? The author of Romans 12:1-2 said: "I beseech you [to] present your bodies a living sacrifice, holy, acceptable unto God, which is your *reasonable* service." That which is *reasonable* when considered choice by choice, with right and wrong as alternatives, is 100% for right and 0% for wrong. It only makes sense to choose that which will give life and good instead of death and evil.

Therefore, knowing that we usually do otherwise, what is the problem? The problem is the rebellious spirit, which needs to be replaced by a willing spirit. We must mobilize within ourselves a spirit of willingness to choose not only that which we know to be right but in the right spirit. Insofar as we are unwilling to make 100% of our choices in accord with that which we know to be right, then we have some spiritual (motivational) growing to do.

To place ourselves on the spiritual path is to make a *general* choice about the direction of our lives with the commitment to choose *specifically* in accord with the ideal. We recognize the rebellious spirit, where we are at this moment in our lives and the problems with which we think we have to deal. We do not condemn ourselves for being where we find ourselves; however, we commit ourselves to get on the path, to begin to make some changes and to work with our lives wherever we can begin to make progress.

A major problem in trying to place ourselves on the spiritual path and still deal with sexuality is our fear that we cannot both obey God and enjoy life. The spiritual path, as we have discerned it from a study of the Cayce readings, invites us to a normal expression of sex in our lives and to see this expression as having a potential for joy and beauty. However, this philosophy also says that *soul development* must take precedence over all other things. At certain times our sexual motivations and our soul development motivations will not be in accord. Then we must choose.

In entering each experience the soul comes for the express purpose of manifesting in materiality under the environs and under those things builded in the experience of the entity, or of hereditary influence of that soul also.

In meeting any experience, as has been given, it, the meeting, whether it be for development or retardment is as to what such an entity does with the knowledge as pertaining to the Creative Forces in all the activity. What the soul, the body, does *about* that it knows, that it may manifest that it, the soul, worships as its ideal.

If that ideal is the Christ Consciousness, well. If that ideal is selfish developments, or the aggrandizing of activities in the carnal forces, then these must bring rather the fruits of such into the experience of the soul.

And, as has been the warning, there is today set before thee life and death, good and evil, and what ye choose with the will of thine own soul—upon that depends what the growth of the soul will be. 288-36, F.29

The strategy for dealing with this situation is to see it as a process rather than a single event and to begin to awaken spiritually based desires. Remember, the spirit of the spiritual path is not "stop doing what is wrong" but rather "start doing what is right." The manner in which we may begin to work with desire is to feed ourselves a diet of mental food that engenders positive attitudes toward the higher priorities demanded of the spiritual life. We can accomplish this not by an act of will in a vacuum but by an active program of meditation, prayer, inspirational reading, listening to music of quality, associating with others who are spiritually minded and especially setting and dwelling upon the spiritual ideal.

For any question, it seemed that the readings' source was centered upon the principle of the individual working with an ideal. For example:

Q-12. *Would it be better for a woman, who desires to marry, to be one of two or more wives to a man in a home rather than to remain unmarried?*

A-12. This is again a matter of *principle;* or the urge within such conditions much be conformative to that set as the ideal.

In the education of individuals as regarding sex relationships, as in every other educational activity, *there must be a standard* or rule to go by or *an ideal state* that has its inception not in the emotions of a physical body but from the *spiritual ideal* which has been set, which was set and given to man in his relation to the Creative Forces.

Then to ask or to seek or to advise or to give suggestions even, that it may be done outside of that, isn't being true to that as is presented. [Author's italics] 826-6, M.24

In working with our motivations, we are invited repeatedly to "study self." We can neither love God nor our fellow man as we should without a better understanding of ourselves.

"Analyze self," the readings told hundreds of people. How are we to do this? One approach to self-analysis is to make an inventory of our motives; this may be done by working with spiritual ideals in a specific written form.

Consider again how [1776] was instructed to study and analyze ideals and to choose his partner according to spiritual ideals, mental aspirations and physical agreements:

Q-5. *With which of these would marriage be successful?*

A-5. This should be determined by the entity itself, in the studying, analyzing, of the purposes and ideals.

For, in consideration of marriage—if it is to be a

success—it must be considered not from merely the outward appearance, a physical attraction; for these soon fade. Rather it should be considered from the angle of spiritual ideals, mental aspirations, and physical agreements. These should be analyzed in the experience of the entity, as in the experience of the companion, in the choice of such relationships.

For, these relationships are representative of the purpose of propagation of specie[s], as well as those ideals that arise from spiritual and mental relationships—see? 1776-2, M.31

Having accomplished this step of writing the ideal (Chapter Two), we are now prepared to deal with the problem of decisions.

A Context for Choices

We may say with surety that no one has a *sexual* problem; everyone's true task is working more in accord with his own spiritual path. It's comparable to a talented and well-trained person who doesn't like to work saying he has a financial problem. As we define *progress on the spiritual path* as the problem and put more of our energy into growth in that area that takes precedence over all others, when we may indeed experience sex as less of a problem in our lives.

One way to progress in the sexual life is to shift a growing portion of our concern toward other constructive and creative activities. As we invest ourselves in the overall health of body, mind and soul, in trying to do something for the other fellow or committing ourselves to a program of learning and study, as we engage ourselves in constructive physical activities (an exercise or recreation program)—in sum, as we invest our lives in projects that make for well-balanced, productive and service-oriented lives—the more chance we have to place our sexual concerns into better perspective. Therefore, anyone who has a sexual problem may take the offensive by beginning to invest heavily in concerns and activities dealing with something other than sex.

A 26-year-old man who had failed to do this was told:

In the [incarnation] before this we find in that first representative sent to this land to represent France, in this as a land. In the name Rau de Claudia. In that experience the entity gained and lost in the application of that as was gained in the MENTAL body, *for the entity knew to do well but allowed the desires of the flesh and of the eye to overcome that as was best in the abilities of the entity.* In the urge as is seen, the love of mystery, and of that not wholly understood—yet the innate doubt as goes with such lack of understanding. The reason, the *lack of basic forces to set self on a firm basis with the correct criterion as the position in the development of self.* [Author's italics]

4145-2, M.26

Many times the overall improvement from a positive action program helps solve what seemed to be simply a sexual problem. Imagine a person concerned about loneliness who desires a compatible sexual partner. If this one with the "sexual" problem sets about a program to make himself more physically fit and, therefore, more attractive; if he sets about learning and studying to make himself more interesting; if he sets himself on a spiritual program of meditation and attunement, then the foundation is laid in the most optimum way for the subsequent meeting of a suitable companion. On the other hand, as long as the problem is defined as not having a partner (which may allow other aspects to go downhill), then the likelihood of finding a suitable partner is lessened. When we consider the soul's journey over thousands, perhaps millions of years in the earth plane, questions of choice of one's partner are not seen as being matters of chance or coincidence. One cannot just go out and meet a good partner; these things are matters of soul patterns that have grown in a series of incarnations. The possibilities present themselves in the meeting of specific and special people who are potentially good partners.

In the same way that we may meet and be drawn to potentially good partners, there are also individuals with whom we have had previous life experiences of such a nature that it could be highly undesirable to start much of a sexual or special relationship in the present incarnation. Granting that these are not matters of chance or coincidence but rather of lawfulness, how many we best begin to put ourselves in attunement with the law? The answer, of course, is through meditation and prayer.

Sexual problems dealing with form can also be met successfully as the individual sets about a more balanced and active life—not just being busy, but actually making progress on the spiritual path in terms of generating a new eagerness to be of service to others, to make attunement to the Divine within, to be creative and productive. The compelling desires of sex's demanding form tend to be relaxed when placed in better perspective. It is possible, then, to be more open to sexual gratification in a wider range of formal expressions.

The major principle, then, for successfully dealing with sexual problems is: By establishing a more holistic and creative pattern for one's life and by investing genuine energies in positive expressions, the individual may thereby gain a better opportunity for sexual enjoyment in a more acceptable form or with a more acceptable partner.

The *spiritual path* program, in contrast with simply a *constructive* program, gives a stronger, more meaningful context in which to work with the problem and a firmer life foundation upon which to build a more fulfilling and acceptable sexual expression.

The readings constitute one source of information and inspiration upon which to begin to build a constructive and holistic program. If it answers to you, you may find it to be uniquely and indescribably rich and helpful. However, it presents a challenge to the pilgrim far beyond a passing interest. It must be given *credence*, yes; but more than that, we are asked to live by it or die with it! Consider this:

The first consideration each individual takes, as they seek either information or association with same, should be the validity of the information—and as to whether or not they themselves are willing, irrespective of comment from without, to stand by same, or to *live* by same wholly, or in another line: Is the information in keeping with the ideal that has been set by such an individual? Is it in keeping with that they (the individual) would live by, or die with? Or, to put in another manner—is the information such that *it* (the information) *gives* the individual *an* ideal, *not* just an idea? Or is the information *ideal*, or just an idea?

As to how each individual is to reach such conclusions, then—as has been outlined—there is seen that first there must be within the information that may be obtained that which corresponds, or which awakens a chord *within* each individual, and that rings true to the individual's own plan, own spiritual desire; for the *spirit* is alive, the *flesh* is weak. The carnal desire must sooner or later, as in nature, *burn* itself out; so, as has been given, "all things are tried so as by fire." *This*, to *some*, will give a new meaning to *many* of the words of old. 254-55

The Will of God

In all my years of discussing and sharing spiritual principles with others, I have found few concepts about which there is more confusion than the notion of the will of God. Most people have a feeling that the will of God implies a narrow, restrictive, moralistic, predetermined course for their lives that robs them of spontaneity and freedom. The readings indicate that God Himself doesn't know from one minute to the next what man will do with his free will. (5749-14) It is clear from this insight that God does not have the predetermined plan in mind for every action of our lives. The purpose of all spiritual teachings, as indicated in the words of Jesus or those of the Buddha, is that we might become *free* and follow a path of liberation. We are not only lost but in bondage. The will of God is not for us to be confined to a narrow and restrictive law;

in giving us free will God wished us to be co-creators with Him, to be truly free. Making choices in accord with His will, then, always moves us to greater freedom.

The problem is that that which may seem to be free—from the point of view of the lower ego—may be more restrictive to the soul itself. Even at the level of our lower ego, though, the law operates in the same manner. Whether we are speaking of physical law, penal law, natural law or spiritual law, the more we make choices that are not in accordance with the law, the more narrow and restricted our subsequent lives and choices become. Conversely, the more we choose in accord with the way things are, the more opportunities open of greater freedom of choice. People whom we regard as truly successful have already learned this lesson. Succeeding generally involves doing what needs to be done. Those who are willing to do what needs to be done *when* it needs to be done have, in turn, tended to reap the rewards of this pattern: greater financial success, greater freedom within their jobs and greater opportunities for creative expression.

At the physical level, the law also works in every aspect of our lives. As stated before, the spiritual path is a path toward greater freedom. Consider this: if in our dietary habits we insist upon more freedom with respect to eating anything we want, in whatever quantity we want, such a life style will eventually work against our overall general health. As our physical condition deteriorates, we might be placed on a very restricted diet and not be able to eat and enjoy, even in moderation, those very items we insisted on earlier. Now the element of freedom that we are addressing is the overall health and energy of the physical body. Therefore, when we impose on ourselves that which may seem to be limiting by following a normal, balanced diet we, in fact, establish a greater physical freedom with the enhanced health, energy and general well-being. In the long run, there is more actual physical enjoyment when the body is optimally healthy than when it is impulsively indulged in by the immediate appetite. The principle of this illustration may be applied to other phases of our lives. Utilizing our free will to place ourselves in accord, instead of out of accord, with God's will is, in truth, putting aside the narrower, more restrictive part of ourselves in favor of the higher. The stakes involve, indeed, the liberation of the soul through eternity.

Decide

People who came to Edgar Cayce with all sorts of questions were sometimes told, "This may best be determined within self." We believe this viewpoint to be not only of the readings, but also of God! God does not have some fixed, obscure plan for us which He hides and dares us to discover! Rather, as co-creators with Him, we have choices to make. The first step in choosing is, in fact, to *decide*. This illustrated in the following response to a young man trying to make decisions about his life work.

In considering the general conditions and the better welfare, it would be well for the body to consider that which has been given respecting the abilities, and that there must be first the choice made in the own mental forces as to what direction is to be taken, what attitude the body would assume or guide self's abilities in. In choosing, then there will of itself be made for the body the greater determination, and will open—as it were—the possibility, the probability; and the *fact*, of making for self an association or connection in that direction . . .

. . . first there must be a determination within self as to what *is* to be the activities: whether sweeping streets, running engines, motors, flying machines, digging ditches, or what! But *choose!* And then stick to that! It's the only way that those abilities that are latent may be developed in *any* entity; anyone that will build; is to apply self *in* the field, *in* the way, *in* that which is *chosen* as the life's work! If it's chosen in the field where the activities are, or have been to some extent expended, then go about to make those activities of such a nature that there will be the opening of more outlets, more channels, more ways in which same will be active! If the activities are to be in other directions, *whatever* is chosen, do THAT!

419-3, M. Adult

Another person, a 52-year-old businessman, was advised to "choose" and to depend upon the Creative Forces.

Q-1. Should this entity continue along the lines of working with metals, salesmanship, etc., as heretofore?

A-1. This, as indicated, must be a choice of the entity. In whatever field of activity the entity is persuaded within itself that it is best fitted for, for the meeting of the material needs and necessities at this time, *that* field engage in.

To say to the entity, "You must not sell cans; you must sell steel," or "You cannot sell steel; you must sell cans," would indicate that the entity's abilities of self-expression were lacking in its associations, its connections with the *source* of *all* truth! Just as all truth, all knowledge, all light, is at the hand of *every* individual. The application of its truth in the experience of an entity must be a *personal* application by self . . .

There must be something *within* that answers, or else the entity is continually either justifying or excusing self at the expense of his *own* development . . .

Whether such is to be chosen or not, this the entity *must* decide.

How has it always been set? "There is set before thee life and death, good and evil. *Choose* THOU!"

. . . Does the entity depend upon *itself* and its abilities and its associations with the Creative Forces? Or must it be led by another?

These are as a choice . . .

If this is the desire, if it is what is wished, then pull up stakes and do it! This *must* be *determined* by *self!* It will *not* be given from here that you should hang *any* hope on *any* tree, on *any* place, on *any* thing, save on *God*—and let Him meet thee in *self!* as to *what* is the choice to be made, *ever*, by self. 333-6, M.52

As we begin to study self, we find that we have many decisions to make, specifically regarding sexual problems. We need to take an inventory to define the problems, to reflect upon alternatives and to choose the direction in which we wish to move to resolve these problems. Then we must decide! Having made the decision, we may then move to the next step.

Guidance from Within

The Cayce readings state that every soul must eventually learn to mediate. What does this mean? Since God is spirit and we are spiritual beings, then we can meet Him only in spirit in the temple within. Eventually, to come to a Oneness with God, we must attune to Him from *within*. We grow most in attunement to the Divine within by practicing the silence.

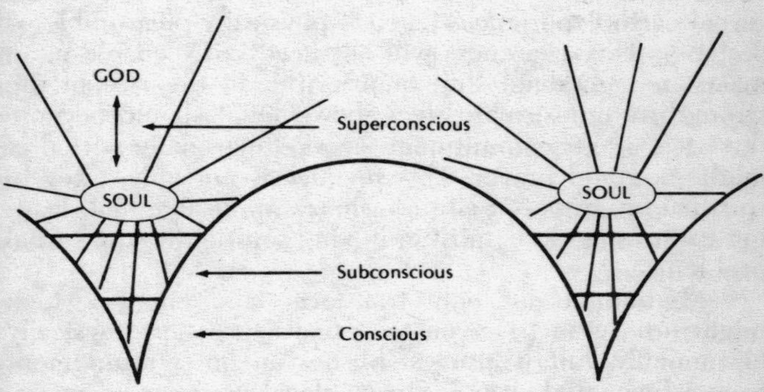

Some people wonder if attuning to the *macrocosmic* God *without* is not superior to attuning to the *macrocosmic* God *within*. That's the whole point. There is only *one* God and He is spirit; therefore, we can become aware of Him only because we are spiritual beings. As spirit, He speaks to us only through *our* spirit—through the *soul*, our spiritual body. And we contact our soul only from within. The superconscious is the soul's potential to be in Oneness with and have an awareness of God.

Prayer is a vital part of meditation. We may truly say that we pray in order to meditate and we meditate in order to pray. In order to meditate, our initial prayers involve working with ourselves. Many times, as we try to enter the period of the silence, there is a great deal of preparation that must be done in putting the mundane concerns and the lower self aside. We must deprogram ourselves, deprogram the conscious mind, as it were, from continuing to return to these preoccupations. Our prayers of confession, prayers of attunement, prayers of praise and thanksgiving prepare us to enter into the silence.

The following is the theme for the whole of our consideration: ". . . how much greater is a day in the house of the Lord—or a moment in His presence—than a thousand years in carnal forces?" (262-57) Considering the implications of this invitation, we may paraphrase it to state that a moment of meditation, in which there is attunement to the Divine, is worth a thousand years of carnal earth experiences (even if physically pleasurable or ecstatic). This awareness will not necessarily enable us to make an immediate shift of priorities in the face of the strength of our sexual drives; however, it should become the basis of our commitment for a regular, daily period of meditation and prayer. This practice is not only a key to spiritual progress but also a primary, applicable tool, leading to the soundest, most gratifying solution to any sexual problems.

Meditation not only transforms the energy which might otherwise be given to sexual expression physically or mentally, but it also establishes an inner attunement from which guided and correct decisions may be made. Furthermore, as we grow in attunement, the energy of the life force of God Himself flows through us, giving us a new quality of motivation and the energy itself to fulfill that which we hope to accomplish on the spiritual path.

Finally, with respect to the soul's sincere desire for love, it must be remembered that God created us out of His desire for companionship. In the depths of our being, we have as our first and deepest love, God. We are invited to direct our sexual energy to return to our first love. (See Revelation 2:4.) As we grow in attunement with the Divine, we begin to sense a relationship with Him beside which all other desires for relationships fade in comparison. Thus, our soul's sincere desire is Oneness with Him, and, to paraphrase St. Augustine, our souls are restless till they find their rest in Him. This is the underlying *reality* of that which may on occasion distort the desires we consider sexual.

Nevertheless, there remain decisions to be made on a day-by-day basis respecting sexual expressions. In the readings we are given extraordinarily promising, detailed and helpful instructions about how to work with meditation in order to be assured of a quality of inner guidance that can be depended upon completely. The following extracts give an idea of how central this practice is to the philosophy of the readings, with assurances of sound guidance for decision making attained by turning to the spirit within.

Q-7. What will help me most in coming to right decisions as to my life?

A-7. Prayer and meditation, to be sure. For, as He has given, "Behold I stand at the door and knock. If ye will open I will enter in."

Then, in thine own mind, decide as to whether this or that direction is right. Then pray on it, and leave it alone. Then suddenly ye will have the answer, yes or no.

Then, with that yes or not, take it again to Him in prayer, "Show me the way." And yes or no will again direct thee from deep within.

***That* is practical direction. 3250-1**

Q-13. How may I know when the will to a course of action is justifiable, or when I am forcing my own personal will which may lead to inaction which is equally unjustifiable?

A-13. By the listening within—there is the answer. For, the answer to every problem, the answer to know His way, is ever within—the answering within to that real desire, that real purpose which motivates activity in the individual.

These appear at times to become contradictory, of course; but know—as the illustration has been used here—attunement, atonement and at-onement are *one;* just as

the inner self is that portion of the infinite, while the self-will or personality is ever at war with the infinite within—for the lack of what may be called stamina, faith, patience or whatnot. Yet each entity, each soul, knows within when it is in an at-onement. 2174-3

Q-4. When confronted with difficult situations, how can I be sure the decision I reach is from the Light and not my own thinking?

A-4. As the body recognizes, there is the body-mind, the body-consciousness, there is also the inner consciousness or soul-mind. Ask the question in self in the physical mind so it may be answered yes or no, and in meditation get the answer. Then closing self to physical consciousness, through the meditation, ask the same question. If these agree, go ahead. If these disagree, analyze the own self and see the problem that lies in the way. 5091-2

As to the choice, as to the determinations—these *must* be made by the soul, the entity itself. 954-4

In choosing, then there will of itself be made for the body the greater determination, and will open—as it were—the possibility, the probability, and the *fact*, of making for self an association or connection in that direction. 419-3

Q-15. It it possible to meditate and obtain needed information?

A-15. On any subject! whether you are going digging for fishing worms or playing a concerto! 1861-12

Q-6. How can one be sure that a decision is in accordance with God's will?

A-6. As indicated here before. Ask self in the own conscious self, "Shall I do this or not?" The voice will answer within. Then meditate, ask the same, yes or no. You may be very sure if thine own conscious self and the divine self is in accord, you are truly in that activity indicated, "My spirit bareth witness with thy spirit." You

can't get far wrong in following the word, as ye call the word of God. 2072-14

From these readings, specific steps may be derived in making decisions that are fully guided by the spirit within.

How to make a decision:

1. Set the spiritual ideal as to purposes.
2. Pose the question so that it may be answered by a yes or a no.
3. Make a rational logical decision, yes or no.
4. Measure the decision by the ideal.
5. Meditate—not on the question but for attunement.
6. Ask the silence, yes or no? Listen!
7. Measure the decision by the ideal.

A Perspective Based on Dreams

The pilgrim on the spiritual path will, for many reasons, want to study his dreams carefully, since these offer an especially rich and instructive perspective in self-study. Dreams constitute a report on the warring between that which we have set as our ideal and that which we are actually living. Nothing of importance happens to us that is not foreshadowed in the dream. Therefore, regarding the sex life, dreams may be very helpful in giving not only feedback on the deeper self's response to thoughts and actions, but also warnings about special significant conditions to be met.

The student of the spiritual path who notes his dreams will find that he will have little difficulty in obtaining a clear "status report" on the direction of his present growth in consciousness. Edgar Cayce gave hundreds of dream interpretations, always encouraging the individuals to observe carefully and to study them. From these sources of information come a number of excellent publications and articles, giving you confidence in growth toward a better understanding of yourself through dream study.

The Edgar Cayce readings, perhaps more than any

other source of spiritual teachings, invite every individual to begin working with his own dreams:

As we see, all visions and dreams are given for the benefit of the individual, [if they would] but interpret them correctly, for we find that visions, or dreams, in whatever character they may come, are the reflection, either of physical condition, with apparitions with same, or of the subconscious, with the conditions relating to the physical body and its action, either through mental or through the elements of the spiritual entity, or a projection from the spiritual forces to the subconscious of the individual, and happy may he be that is able to say they have been spoken to through the dream or vision. 294-15

The following two dreams and their interpretations by Cayce are not only illustrative of the way in which the source dealt with dreams, but also very instructive with respect to our considerations of sex and the spiritual path.

Q-5. Morning of September 7, 1926. "My father appeared. Many were in our house. I was attracted to a woman by virtue of sex appeal. When I was a boy she had so attracted and appealed to me. I legitimized my relations to her by deserting my own wife and marrying her. I said: 'Now it is all right. I am divorced and have married, so my relations are justified.' My father denied that. I heard him in the bathroom, and when I wanted to get in, I couldn't. I carried on my relations. The scene changed. The moon was shining upon the earth. I saw its rays break through the clouds. Then my father or the voice spoke: 'Redeemers are not meant to go about dreaming and romancing and idling under the moon. The next time you do this, I will take your sight away from you. You will lose your vision!'"

A-5. In this there are seen, as has been given or forewarned in that just as given—through that presentation from the father of those forces through which the mental mind of the entity has been guiding or directing its mental forces as pertaining to various conditions as are seen in the earth's plane—through those relations as

are seen—these are of those conditions on which the entity has dwelt in mental forces, and, as is seen through the experience and through that of the voice, and through that of the action of the father and of relations as are seen, the elements as enter in are as seen, that sex is as of the carnal mind, and of the earth earthy. Then, as applied in that way and manner as lessons, as given, there is seen that there is taken from *any* entity—this entity as well as others—that spiritual insight into the conditions as are of the spiritual nature, through indulgence in carnal conditions. Hence the rule, the lessons as have been given, in being in that way of that as is the showing self to be in the position of not an extremist in any nature or sense, for all force is of one force, but may be carried to the extreme to such an extent as to destroy the insight or the relations as one element of force to another. See? 900-268

Q-8. "Physical forces as related to [4855]. Voice: 'Adultery is a matter of the heart and not action.'"

A-8. This is the intent of the subconscious in gaining to the entity that clearer understanding of the precepts as laid down by the Master: "As the hart panteth after water in the brook, so panteth my heart after thee," or, as is given in the understanding, "He that looketh on a woman to lust after her hath committed adultery already," see? An act and an intent, or "the thoughts are deeds, and may become crimes or miracles."

Q-9. This either absolved or censured me—what is indicated?

A-9. Neither. As is given, the lesson that entity may gain, as is seen, that self-condemnation may not be a hindering element in the development of the entity for past experience. Then learn how that one is absolved from intent and purpose as set, by turning about and making whole body, mind, spirit, soul, in accord with the will of the entity, of the Whole, see? 900-201

This information assures us that we may be helped physically, mentally, spiritually, financially and otherwise if we properly interpret our dreams. Dreams have the potential for tuning us in to almost any level of our inner being. On occasion, they simply reveal desire patterns in the unconscious, therefore giving us the opportunity of seeing ourselves in a way which may not be consistent with our waking self-image. For example, one who has difficulty accepting homosexuality in others may, to his dismay, have a homosexually oriented dream, and even enjoy the activity. This type of dream may provoke anxiety that one is latently homosexual. Such may not be the case at all; however, the dream does offer potential for the one offended by such behavior to understand better how others may be drawn to it. The instructive potential of such dreams is tremendous if the individual is willing to work with the reservoir of perspectives in understanding many of life's dimensions portrayed in dreams.

With respect to present life relationships, dreams offer excellent avenues for viewing past life bases of relationships. For anyone truly seeking to understand the reincarnation origins of present life difficulties, dreams afford an invaluable resource. If we are having a problem with a certain individual, we can, through our dreams, begin to see that individual in relationships other than the present one, thus gaining insights on the present problem.

An interesting and instructive potential of the dream is its *forward-looking* or *prospective* function. (Carl Jung called this the *prospective* function.) The readings indicate that nothing of importance happens to us that is not first previewed in a dream. More usually we consider the dream's origin, but the prospective function of dreams orients us toward the future instead of the past. In working with a dream, we should consider how it may be altering us to something forthcoming in our external life and in our relationships, or in the development of our inner life, inner growth and transformation.

Suppose we awaken with a dream dealing with sex. We may wonder what we have *done* that led to the dream, or we may assume that some biological energies are beginning to seek expression. This may be the case; however, if we approach the dream with a view of its *prospective function*, we may glimpse in direction in which we are being impelled by the forces operating in our lives. Later these inner experiences may come more fully into waking consciousness. Sometimes they come as promises or as warnings. The latter may depict undesirable outcomes, a result of our continuance along present lines of thinking and experience. For example, if any sexual excesses or exaggerations appear in the dream, these may warn us of the direction we are building and of the consequences of such a direction for the future.

A great deal might be said about the usefulness of dreams in understanding ourselves, particularly with respect to a deeper understanding of our sexual motives and propensities. However, at present, we are mainly concerned with the contribution of dream study to the decision-making process. If nothing of importance happens to us that is not already foreshadowed in a dream, then we may find in our dreams regular previews of experiences later to be encountered at the physical level in waking consciousness. If we monitor these as future experiences or temptations, we may reflect upon and make decisions relevant to these possibilities. Here is an example:

John, a handsome, pre-law student, was seeking *the* partner from among many with whom he came in contact. Finally came one who seemed to meet all criteria *except* a shared interest in the spiritual path. Her father was a very successful distributor of a certain food product. One night in the course of his decision-making trials, he dreamed that he was choking to death on this food product. He subsequently, though perhaps still ambivalently, married this one. Was the dream a result of natural anxiety which usually would accompany such a decision or was it a warning against the choice? Such dreams become a special source of hypotheses which may be taken into the inner temple and placed on the altar in meditation with a prayer for guidance.

Sometimes we may use these dream opportunities in opposition to their instructive potential. A dream of a sexual experience with another person may warn us to be on guard against such a temptation; however, it may be permitted to become a basis for a new thought stimulation respecting such a prospect. We may, therefore, use the warning itself as a stumbling block instead of a stepping-stone.

If we fail to observe our dreams and to consider our sexual dreams instructive with respect to future choices, we may rob ourselves of a great opportunity of preparation for decision making. Without the forward look, we put our lives more in a position of being *reactive* to circumstances. The *prospective* quality of dreams given the pilgrim on the spiritual path a pair of binoculars through which to view to road signs and possible detours ahead so that determination of ideals and clarification of purposes may be made well in advance of the physical occasion for confrontation with the decision.

Free Will

One of the most remarkable qualities concerning man's nature as a spiritual being is his free will, God's gift to us, His children. Regardless of the many debates and rationalizations we may develop to try to talk ourselves *out* of seeing clearly the responsibility accompanying such a gift, the readings indicate that the will is indeed far more significant and potentially far more free than we have ever imagined. Just how free is the will in respect to other determining factors? The following reading indicates that it may overome any or all factors if—and only if—the choice is made in accord with the "pattern."

Q-15. Are heredity, environment and will equal factors in aiding or retarding the entity's development?

A-15. Will is the greater factor, for it may overcome any or all of the others; provided that will is made one with the pattern, see? For, no influence of heredity, environment or whatnot, surpasses the will; else why would there have been that pattern shown in which the individual soul, no matter how far astray it may have gone, may enter with Him into the holy of holies? 5749-14

The argument *against* free will constitutes an argument against individual responsibility. The argument *for* free will is an argument for a fuller assumption of responsibilities for ourselves, our choices, our actions, the nature of our relationships with others, and the nature of the impact of our choices and actions on others' lives. There is no doubt, from the point of view of the readings, that we are responsible for our choices regarding sexual behavior, with respect to the question both of *what* and of *with whom*. We are then assured that whatever the strength of the attraction or the compulsive quality of the impulse, we have, nevertheless, a responsibility in that we may choose *to* or *not to* put our thoughts and actions in accord with the ideals we have set.

In the application of the will the entity's experience—these, as we shall see, have been used in a way and manner so that the development has been both good and bad, or an advancement as well as a retarding, making for the necessity of those surroundings for the entity in the present—as to its mental, as to its love influence, as to its desires—that may be made either of the carnal nature or of the spiritual influences. Made in the spiritual, there will be the development in the present; *while those of the purely carnal or of material forces ruling will bring for those in the end of a dissatisfaction that must bring consternation, turmoil, strife, and dissension in the experience in the present influence;* yet these, as we see, guided aright—these, as we see, used in the manner as a stepping-stone—that is, those that have been of hindrances used as stepping-stones rather than stones about the self that would drag down—they may be builded up. In the will's application, make that as is innate in the experience of the entity. Be not high-minded, but condescending to, harkening to, counsel of those—not *worldly* wise, but spiritually wise—and spiritually minded, heeding in a manner that those lessons that are given may be as experiences in the balance of the entity's mental forces, as to gain by those experiences, and passing under the rod in a manner that will make for a *glorious* influence in the entity's experience in the present force. [Author's italics]

1912-1, M.18

There is no impulse of form or relationship that cannot be aligned with the ideal by virtue of God's love, which may be channeled through the spiritual ideal we have set.

Hence beauty, love, music, nature, are those things that answer the most to the entity. The beauty of friendship, the beauty of associations, the beauty of the landscape, the beauty of the storm, and yet a fear creeps in when there is a closing in about the entity—as we shall see—from the *lack of the full trust in Him.*

The experiences in the earth are indicated not merely as periods of sojourn but as periods in which the soul has grown or been *warped by what men would call circumstance or environ. Yet the will of a soul attuned to God may change the circumstance or the environment*, as indicated in the lily; in fact, all the forces even in nature itself. For all the beauty is of God, all the love is of God. All of those that abide in same, then, are manifestations of His love. These nourish, these cherish in all of thy dealings with thy fellow men. [Author's italics]

3374-1, F.35

Discipline and Obedience

Once we convince ourselves that our lives may be controlled more by our own choices than by others' influences or internal predispositions beyond our control—once we understand that we can make choices which may withstand these contrary influences—then we have seemingly the more difficult problem of continually living out these choices; i.e., *application*.

We are advised to take control of our own lives by bringing ourselves *forcibly*, if necessary, into courses of action consistent with our higher ideals. How can we do this?

A-4. How can I discipline myself at my age to do what is mine to do?

A-4. Repeat three times every day, and then listen

"Lord, what would Thou have me do today?"

Have this not as rote. Mean it! For as He has spoken, as He has promised, "If ye call I will hear, and answer speedily." He meant it! Believe it! 3003-1, F.61

Our particular society seems especially disinclined to the appropriateness of *making* ourselves do something. Even the emphasis that is being given to assertiveness tends to feature self-assertiveness rather than one based upon spiritual ideals. We may even say, to dramatize this point, that the real taboo word of our society is *obedience*. I once has a pastor who asked the congregation for suggestions for sermon topics. I told him that I would like to hear a sermon on obedience because I had never heard such. I *still* have not heard a sermon on obedience.

I speak of obedience as a taboo word because the new psychology of our time has tended to stress "getting in touch with" and "expressing" our *feelings*, rather than disciplining ourselves to adhere to that which we have set as a standard. Some of our contemporary emphasis on freedom enhances the rebellious spirit and, therefore, leads to greater imprisonment rather than true freedom. It has become most interesting to me that in all of the New Testament we find *only one* reference which suggests that Jesus had anything *to learn:* He learned *obedience* by the things that He suffered. (Hebrews 5:8) If indeed the Master Himself was learning *obedience*, then we may see it as the final, most critical and ultimately required lesson for us to learn also. This virtue is so vitally and centrally important because it affirms the spirit respecting God's law in contrast to the soul's basic problem, the spirit of rebellion. One of the special forms of this problem occurs in considering and confronting our sexual attitudes and actions. Clearly, the spiritual path requires us to be in firm control of these rather than to allow them to be in control of us.

. . . be the control even of the mind, rather than any desires from without controlling the body! Make the self do that what it *wants* to do! Know that the body is thine.

Know that the mind is thine. Make its will one with that as is set as the body's ideal, and make them conform to those rules and regulations of *that* ideal! 768-2, F.15

By What Power?

Some of us may be dealing with sexual temptations or impulses that seem so compelling that we see little promise of release from these predisposing patterns. Some with sexual problems battle most of their lives against impulses so deeply innate that they often question whether there is any power that would enable them to change or to resist and not to give in. The urge to give expression to such is so strong or alternative relationships seem so repugnant that the individual may feel it too innately a part of himself to be battled or controlled. Such a one is confronted with a specific instance of the greater problem with which we all have to deal. The basic condition of man in the earth plane is that we are *lost*—we may even say *dead*. We are cut off from the source of life which would bring us the information, the healing, the energy and a sense of relationship to the Divine that would enable us to truly *live*.

When we look at the magnitude of the need for healing a serious and chronic disorder, it may seem too overwhelming and beyond our control to take any meaningful, corrective action. On the other hand, we are given true hope in the understanding that there is only one force, that force is God and God is love. By the very nature of our beings we have the potential for that power and love to flow through us, giving us what we need to bring about the change or transformation that seems so beyond our conscious ability to control. It is only and always by the love and grace of God that we are enabled to grow, to change and to be transformed. It is never by virtue of any power on our part that we are required to heal ourselves. That which empowers us to be healed, to be transformed, is not of ourselves; it is a gift of God. But this rarely occurs in any enduring way by the simple evangelical expediency of being "saved." It is certainly true that Jesus came "that ye may know that the Son of man hath power on earth to forgive sins." (Matthew 9:6)

But we must grow, even in grace. Our bodies carry within them the points of contact, our minds carry the Pattern through which in time, with a growing commitment to attunement and application of His power, we may be assured of being healed and indeed made fully whole. But how much longer will this take?

If it's a day or a year, what's the difference if it's accomplished! There is no time! If thou art weary in that thou art doing, then turn back! 281-5

Choice and Grace

Many people talk about the laws of karma and grace without gaining clarity of how these may work with each other. A simple analogy may be helpful. Consider an airplane as it flies. Does it defy the law of gravity? No. However, it *appears* to defy this law because *another* law has been brought into effect—the law of aerodynamics. Once the wing can be brought to a certain speed through the air, then another set of forces is made operative; the result appears to be a contradiction of the law of gravity, making it appear ineffective.

The same may be said of the laws of grace and karma: The law of grace may make the law of karma ineffective. However, just as the airplane's wing must be made to move through the air, so must we make the choices and applications that constitute a viable invitation for God's love to come into our lives in a healing and transforming manner. Then we may be assured that in grace "we may do all things through Christ which strengthens . . ." (Philippians 4:13) Let us study several examples of the way in which the readings invite us to move from karma to grace:

Q-2. Considering my ideals, purposes and karmic pattern, as well as the conditions which I face at present,

in what specific direction should I seek expression for my talents and abilities in order to render the greatest possible service?

A-2. This is rather a compound question, for it presumes or presupposes as to ideals, as to purposes, and as to self's concept of karma.

What *is* karma? and what *is* the pattern?

He alone is each soul pattern. He *alone* is each soul pattern! *He* is thy *karma*, if ye put thy trust *wholly* in Him! See? **2067-2, F.52**

Q-3. What is the karma which follows me?

A-3. This—find it in self. Know, so long as we *feel* there is karma, it *is* cause and effect. But in righteousness we may be justified before the Throne; thus we may *pass from cause and effect, or karma, to that of grace.*

This is the attitude; not of self-righteousness, no, but of blessed assurance that He is able to take all that we may commit unto Him against any experience in our lives. [Author's italics] **3177-1, F.68**

For, as ye condemn, so *are* ye condemned. As ye forgive, so may ye be forgiven. As ye do unto the least of thy brethren, so ye do unto thy Maker. These as laws, as truths, are unfailing. And because He may oft appear slow in meting out the results of such activity does not alter or change the law, save as may be understood in the law of forgiveness. Yet any error, or a fault, or failure, *must* be met! For as given, though the heavens, the earth may pass away, His word will *not* pass away! His word, then, is the way, the truth, the light. And each entity, each soul—*as himself*—must pay to the last jot or tittle!

Yes, forgiveness and karma may at times appear to be extremes; and yet know that *only* in Him—the Christ—do extremes meet. But that each soul may know, and not lose the way, these *are* experiences—in the meeting of such—as may be borne or understood, or even comprehended, in and with His presence, His purpose, His love. **2449-1, M.60**

For what one sows that must one reap. This is unchangeable law. Know that this law may be turned into law of grace and mercy by the individual, through living and acting in their lives in relationships to others.
5233-1, M.79

That as has been builded must be met every whit, until there is the whole trust of self in that that makes the law of recompense, or of karma, of none effect. It's in him [218]! 281-6

Karma can be met in the ideal and, as a law, changed from law as penal law to grace, mercy. But this you show, this you manifest not by bragging, not by applauding, but by daily living. 5224-1, M.47

For the law of the Lord is perfect, and whatsoever an entity, an individual sows, that must he reap. That as law cannot be changed. As to whether one meets it in the letter of the law or in mercy, in grace, becomes the choice of the entity. If one would have mercy, grace, love, friends, one must show self in such a manner to those with whom one becomes associated. For like begets like.

There are barriers builded, yes. These may be taken away in Him, who has paid the price for thee; not of thyself but in faith, in love, in patience, in kindness, in gentleness may it be met.

That these have been the experience may appear to the entity as rather unfair. Is it? The law of the Lord is perfect. His grace is sufficient, if thy patience will be sufficient also. 5001-1, M.32

We would minimize the faults, we would magnify the virtues. There is within the ability of the entity the choice through that which is the gift of light or knowledge to man, through that which is a part of man's consciousness in the Mind (or the Son) making intercession for man to the Creative Forces or God—*will.*

So, no urge arising from astrological aspects or from

sojourns of the entity in the earth surpasses the will of the individual entity, when its trust, its hope, its desire is put in the mind of God or the Christ Consciousness. 5000-1, M.20

A Companion on the Way

As we set out on the spiritual path, the most important insight to be gained is to know and accept the promise that we do not travel alone. The *way* is not only a path but more importantly a Person. At our instant invitation we are immediately joined by our Elder Brother, who indeed becomes our guide and the enabler of our progress along the path. Through Him, we are assured of the ability to transform stumbling blocks into stepping-stones. The position of the Cayce readings and the magnitude and greatness of this promise and invitation is presented again and again, as in the following quotations:

Q-18. What leader or teacher could guide the body along the path?

A-18. *Him.* In Him! Along the ways that were given by Him! Be satisfied with nothing less than He as thy guide, by day and by night! Let ever that mind be in thee: *"If His presence abides not with me day by day, may I not be lifted up!"* 452-6, M.28

Remember the sources, as we have indicated are the meeting of one's own self; thus are karmic. These can be met most in Him who, taking away the law of cause and effect by fulfilling the law, establishes the law of grace. Thus the needs for the entity to lean upon the arm of Him who is the law, and the truth and the light.

For, while these may be sought to be explained through the defects in the body, read carefully—who healeth all thy diseases, who bringeth this or that to pass in thy experience? that, through thy experience ye may learn the more of the law of the Lord, that it is perfect. Thus ye apply those things of which ye thyself are a part. 2828-4, M.41

No soul-entity enters by chance. For God, having not willed that any soul should perish, has given the entity the will to choose that which if applied in the experience in the earth enables individuals to meet that wherein they have fallen short of the higher calling as set in Him. Thus an entity enters into life meeting self as an individual. And as the relationships are one with another, so is it met in the relationships to God. For as is illustrated, the debt the Son paid for the earth was in the earth and among men. 3394-2, M.54

It is never too late to mend thy ways. For life is eternal and ye are today what ye are because of what ye have been. For ye are the co-creator with thy Maker, that ye may one day be present with all of those who love His coming. [Author's italics] 5284-1, F.38

Be ye joyous in thy service to thy fellow man, in the *name* of Him who is able to keep thy ways. Count thy hardships, thy troubles, even thy disappointments, rather as stepping-stones to know His way better. Be ye joyous; be ye happy in *His love*. For He hath loved us, even when afar. How much more when we try, though we may stumble and fail! For the trial, the test, the *determination* creates that which will rise as faithful, true, and as righteousness before the throne of grace. For thou art under a dispensation of mercy. Be ye merciful. Be ye unhurt by hard words. For *thy* hurts are His! Bear them, then, with Him in thy dealings with thy fellow man. If ye would have love, show thyself lovely; not only to those that speak kindly to thee—for what profit have ye? Are ye seeking the easy way? Did He? Come! Be joyous in thy love for thy friend, thy foe, thy loved ones, thy enemies. For *all* are His; and as ye do it unto the least ye do it unto Him. 262-83

Q-9. . . . Am I still on the straight and narrow path?

A-9. That must be answered from within, to Him in whom thou hast put thy faith, thy trust, thy hope, thy

hereafter. WHO am *I* to judge thee? "*Who* is good?" as He gave, "*None* save the Father," not even the Son of man. Rather in *Him* is the way, and "My Spirit," saith He, "beareth witness with thy spirit whether ye be the sons of God or not." 262-19

Appendix

As background study for Chapter One, "Sex! And How It Got That Way," the following reading is invaluable. This reading became the basis for the philosophy chapter in *There Is a River.*

Hugh Lynn Cayce: You will have before you the enquiring mind of the entity, Thomas Sugrue, present in this room, and certain of the problems which confront him in composing the manuscript of There Is a River.

The entity is now ready to describe the philosophical concepts which have been given through this source, and wishes to parallel and align them with known religious tenets, especially those of Christian theology.

The entity does not wish to set forth a system of thought, nor imply that all questions of a philosophical nature can be answered through this source—the limitations of the finite mind prevent this.

But the entity wishes to answer those questions which will naturally arise in the mind of the reader, and many of the questions which are being asked by all people in the world today.

Therefore the entity presents certain problems and questions, which you will answer as befits the entity's understanding and the task of interpretation before him.

Mr. Cayce: Yes, we have the enquiring mind, Thomas Sugrue, and those problems, those questions that arise in the mind of the entity at this period. Ready for questions.

Q-1. The first problem concerns the reason for creation. Should this be given as God's desire to experience Himself, God's desire for companionship, God's desire for expression, or in some other way?

A-1. God's desire for companionship and expression.

Q-2. The second problem concerns that which is variously called evil, darkness, negation, sin. Should it be said that this condition existed as a necessary element of creation, and the soul, given free will, found itself with the power to indulge in it, or lose itself in it? Or should it be said that this is a condition created by the activity of the soul itself? Should it be described, in either case, as a state of consciousness, a gradual lack of awareness of self and self's relation to God?

A-2. It is the free will and its losing itself in its relationship to God.

Q-3. The third problem has to do with the fall of man. Should this be described as something which was inevitable in the destiny of souls, or something which God did not desire, but which He did not prevent once He had given free will? The problem here is to reconcile the omniscience of God and His knowledge of all things with the free will of the soul and the soul's fall from grace.

A-3. He did not prevent, once having given free will. For, He made the individual entities or souls in the beginning. For, the beginnings of sin, of course, were in seeking expression of themselves outside of the plan or the way in which God had expressed same. Thus it was the individual, see?

Having given free will, then—though having the foreknowledge, though being omnipotent and omnipresent—it is only when the soul that is a portion of God *chooses* that God knows the end thereof.

Q-4. The fourth problem concerns man's tenancy on earth. Was it originally intended that souls remain out of earthly forms, and were the races originated as a necessity resulting from error?

A-4. The earth and its manifestations were only the expression of God and not necessarily as a place of tenancy for the souls of men, until man was created—to meet the needs of existing conditions.

Q-5. The fifth problem concerns an explanation of the life readings. From a study of these it seems that there is a trend downward, from early incarnations, toward greater earthliness and less mentality. Then there is a swing upward, accompanied by suffering, patience, and understanding. Is this the normal pattern, which results in virtue and Oneness with God obtained by free will and mind?

A-5. This is correct. It is the pattern as it is set in Him.

Q-6. The sixth problem concerns interplanetary and intersystem dwelling, between earthly lives. It was given through this source that the entity Edgar Cayce, after the experience as Uhjltd, went to the system of Arcturus, and then returned to earth. Does this indicate a usual or an unusual step in soul evolution?

A-6. As indicated, or as has been indicated in other sources besides this as respecting this very problem—Arcturus is that which may be called the center of this universe, through which individuals pass and at which period there comes the choice of the individual as to whether it is to return to complete there—that is, in this planetary system, our sun, the earth sun and its planetary system—or to pass on to others. This was an unusual step, and yet a usual one.

Q-7. The seventh problem concerns implications from the sixth problem. It is necessary to finish the solar system cycle before going to other systems?

A-7. Necessary to finish the solar cycle.

Q-8. Can Oneness be attained—or the finish of evolution reached—on any system, or must it be in a particular one?

A-8. Depending upon what system the entity has entered, to be sure. It may be completed in any of the many systems.

Q-9. Must the solar cycle be finished on earth, or can it be completed on another planet, or does each planet have a cycle of its own which must be finished?

A-9. If it is begun on earth it must be finished on the earth. The solar system of which the earth is a part is only a portion of the whole. For, as indicated in the number of planets about the earth, they are of one and the same—and they are relative one to another. It is the cycle of the whole system that is finished, see?

Q-10. The eighth problem concerns the pattern made by parents at conception. Should it be said that this pattern attracts a certain soul because it approximates conditions which that soul wishes to work with?

A-10. It approximates conditions. It does not set. For, the individual entity or soul, given the opportunity, has its own free will to work in or out of those problems as presented by that very union. Yet the very union, of course, attracts or brings a channel or an opportunity for the expression of an individual entity.

Q-11. Does the incoming soul take on of necessity some of the parents' karma?

A-11. Because of its relative relationship to same, yes. Otherwise, no.

Q-12. Does the soul itself have an earthly pattern which fits back into the one created by the parents?

A-12. Just as indicated, it is relative—as one related to another; and because of the union of activities they are brought in the pattern. For in such there is the explanation of universal or divine laws, which are ever one and the same; as indicated in the expression that God moved within Himself and then He didn't change, though did bring to Himself that of His own being made crucified even in the flesh.

Q-13. Are there several patterns which a soul might take on, depending on what phase of development it wished to work upon—i.e., could a soul choose to be one of several personalities, any of which would fit its individuality?

A-13. Correct.

Q-14. Is the average fulfillment of the soul's expectation more or less than fifty percent?

A-14. It's a continuous advancement, so it is more than fifty percent.

Q-15. Are heredity, environment and will equal factors in aiding or retarding the entity's development?

A-15. Will is the greater factor, for it may overcome any or all of the others; provided that will is made one with the pattern, see? For, no influence of heredity, environment or whatnot, surpasses the will; else why would there have been that pattern shown in which the individual soul, no matter how far astray it may have gone, may enter with Him into the holy of holies?

Q-16. The ninth problem concerns the proper symbols, or similies, for the Master, the Christ. Should Jesus be described as the soul who first went throught the cycle of earthly lives to attain perfection, including perfection in the planetary lives also?

A-16. He should be. This is as the man, see?

Q-17. Should this be described as a voluntary mission [of] One who was already perfected and returned to God, having accomplished His Oneness in other planes and systems?

A-17. Correct.

Q-18. Should the Christ Consciousness be described as the awareness within each soul, imprinted in pattern on the mind and waiting to be awakened by the will, of the soul's Oneness with God?

A-18. Correct. That's the idea exactly!

Q-19. Please list the names of the incarnations of the Christ, and of Jesus, indicating where the development of the man Jesus began.

A-19. First, in the beginning, of course; and then as Enoch, Melchizedek, in the perfection. Then in the earth of Joseph, Joshua, Jeshua, Jesus.

Q-20. The tenth problem concerns the factors of soul evolution. Should mind, the builder, be described as the last development because it should not unfold until it has a firm foundation of emotional virtues?

A-20. This might be answered Yes and No, both. But if it is presented in that there is dept, willfully, see, that desire to be in the at-onement, then it is necessary for that attainment before it recognizes mind as the way.

Q-21. The eleventh problem concerns a parallel with

Christianity. Is Gnosticism the closest type of Christianity to that which is given through this source?

A-21. This is a parallel, and was the commonly accepted one until there began to be set rules in which there were the attempts to take shortcuts. And there are none in Christianity!

Q-22. What action of the early church, or council, can be mentioned as that which ruled reincarnation from Christian theology?

A-22. Just as indicated—the attempts of individuals to accept or take advantage of, because of this knowledge, see?

Q-23. Do souls become entangled in other systems as they did in this system?

A-23. In other systems that represent the same as the earth does in this system, yes.

Q-24. Is there any other advice which may be given to this entity at this time in the preparation of these chapters?

A-24. Hold fast to that ideal, and using Him ever as the Ideal. And hold up the *necessity* for each to meet the same problems. And *do not* attempt to shed or to surpass or go around the cross. *This* is that upon which each and every soul *must* look and know it is to be borne in self *with* Him.

We are through for the present. 5749-14

C. Austin Rice, a 34-year-old lawyer, was encouraged by the readings to write a book on sex education entitled *A Timely Warning;* it was published in 1935. By today's consciousness the contents appear rather moralistic. Nevertheless, the following two readings, 5747-3 and 826-6, are very contemporary and relevant; they are the only two discourses given on the general question of sex education, calling for a deep and serious restructuring of our approach to it and to conception.

Mrs. Cayce: You will have before you the question of sex and sex relations as related to delinquency of the teens and younger ages. You will give such information on this subject as indicated could be given through this channel as a warning at this time. Indicate that which should be used for publication and application by Charles Austin Rice and A.K. Swartz present here. You will answer the questions that may be asked:

Mr. Cayce [After repeating suggestion in an undertone]:

Yes, we have the question here regarding sex and sex relationships, the influence that is manifested in the lives of the peoples as a whole in this country; with relationship to delinquency in the teen age.

In giving, then, that as we find from here, it is well that you who are considering being of aid to others in meeting or facing this problem at this time be given something not exactly as a history but as a review—for the moment—of the causes, and how these causes apply in the experience of the individuals and the nations as a whole.

First, we would begin then at the beginnings; man's advent into materiality or into a material world and becoming as individual bodies of the world, who became observing of this fact in the material world from that he (man and woman) saw in the earth. Hence it is given in thy writings of Scripture (although in a hidden manner, ye may observe if ye will look) how Adam named those that were brought before him in creation. Their *name* indicates to the carnal mind their relationships in the sex condition or question. Hence the question ye seek is as old as or older than man.

This has been the problem throughout man's experience or man's sojourn in the earth; since taking bodily form, with the attributes of the animal in which he had *projected* himself as a portion of, that he might through the self gain that activity which was visualized to him in those relationships in the earth.

Hence slow has been the progress through the ages. And as has been seen, and as may be gained by a study of man's development, this question of the causes, of the relationships in those directions, has ever been a problem before man.

This is ever, and will ever be, a question, a problem, until there is the greater spiritual awakening within man's experience that this phase biologically, sociologically, or even from the analogical experience, must be as a stepping-stone for the greater awakening; and as the exercising of an influence in man's experience in the Creative Forces for the reproduction of species, rather than for the satisfying or gratifying of a biological urge within the individual that partakes or has partaken of the first causes of man's encasement in body in the earth.

These conditions, then, as a very sketch, are the problems to be met that exist in this country, this land. As we find, they, the conditions in the social life, in the marital life, in the experience of groups of various characters, confront the world, the country, the home, the individual, today. Various problems of the same nature are in various lands, because of *their* own individual aspect of such conditions, owing to the role by certain political or so-called religious influences that are a portion of the laws or rules or regulations under which these attempt to direct or to govern the social relationships of man and woman. Then, what is the condition, what is wrong, and how may same be corrected—*under* the existent conditions?

For these that would be of a help must of necessity take the conditions as they *exist*, and not as they would *like* to have them. These *exist* because of certain definite facts that have been indicated, in how that first there was seen that which brought about desire. This awoke within the various forms or manners the result of such relationships in individuals, and brought about certain relationships—and eventually man's encasement within a body which through the ages has gradually developed, with the varied activities that have influenced and been influenced by those very same questions—as they exist today.

So, then, give ye unto men as this: Train ye the child when he is young, and when he is old he will not depart from the Lord. Train *him*, train *her*, train *them* rather in the sacredness of that which has come to them as a privilege, which has come to them as a heritage; from a falling away, to be sure, but through the purifying of the body in thought, in act, in certainty, it may make for a peoples, a state, a nation that may indeed herald the coming of the Lord, For this is the problem, that ye keep the law and present same as holy to those who seek. Who seeks? *Every* child born into the earth, from the age of 2½ to 3 years begins to find there is something that takes place within its *body,* and that it is *different;* not as animals, though the *animal* instinct is there, of the biological urge, that is a law! For that is the source of man's undoing. But ye who set yourselves as examples in the order of society, education, Christian principles, religious thought, religious ideals, hold rather than to anything else to that *love* which is *un*sexed! For He hath given that in the heavenly state, in the higher forces, there is neither marriage nor giving in marriage; for they are as *one!* Yet ye say ye are in the earth, ye are born with the urge! The awakening, then, must come from within; here a little, there a little. Each soul, each body, that is preserved unto Him as a channel of blessings has received and does receive that within itself which makes for the greater abilities for awakening within the hearts, minds, souls and bodies of the young who question, "What will I do with the biological urge that arises?" *Purify* same in service to Him, in expressions of love; in expressions of the fruits of the spirit, which are: gentleness, kindness, brotherly love, long-suffering. *These* are the fruits, and these as the urge of sex are in the nature of the association of ideas, conditions or positions as related to the various conditions about the body. Then set the activity in motion and these become either that which takes hold on hell or that which builds to the kingdom within.

Q-1. Are there any sex practices that should be abolished—

A-1. [Interrupting] There are many sex *practices* in the various portions of this land, as in other lands, that should be—*must* be abolished. *How?* Only through the education of the *young!* Not in their teen age, for *then* they are set! When there are activities or speech not explained within the sound or sight of those in their formative years, they *too* must one day satisfy that which caused men to come into body-form—*experience* same *themselves!* Then, by word and by act keep the life *clean!* The urge is inborn, to be sure; but if the purpose of those who bring individuals into being is only for expressing the beauty and love of the Creative Forces or God, the urge is different with such individuals. Why? It's the law; it's the *law!*

Q-2. Should anything about this sex teaching be included in the book by [826]?

A-2. There has been a presentation of same in that already given—but this must of necessity be cut, changed—edited in such a manner that those *principles* as here presented may be the basis of that given to the public. In *that* manner yes, give same. Much may be given on any phase—but these would only be as a phase or a portion of the whole. Prepare or present that which has been given that is may be *as it is* a *practical* thing. For unless it is sanctioned by the powers that *rule* and influence the God-given forces of man, little may be accomplished.

We are through for the present. 5747-3

Mrs. Cayce: You will have before you the enquiring mind of [826], present in this room, and his desire to comply with the advice given him through these sources; that is, to "cleanse the minds of the moral practices and social relationships in sex." Will you explain in detail the sex practices and sex thoughts of the people which are destructive, pointing out those which should be abolished, and others which should be substituted therefor. Explain particularly with relation to adults over 20 years old, because by education and example they teach the young. Point out those harmful factors about the moral and social relationships in sex and the remedies for them which should be dealt with in the book A Timely Warning *which is present in this room. You will answer the questions he will submit, as I ask them:*

Mr. Cayce: Yes, we have the enquiring mind of [826], also those desires of presenting the conditions as timely warnings for the young in this age and this experience.

As we find, in presenting what may be helpful in the educational way and manner, as we have indicated, the condition that exists in the present as related to the relationships in sex—or the greater cause for the lack of judgment, the lack of proper consideration, the lack of those things necessary to prevent the laxness and the practice of those conditions and experiences as related to same—is from the lack of education in the young *before* their teen-age years!

For few there be who have the proper understanding, as we have indicated, of what the biological urge produces in the body!

Now whether such an education is to be undertaken in the home or in the school is the greater problem.

To be sure, there are conditions existent in relationship to many of the denominational activities religiously that prohibit, bar or prevent sufficient consideration of these problems in the public schools or even in the private schools.

And little has there been of the proper education of the mother, the father of those who need such instruction.

But these are the places to begin. And the warnings as would be presented are *not* as to the practices of this or the manner of that, or the association of this or that in the adult life. But there should be those precautions, understandings, relationships as to how and in what manner there becomes the biological urge; which through the proper training may become a *pathological* condition in the body of the individual. For it is as from the beginning of puberty the essence of the Creative Forces or Energies within the body of the individual.

And if such forces are turned to those channels for the aggrandizement of selfish motives, or for the satisfying of that within the urge for the gratification of *emotions*, they become destructive; not only in the manner of the offspring but also in the very *physical body* of the offspring, as well as in the energies of the bodies so producing same.

These are the approaches that *should* be given as timely warnings to the mother, the father; and as for the *young* these should be rather as the suggestions for the instructors, the warnings to the mother, the parents as to the conversation of the nurse, the maid, or as to the exercisings of the children in their formative years—in *whatever* relationships there may be.

And then, as these grow and become a portion of the politic body for public education, there should be the greater stress laid upon the educations in these directions; and not wait until they have reached or arrived at that position where they begin to study physiology, anatomy or hygiene. But even in the *formative* years there should be the training in these directions, as a portion of the material things. Even as the child studies its letters, let a portion of the instructions be in the care of the body, and more and more the stress upon the care in relation to the sex of the body and in the preservation of that as to its relationships to its Creator.

For it is through such factors, through such bodies of activity, that there may become a manifestation of the spiritual forces such as to bring *into being* those of one's own flesh and blood.

These are the approaches. There are the conditions.

Do not begin halfway. Do not begin after there has been already begun the practice of the conditions that make for destructive forces, or for the issue of the body to become as a burning within the very elements of the body itself—and to find expression in the gratifying of the emotions of the body!

For, to be sure, relationships in the sex are the exercising of the highest emotions in which a physical body may indulge. And *only* in man is there found that such are used as that of *destruction* to the body-offspring!

This, then, is the approach; this is the manner.

Ready for questions.

Q-1. Is monogamy the best form of home relationship?

A-1. Let the teachings be rather toward the spiritual intent. Whether it's monogamy, polygamy, or whatnot, let it be the answering of the spiritual *within* the individual!

But monogamy is the best, of course, as indicated from the Scripture itself—*One—ONE!* For the union of one should ever be *One*.

Q-2. Is marriage as we have it necessary and advisable?

A-2. It is!

Q-3. Should divorces be encouraged by making them easier to obtain?

A-3. This depends upon first the education of the body. Once united, once understood that the relationships are to be as one, less and less is there the necessity of such conditions. Man may learn a great deal from a study of the goose in this direction. Once it has mated, *never* is there a mating with any other—either the male or female, no matter how soon the destruction of the mate may occur—unless *forced* by *man's* intervention.

This does not indicate that this is the *end*, and should *only* remain as such. For, as we have indicated, *this* is indicated by the name and the *meaning* of the name itself. For this is the *extreme*. Just as indicated in all of the animals—the fowl or those that have become the closer related to man, and man's intervention in their surroundings and their activities and their adaptabilities; in their *natural* state these are in the forms as their *names* indicate. And from these man may learn many lessons; which *was* attempted in the beginning. And yet, as we have indicated, in same he lost self in that he found that he could satisfy those emotions or *gratify* what might be builded as emotions from experience to experience. Thus there were gradually brought on the various polygamous relationships that have existed throughout the ages in many periods. And, as indicated in the lives of groups and nations, these become the stumbling blocks that are ever kept within the background—but that have made for the destructive influence that arose within the activities of such groups and nations, in such relationships.

Hence to begin, begin with the *Mind*. For, as we have said, to build the perfect relationship in *any* direction that there may be brought a union is to begin before the parents of such are born! in *their* own minds!

Hence to begin with the teen-age, or at twenty, or at fifty, or with an older individual, is only to have the tail end of something! and does not tend to be constructive *at all!* Only does it become a *form*.

But begin with those when they are *choosing* their mate, see?

Q-4. Should nudism be encouraged?

A-4. That should be a matter of principle within the

individuals as there is the training as to what is the purpose of those parts covered. Nudism or clothing or whatnot, as we have *oft* indicated, should be *rather* the matter of the environ—and not a matter of moral principle in *any* sense!

Q-5. Is the broadcasting of birth control information advantageous in improving the race?

A-5. It is like shooting feathers at an eagle: It's a move in the right direction, but that's about as much as might be said. This should be rather the *training* of those that are in the positions of *being* the mothers and fathers *of* the nation, of the peoples!

What are the factors in the lives of those that broadcast such? Look into those and ye may easily find the answer to your question. Not all, but *most* are prompted by something that is lacking in their *own* makeup.

Who giveth the increase? Man may plant, man may sow. Man understanding, then, the varied activities of a given condition—through the education in the character of the soil, in the elements going to make up the body of that sought to be produced—*prepares* for same. But who giveth the increase? *Who* maketh for that which bringeth the returns? Man in his preparation, or the source from which it arises?

So with the education, so with that which does the prompting, let it be from not that which is *lacking* in an urge, but rather from *what* is to be done by the individual *with* the urge! See? and leave the results with the *Giver* of Life!

For *Life* is of, and is, the Creative Force; it is that ye worship as God.

Those then that besmirch same by overindulgence besmirch that which is best within themselves. And that should be the key to birth control or sex relations, or every phase of the relationships between the sons and daughters of men—that would become the sons and daughter of God.

Q-6. You suggested that I should publish this book myself and also to have it published by a firm such as

*Macmillan or Simon & Schuster. If I publish it myself, Macmillan or Simon & Schuster will not print and mail it, and if one of these firms publishes, I cannot do so myself. Which course should I follow?**

A-6. Present it, as indicated, to a publisher for consideration, see? If it is accepted, then there is no need to attempt publishing it yourself. If it is not accepted, then make arrangements with the publishers to publish it yourself for distribution in various ways and manners that may be made. There are three forms of printing such. It may either be accepted altogether on its merits, or obtain a presubscription for such a publication by the activities of self—in which the publisher publishes same, and then the own advertising from that accompanying the list of those who have presubscribed; or the individual (self) assumes the whole responsibility. Use some consideration or judgment or ability in these directions! You have it!

Q-7. The selling price of this series of books under one volume should be $1 or $1.25. Is that right?

A-7. One twenty-five ($1.25).

Q-8. Should I explain in this book the powers of Mr. Edgar Cayce with reference to the cure of disease, and his powers relating to psychic and life readings?

A-8. It may be made a chapter, but should be presented *not* as Edgar Cayce but as a possibility; or rather through mentioning an association or connection made by self and stated as a fact. But, we we find, this would be better presented as a separate and distinct presentation, rather than a portion of such a *broad* field as covered in this series.

Q-9. Is continence in marriage advisable except when mating to produce offspring?

A-9. This should be, and is, as we have indicated in the matter of education, the *outcome* of the *universal* sources of supply of the individuals. For some, yes; in other cases it would be *very* bad on the part of each, while in others it would be bad on one or the other, see?

---

*He published the book himself later that year—1935.

There should be, then, rather the educating as to the *purposes*, and *how—HOW* that the force, the vitality, that goes for the gratifying of emotions may be centralized in creating—in the lives of others about the body in all its various phases—spiritual blessings.

Q-10. Should men or women who do not have the opportunity to marry have sex relationships outside of marriage?

A-10. This again is a matter of principle within the individual. The sex organs, the sex demands of every individual, must be gratified in *some* manner as a portion of the biological urge within the individual. These *begin* in the present with curiosity. For it is as natural for there to be sexual relations between man and woman, when drawn together in their regular relations or activities, as it is for the flowers to bloom in the spring, or for the snows to come in the winter, when the atmospheric conditions are conducive or inducive to such conditions.

When a man or woman has chosen (for it must be choice, and is only by choice that one remains out of relationships with the opposite sex in marriage)—if it has chosen to not be in such relationships, then be true to the choice; or else it is to self a sin! For that which one would pretend to be and isn't is indeed sin!

Q-11. Should they raise children outside of marriage?

A.11. It answers itself.

Q-12. Would it be better for a woman, who desires to marry, to be one of two or more wives to a man in a home rather than to remain unmarried?

A-12. This is again a matter of *principle;* or the urge within such conditions must be conformative to the set as the ideal.

In the education of individuals as regarding sex relationships, as in every other educational activity, there must be a standard or a rule to go by or an ideal state that has its inception not in the emotions of a physical body but from the spiritual ideal which has been set, which was set and given to man in his relation to the Creative Forces.

Then to ask or to seek or to advise or to give suggestions even, that is may be done outside of that, isn't being true to that as is presented.

We are through for the present. 826-6

The following two readings were for expectant mothers. The first, 457-10, was given for a 34-year-old woman who was seeking to prepare herself mentally and spiritually for the best development of her unborn child. The second, 4926-1, was for an unmarried teen-aged girl, who was instructed not only to have her child but to make arrangements so that she would eventually assume her responsibilities as the child's mother.

Mrs. Cayce: You will have before you the entity, [457] . . .N.Y.C., who seeks a mental and spiritual reading, keeping in mind preparation of the entity's mind and spiritual forces for the creation the best development of a child; answering the questions she has submitted, as I ask them:

Mr. Cayce: Yes, we have the body, the entity's mind and body, the desires and purposes and aims.

In giving information, or in answering questions respecting mental and spiritual attitudes, all of these should be approached from *this* basis of reasoning—especially as preparations are made in body, mind and spirit for a soul's entrance into the material plane.

While as an individual entity, [457], presents the fact of a body, a mind, a soul—it has been given as a promise, as an opportunity to man through coition, to furnish, to create a channel through which the Creator, God, may give to individuals the opportunity of seeing, experiencing His handiwork.

Thus the greater preparation that may be made, in earnest, in truth in offering self as a channel, is first physical, then the mental attitude; knowing that God, the Creator, will supply that character, that nature may have its course in being and in bringing into material manifestation a soul. For, in being absent from a physical body a soul is in the presence of its Maker.

Then, know the attitude of mind of self, of the companion, in creating the opportunity; for it depends upon the state of attitude as to the nature, the character that may be brought into material experience.

Leave *then* the spiritual aspects to God. Prepare the mental and the physical body, according to the nature, the character of that soul being sought.

The fact that there has been in the experience of this entity and its companion the mind of doubt, because of material needs and because of mental aspects as may have been or might be a heritage physically, has delayed or prevented such activities. Remember, there is an example of such in the Scripture that the entity would do well to study, to analyze; not merely as a historical fact but the attitude not only of Hannah but of those about the entity who doubted the purpose.

Then, in that same attitude as that entity may this entity in that way bring those activities as may best endow self, as well as the offspring, to be a messenger, a channel to the glory of God and to the honor of self.

Ready for questions.

Q-1. Is it right to bring a child into being in a world such as we have today, even though it may never know a normal life but only one of war and killing and anger and hate?

A-1. The doubt as created in the self, from the very asking of such a question, may be answered best in considering the attitude, the conditions which existed in those people's minds and activities at the period given as an example. If that does not answer, then to this entity it cannot be answered.

Q-2. Should any thought be given the the possibility of draft of the [planned baby's] father [Mr. 412]?

A-2. Whether this has the correct attitude, in whether this is to be a duty, an obligation or an opportunity of the father—this, too, must be settled in self's own mind.

Q-3. Has there been much lost in spiritual development in these past years of absorption in material existence, or was this experience a necessary foundation for that yet to come?

A-3. It can be *made* such, as an experience needed. If it is used as an excuse, if it is used as something to shield self and companion, then it is lost. If it is used as the opportunity, now, for fulfilling the purpose, it is gain. For, what is the first command by the Creator to man? "Be thou fruitful and multiply." Yet this sets a natural law, a mental law, a spiritual law in motion, according to whether such activity is for the gratification of the flesh, of the mental self, or the fulfilling of a *complete* relationship to the Creative Forces.

Q-4. Should I read any book for my spiritual development besides A Search for God?

A-4. Read the Book of all books—especially Deuteronomy 30, and Samuel—considering especially the attitude of Hannah, the conditions, the circumstances which existed not only as to its relationship to its husband and to other companions, but as to the needs for spiritual awakening in that experience—which exist in the world and the earth today.

If the entity can and will so place self, and then studying John 14, 15, 16, and 17—can ye make yourself as one with Him? These, as combined with the study of the preparation physically, may give the understanding; not as duty but an *opportunity* to be a handmaid of the Lord.

Q-5. Do thoughts of future mother have any direct effect or influence on soul attracted to be her child?

A-5. This should be, as ever, left in the hands of the Creator. Prepare the self mentally and physically, and leave that to the Lord; not merely passively but actively, knowing that in the same measure ye mete to others ye mete to thy Maker. Then, what manner of soul are ye attracting?

Q-6. Does soul enter child at conception or birth or in between?

A-6. It may at the first moment of breath; it may some hours before birth; it may many hours after birth. This depends upon that condition, that environ surrounding the circumstance.

Q-7. Are there souls waiting on the other side to come to this world as my children?

A-7. If the opportunity is offered, they will come.

Q-8. Is it possible to influence this selection by the mental or spiritual thoughts of the prospective mother?

A-8. These should be, as indicated, left to the will, the purpose of the Father-God. What do ye seek? That such shall be a channel of blessings to others, or to satisfy or gratify thine own desires, or that ye in thy desire may fulfill the whole purpose *He*, thy Maker, may have with thee? Art thou willing to pay the price for such?

Q-9. While carrying the child do thoughts and impressions have any effect on the child?

A-9. To be sure. Thus, if surrounded with beauty, the more beauty there may be. Hast thou not read how that when Mary spoke to Elizabeth, the child leaped within the womb?

Q-10. Do emotions such as fright, excitement, etc., have any effect on the child?

A-10. Depends upon how much of this goes beyond the real purpose of the individual entity caring for, or carrying, the child.

Q-11. Is not the mother when carrying a child very close to God?

A-11. If she puts herself so! If not, it is merely a physical condition. It's a law—universal law, mental *and* material. It may be either, or any, or all. Remember, the Lord thy God is One.

Q-12. What is the meaning of names? I have been told that Martha should be my real name. Is there a reason why?

A-12. This comes rather as to the minds and purposes of those who give names to their offspring. Names, to be sure, have their meaning, but as given by the poet, a rose by any other name would be just as beautiful or just as sweet. So may such be said of these. Yet, as given by Him, names have their meaning, and these depend upon the purposes when such are bestowed upon an individual entity entering the earth's plane.

Have ye not understood how that in various experiences individuals, as their purposes or attitudes or desires were indicated, had their names henceforth called a complete or full name meaning or indicating the purpose to which the individual entity or soul had been called? So, all of these have their part. They are not *all*, as indicated. For, *all* is one. One is all, but each individual is impressed by the various phases of man's consciousness in materiality. These, as we find, have varying degrees of effect upon the consciousness or the awareness of individuals.

For, "My Spirit beareth witness with thy spirit" is complete in itself.

Q-13. Do names have a spiritual influence on people?

A-13. As has just been given.

Q-14. Would it make any difference to me whether called [457] or Martha?

A-14. Depends upon how the individual associates names with same.

Q-15. When would it be best to choose a name for the child?

A-15. When ye have determined as to the purpose to which ye hope, and which ye will, which ye are willing to dedicate same.

Q-16. Does this have anything to do with the time when soul enters new body?

A-16. Nothing.

Q-17. Is the little boy Mr. Cayce saw, as a vision, with me, still waiting to come as my child?

A-17. This may depend upon the attitude of the individual.

Q-18. Is there anything besides prayer and meditation which I can do for my spiritual development and for this new soul?

A-18. As has been outlined, the study of various phases of experiences of individuals through their relationship to Creative Forces, and their relationship to their fellow man.

For, remember, the soul that is brought into the earth is only lent to thee by the Lord. And the impressions, and that purpose that ye build into that, is that ye send back to thy Maker in the end.

We are through for the present. 457-10

Mrs. Cayce: You will have before you [4926] who is at the Allen Memorial Hospital . . . Alabama, and all the conditions surrounding her moral, parental and home relations. You will answer the questions which have been submitted by her mother in regard to these, as I ask them.

Mr. Cayce: Yes, we have the body, [4926], those conditions of every nature that surround the body in the present. Ready for questions.

Q-1. What caused first evidence of weakness in moral nature? If weakness of nature exists, how may it be corrected?

A-1. In the light of existent conditions there was a weakness from many a standpoint, as morals would be judged.

The cause, as we find, was in the general surroundings, that may be considered from the attitude of the associations and from the enviromentals that were thrown about the body.

The condition, as we see, was not from innately immoral attitudes; nor was the body innately given to those states of body or mind that would lead to such a condition; for, by *nature* the body or body-mind is not so inclined.

Rather, there was the trusting indiscretion on the part of the body.

Then, as to how this situation may be handled—or what may be done about same:

We would change this attitude, this environment, this *manner* of association; through throwing about the body those influences of love, not the manner as of *condonement* but not as of silent or open condemnation. Rather in the manner that the lesson, though very grave, is very deep in the mind and in the heart of the body. And through that manner shown by the Giver of all good and perfect gifts, who gave: *Sin* no more! I *condemn* thee not for thy weakness!"

And, if these conditions and environs will be put about the body, there may come in the experience of the body, [4926], that of a usefulness and a service to *many* another.

But, with silent or open rebellion there must grow

that of hate of self and of others; and be brought rather the gratifying of all *unseeming* desires in the experience of a body!

Q-2. What should be done with, or about, the baby?

A-2. There should be the completion of the preparation in the mental body of the young mother for the general aptitudes, the physical preparations of mind and body, for the vicissitudes of life; or, at least one more session or season in study and associations.

While, unless there is every love and precaution put about the body, the mother desire will not allow such a change to come about—but this, as we find, would be the better for the body.

Then, with one that may choose to give his love, his protection, his every effort in bringing about the body the proper surroundings, proper relations (that exist deep in the make-up of a *friend;* yea, more than the friend!), the baby may be taken—as by the outward aspects of the penal law—as one with, one among, those of the household.

Then do not, under *any* circumstance, put the child in such a place that it may not *some* day know the true mother love, the true mother affection that may be its—and is *every* soul's—birthright!

Make, then, some arrangements whereby—for the one year—it may be cared for, in an institution; whereby there is given every care, every protection. But with the stipulation that at the end of the period the *mother* will claim same, under the law, as her own.

Q-3. Please give name and location of such an institution, that would be the best under the present circumstances and conditions with this body?

A-3. In the foundlings home in Birmingham, Mobile or New Orleans. All have such institutions. But let it be *definitely* settled (for this child that has suffered so in every manner) that it, the baby, *will* be her very own. Let it be embued from day to day in the mind, in the heart, that it is a living duty, a living obligation; and that the child has that right as of a soul dependent upon the activities of the body itself who brought same into being.

For, a soul is *here*—that may go *far,* in bringing much

to many. *Dedicate* this precious life to a service of the Creative Forces, to God, through Him who suffered little children to come unto Him; for "of such is the kingdom."

Else we will find it will be as a canker in the heart and mind of everyone concerned, and will *eat*—and *EAT*—and rust!

Q-4. What is proper attitude to be taken toward father of baby?

A-4. As loving indifference.

Q-5. Is there danger for him and . . . to be thrown together in same town?

A-5. As we have given, the environs should be changed for the body.

Q-6. Where should [4926] go from . . . or where would be the best place?

A-6. Around those surroundings that are pleasant, and where there may be *instilled* those true relationships of men and women—and of the love of God for those even who falter, according to men's morals, in their activities in this material world! Or, where there are true friends to be found.

Q-7. Would . . . Alabama, be advised?

A-7. Be well.

Q-8. Should her mother go to . . . for her, regardless of where she should go?

A-8. She should.

Q-9. Where would be the best place for her to finish high school?

A-9. In any of those environs where there may be the better attitudes held for the body. For, *face* the issue! Face the circumstance, and so give the body—[4926]—that insight into the forgiveness of the Father, that she may even be able to forgive slights spoken here and there.

Then, in whatever surroundings that may make for the *better* conditions in *that* direction, whether in the same schools from which she has gone or those nearby.

Q-10. Would it be best for her to take any part of business course now, if she should be in . . . for present?

A-10. Best that the preparations for a *home* life be

made; making those associations, those connections, with that portion of life that fits her for such.

Q-11. Should present relation exist between her and . . .?

A-11. Be well that, at the end of the year, the union be such that the home may be established, for this—*HER*—baby!

Q-12. What would be best for her protection and happiness in future as compared to past attitudes of those who have loved and cared for her?

A-12. Those relationships that we have given. There must be thrown about the body the atmosphere that it is the *duty,* it is the obligation, for everyone who has loved and cared for her, to act in that same manner as did Him towards such relations; that they show that love in reality. As given, not condoning—but *never* condemning, in act, in word, in heart. Be the real *friend—everyone,* as ye seek for the Christ to be *your* Friend.

For, he that aideth not one in a moment has been weak—how can he expect forgiveness and love from Him who *is* Love, and Mercy, *and* LIFE!

We are through. 4926-1

In the following a 27-year-old woman [1436] was told she had been Tamar. (See Genesis 38.) The Biblical story concerns Judah, his sons Er and Onan, and Er's wife Tamar.

One of the perspectives on sex which has influenced our culture most deeply is that which comes from church traditions and their interpretation of the Bible. The only Biblical reference which can be construed as relating to masturbation is in the story of Onan. It was the tradition of the time for a widow to be cared for by the brothers of her former husband, especially with respect to assuring that she had children. It was socially undesirable for a married woman or a widow to be barren; this condition was interpreted as a lack of God's favor or blessing. Judah's son, Er, was wicked and the Lord slew him. Tamar, the widow, asked her father-in-law, Judah, about the requirement of her brother-in-law to provide her with children. Onan had been lax in fulfilling this duty for several years. At her insistence, Judah then instructed his son to fulfill his duty which tradition required. Reluctantly Onan went in to Tamar, pretending to fulfill his obligation; however, he withdrew before ejaculation and "spilled it on the ground." This displeased the Lord and He slew him. Because of the Lord's reported anger, many Biblical interpreters have used this passage as a basis for attitudes about masturbation. It seems much more likely that the Lord's wrath was in response to the failure of Onan to provide her with a child than the manner in which he avoided such. Therefore, this passage seems not at all relevant to the Biblical attitude about masturbation.

As the story continues, Tamar deceives her father-in-law by pretending to be a harlot and has twins by him. An interesting karmic twist is that her present father was Er, Tamar's husband.

Mr. Cayce: Yes, we have the body here, [1436].

Now, as we find, there needs be consideration given for the physical forces of the body. For the body *must* manifest that which *is* a growth of the mental self.

So much is expected, so much required of this body-mind, it is well that the spiritual and the mental be included with the physical forces of the body in the present.

First, then, for the physical forces:

Here we have disturbing forces owing to an unbalanced condition between the purely physical and the mental and spiritual self.

Hence we have conflicting influences and thus, as has been indicated, a crystallizing in the physical of the physical deficiencies through inabilities of the body to assimilate that which has been the diet with sufficient of the elements to keep an equal balance in the physical body.

Thus the disturbances through the digestive system, the inclinations for the functionings of the vibratory forces of the organs through the pelvis and the activities of the system, bring about the inefficiency of the replenishing forces, by the activity of the glandular system to supply the elements necessary for the bodily functions.

First, then, from the basis of activity of the spiritual in a physical and mental body:

Spiritual is, to be sure, eternal; and thus is the image of that which is creative—or that is termed in materiality Godlike in its nature.

Then, there must be—and are—contacts within the physical to the points from which, through which, the spiritual and mental must coordinate for the activities of a physical body.

The vibrations of the body, then, have *not* kept (in the physical) in accord or attune to the vibrations of the mental and the spiritual self—to the detriment of the physical self, as indicated from the points of accumulations or those points where segregations form in cysts, tumor and the like in the body.

Then, mind being the builder—yet physical activities and the spiritual or life elements of same in the form of that assimilated—is the contact for the life forces in materiality or physical body.

Hence we have in the analysis the acids, alkalines, potashes, in their natural forms; and these are assimilations from the diets of the body. These through their deficiencies have produced that effect upon the vibratory centers of the body. The glands of the system become then deficient in their activities.

These then, as we find, make for hindrances that have brought and do bring about these disturbing conditions—physically.

Then, the body-mental being incoordinant or not coordinating, *with* a deficient physical being, the *high mental* efficiency and activity, with the environs about the body there is created then an added disturbance for the mental forces—and all have their effect upon the bodily functions.

Know this: that all healing of every nature must come from a mental attitude created by either that activity within the system as food, as medicine, as activities, the principle of which is constructive in aiding those deficient portions to become coordinant with the rest of the system for constructive forces.

Whether this is taken internally, mechanically applied, laying on of hands of by the spoken word, the *effect* must be the same; but each in its sphere of activity.

Do not judge, then, *mental* things *only* by material reaction or activity; nor judge spiritual things except as the patterns or reflections of those things in a material world.

Hence for this body, we would add first as these:

That which will first arouse or cleanse the system for the activity of the glandular forces of the body.

Take, then, one minim of atomic iodine (Atomidine) —do not take more than this at a time—in half a glass of water before the morning meal, for three mornings; then leave off for three mornings; then take again for three mornings. Or, take it three days each week, Mondays, Tuesdays, Wednesdays, leaving off until the next Monday and then take again. Do this for a period of three weeks.

This will raise that activity to the pulsation, to the heart's activity, cleansing the thyroid, the thymus, the glandular forces of the digestive system; arousing an activity in the hepatic circulation, changing the order of vibration through the adrenals, and making through the caecum, through the ileum activity or plexus a reduction in irritation as aroused by the improper coagulation in the blood supply.

Also we would begin immediately with using each day for thirty minutes (not longer for the first thirty days) the vibrations from the Radio-active Appliance; that we may create the coordinant vibratory forces of the body to the *functioning* of the bodily forces in the physical activities.

And make this thirty-minute period each day as the period of meditation. Let the meditation be put in the body's own words, but following as this:

"Great Creative Forces, I am Thy servant; and would give myself in body, in mind, in spirit, to the service of my fellow man that the Creative Forces may be the better understood, and man's relationship to same known in the heart of men.

"*Make Thou, then, my body* whole *in the ways, the manners, in which I may serve this purpose the better.*"

And *mean* what is said, and *act* that way.

Then after the three weeks of taking the Atomidine and using the Appliance as indicated:

We would begin then with the mechanical applications as may be applied through the *osteopathic* profession. Mechanical adjustments are necessary, then, in the coccyx area, in the last dorsal area, in the 9th dorsal area, and through the upper dorsal and cervical; such as may be had in the Dobbins' method. These would only be twice a week for six such treatments, rest a whole month before they would be applied again for some three or four treatments—unless emergencies should arise.

In the matter of the diet: Here we find there have been extremes applied in the experience of the body. At times there have come doubts, and again there was assurance, and a mental condition wherein the call of the bodily forces was not coordinant with the needs of the physical body.

At least have two meals of cooked food each day, and one meal at which there is *no* cooked food. Meats should be taboo, save that occasionally of fowl or fish. Citrus fruit juices *or* cereals (not the two together or at the same meal). Whole wheat *well*-cooked, rye and barley mixed—these are well to be taken for the body under the existent conditions.

And as we find we will bring for this body a *new understanding*, a *new* coordination, in the physical and the mental and the spiritual being.

For the spiritual and mental body:

Each entity, each soul, enters the material experience for purposes. These are not individual or of a selfish nature, though they are very personal in their application and their practice.

Each soul meets *constantly* itself; not alone in what is called at times karma or karmic influences. For remember Life is God; that which is constructive grows; that which is destructive deteriorates.

Then, *karmic* forces—if the life application in the

experience of an individual is made towards constructiveness, it grows and grows. For the individual entity *grows* to a haven of peace and harmony and understanding; or ye *grow* to heaven of peace and harmony and understanding; or ye *grow* to heaven, rather than going to heaven. Ye grow in grace, in knowledge, in understanding.

Then, what is the purpose of this entity's experience in this particular phase and time and period?

To many the entity is far in advance of its time, its period; it having caught a vision as from the mount, and the vibration or the sun of light has risen for the entity, only to be shaded by selfish indulgences in the *minds* of those that have directed—*not* the entity!

Remember then as this: There are promises made by the Creative Forces or God to the children of men, that "If ye will be my daughter, my son, my child, I will indeed be thy God."

This is an individual promise. Hence the purposes are for an entrance that the *soul* may be prepared for an indwelling with the soul, the mind of a living God.

How, then, ye ask, are we to know when ye are on the straight and narrow way?

"My Spirit beareth witness with thy spirit that ye are indeed the children of God."

How? Thy God Consciousness, thy soul, either condemns, rejects or falters before conditions that exist in the experience of the mental and material self. Mind ever is the builder.

Then, as ye show forth the fruits of the spirit. What are these? Faith, hope, patience, long-suffering, kindness, gentleness, brotherly love—these be those over which so many stumble; yet they are the very voices, yea the very morning sun's light in which the entity has caught that vision of the *new age*, the new understanding, the new seeking for the relationships of a Creative Force to the sons of men.

And indeed then the purposes are to manifest in such measures those fruits that they who are weak take hope, they who have faltered gain new courage, they who are disappointed and disheartened gain a new concept of hope that springs eternally within the human breast.

For God is not mocked, and whatsoever a man soweth, that shall he also reap.

Remember above all, as He hath given, "As ye do it unto the least of thy brethren, of thy associates, of thy companions, day by day, ye do it unto thy God; yea, the God within *thyself!*"

For unless the answer is "My spirit beareth witness with that which is my hope for life, my conception of eternity, my conception of life that is *thy* conception" —unless it beareth witness with these, ye are indeed wandering far afield. But His promises have been, "Seek and ye shall find; knock and it shall be opened unto thee."

And these become then thy mission. Open the door for those that cry aloud for a knowledge that God is within the reach of those that will put their hand to *doing;* just being kind—not a great deed as men count greatness, but just being gentle and patient and loving even with those that would despitefully use thee. For the beauties of the Lord are with those that seek to know and *witness* for Him among men.

That is thy mission, that is thy purpose, in this material experience.

What then is the mental attitude to be? In keeping with that which has been given, "Lo, Lord, I am Thine—to be directed as *Thou*—not my fellow man, but *Thou*—would direct."

For He hath given His angels charge concerning thee, that ye faint not by the way. For He stands—*stands*—at the door and knocks, and if ye will open He will come and sup with thee. For He *is* life and light and immortality; and the way is good.

Ready for questions.

Q-1. How can I maintain a physical and mental balance without so much physical exercise, and produce a normal balance in my sex urges?

A-1. As has been indicated, the glandular system has been disturbed. Now: By the creating of a normal balance within the body for its physical and mental and spiritual well-being, we not only create a normal physical balance but then give—in the expressions of what has been indicated for the physical and mental body—an *outlet* for the beauty of sex.

Do not look upon sex as merely a *physical* expression! There is a physical expression that is beauty within itself, if it is considered from that angle; but when the mental and the spiritual are guiding, then the outlet for beauty becomes a *normal* expression of a *normal*, healthy body.

Q-2. When did this condition begin?

A-2. About a year and a half ago, it began—when there were excesses as to leaving off of energies that found expression in the minds of others rather than in the expression of doing for others.

Q-3. Has my diet harmed me?

A-3. As has been indicated, this has grown gradually to an extreme, and hence has at times—with the outward expression of so much of energies of self—*broken* the coordination between physical *and* the spiritual and mental well-being.

Now when we speak of the mental, know that it is a channel; that is, it is both material and spiritual, and hence is the builder. For when there is an excess of energies used in any direction, without the supplying in each of its phases the material and the spiritual, it becomes unbalanced and incoordinant—not cooperation or coordination.

Q-4. Please explain the cause of the growth on my body and what should be done for it.

A-4. As we find, it is from the accumulations of the energies not expended in their proper channels. Hence, apply those applications that have been indicated first for the *general* health.

Then as these alter, locally apply that which would create a dissipation of same; or an equal combination of Mutton Suet, Turpentine and Spirits of Camphor—gently massaged. This should be done only *after* there has been set to work those activities through the general physical system, through the things or treatments indicated.

Q-5. Is this a cyst or what?

A-5. A cyst, as has been first indicated.

Q-6. I am particularly disturbed at times with conditions of the female organs. Please explain.

A-6. As has been indicated in the activity of the glandular system, these are a portion of the mental and physical and spiritual being. Those channels through which procreation in the activity of the material forces becomes active, the central organizations through which the vibrations may be consciously raised within the body *for* activities in the deeper meditations—these have *overcharged* by lack of applying the conditions or supplying the physical emergencies or physical conditions and the using of the energies by the activities of the body in deeper meditations, the breathings and other activities which have been a portion of the body-physical's resources.

Then, when we make these corrections as indicated, we should find normal conditions coming about.

First, as indicated, an arousing of the glandular forces of the body to activity—through the Atomidine.

Second, the vibratory forces of the Radio-active Appliance, in which there is a union of purposes within the consciousness and the superconsciousness for the use of the body, mind and soul for constructive forces.

Then, thirdly, the activities of the mechanical manipulations, *osteopathically*, for a distribution or dissemination of energies through the body by the correct coordination of the physical energies.

And then the use of the self in body, in mind, for those purposes for which it has entered; and we will find the body regaining its equilibrium in *every* sense. Do that.

Q-7. I have not menstruated in a year.

A-7. This is a stoppage of those very influences that have become as a part of the activities in the attempts for the system to eliminate that which should go through the normal channels.

And we will find after the periods indicated there should be the beginning, not normal at first but gradually the growing towards normalcy in all directions.

Q-8. Have I been wrong not to have sexual contact? Would it do me any good?

A-8. The body has not been wrong! The body would *not* be physically benefited by such—until there are the activities within the physical, the mental, the spiritual self for the proper balance in activities in the Creative Forces as well as the mental and material things for the better coordination in all.

Do the first things first, as has been indicated for the body; following same with the mental attitudes, putting self within the care, the keeping of the Infinite Love that is thine, that ye may show forth the love of the Father, the beauty of a life lived that the glory of the Son may be manifested in the lives of thy fellow men.

Not unto thyself but in Him is all might, all power, all glory.

We are through for the present. 1436-

Mr. Cayce: [Going back over years from present— "1937—'36—'27—the greater change came—'26, '25—'1' —that impressionable change—'16—" etc., on back to birth date.]

The entity as we find, we have the records here that are written upon time and space—as ye would term same.

In giving the interpretations of same, as we find *so much* may be given.

For the experiences of the entity in the earth plane and the application of will as respecting Creative Forces and influences through the activity of the mental forces of the body, have so changed the innate and manifested activities as for the astrological urges to mean so very little.

For the entity's interpretation of the astrological urges, as we find, the name chosen is very well. For this not only in its vibrations from the numerological aspects makes for better influences but comes more in keeping with the Creative Forces or activities of the mental self as related to the materiality.

But as to those from its *spiritual* development, these would come closer to other vibrations.

But we would keep same for the present, the vibrations of the name chosen, [1436], at least until there is a change in the abilities of self to make for the closer communion with self in the inmost being.

In the astrological aspects, the entity in itself finds the Jupiterian the greater influence; and makes for the *world* of meaning, or the activities of the entity combining with or for a *broader* vision; and it is also a protective influence.

As for the other astrological aspects, these we would ignore, from the very nature of the entity's experiences in the earth.

For most every appearance stands out not only as unusual but as one in which the very activities of the entity influenced the world in its choice of action.

In interpreting these, then, as we find these become rather intrinsic; or there is the necessity of giving much of the activities in the experiences in the earth.

For the *confusions* that have arisen in the experience in the present, for the better soul development, must be made not as easy ways but rather as *understandable*!

For if an entity, a body, understands the causes, the purposes of the experiences, then the lesson as an experience for development may be made much more applicable in the experiences of an entity day by day.

And it is Creative Forces' or God's way, God's choice.

For so oft has the entity touched the very influences in which there has been termed by the world, termed by many, that the hand of God was shown in the affairs of many, that it is no wonder that those who have interpreted the records of the entity in or through their own psychic experience have seen the fires of nature, have seen the glories of the Lord, have seen the closer associations of the entity with the holy ones that have trod the earth among the children of men.

For the entity in its activities, though in the ways of man often has been questioned, yet the purposes that were deep-rooted within the heart, the soul, the being of the entity in its progress through the activities, have brought *never* condemnation from the Father-God.

Not that He condemns any, but rather has He looked upon the soul as one through which many blessings have come to the children of men.

Is it a wonder then that oft has it been said, and may it be said oft again, much is expected of the entity? and the way is to be opened by same in its dealings and in its relationships with the children of men?

For the Lord, thy God, will lead, if ye will but put thyself *wholly* into His hands.

Each appearance of the entity in the earth needs its individual analysis, that the temperaments, the latent urges, the influences wrought by the vibrations, by the color, by the harmony, yea by the very *inharmony* among associates, may be understood as to the effect had upon the feelings of the entity.

For the experience becomes rather as a very delicate instrument of music upon which the chords of life (which is God) are played.

Hence it becomes so necessary that the entity be stabilized in those very things that have through its experiences in the earth been as the voice of God unto the soul, "Daughter, I do not condemn thee—sin no more."

Keep in the ways of life, of patience, of earnestness, of sincerity; knowing in *whom* ye have believed, rather than in just what ye believe.

And know that He in whom ye believe is able to keep that committed unto Him against any experience in thy life, thy expressions of life, thy consciousness of activity in any associations.

For these have come as words into the soul of this entity, when the *world* condemned her!

As to the appearances then that become as influences, these are not all, but the outstanding influences in the experience of the entity in the present, and in its activity in the immediate for its finding itself and its relationships to its Maker.

Before this we find the entity was in that land now known as a portion of the French and German land, in that portion called Alsace—in the name Audrie Cordieur.

In the experience the entity acted in the capacity of

the designer for the courts of Louis 13th, 14th, 15th, to those that were in the positions of loyalty and royalty.

The entity was *not* known to man in carnal manner, for there had been those impressions, those needs in its bodily association to keep itself pure *for a purpose*—as had been the calls before.

In the experience the entity gained, yet saw the vileness of intrigue, saw the disappointments of material desires, saw all the activities through which the peoples passed that were oppressed that there might be the gratifying of those in the lusts of the flesh and the body during the experience.

Yet the entity kept itself as the leaven that made for hope to arise within the hearts of many.

For though the entity acted in the capacity of making the pleasures more gratifying in individuals in high places, its heart went out to those that were oppressed; and through the very teachings and activities made for that of hope to spring eternal within the breast for the crying unto and for the justness of a Creator, that took in consideration the affairs of men.

Before that we find the entity was in the land when the Master of Masters walked in the earth, when there were those trials, those temptations, those activities and those desires for the ability of those in authority to trap Him.

The entity was that maid brought before the Master in the temple that was condemned as one taken in adultery; and because of the judgment passed upon that entity according to the law, the peoples or the high priest or those of the Sanhedrin declared that He must make a statement.

And He gave, "Let him that is without sin cast the first stone." Let him that has been guiltless make the first move for the fulfilling of the *letter* of the law.

And lo, they all went their way! And as He wrote upon the ground, "Medi [?] Medici [?] Cui [?]" these meant—in the experience of they that looked on—that which showed the awakening in the heart of the entity of hope, and as the cry came, "Master, what sayest thou?"

the answer came, "I condemn thee not, daughter—go and sin no more."

Is it any wonder, then, that those days that followed made for a remoulding of the entity? though the entity kept afar, and not until after those periods when the persecutions began did she venture to come nigh unto those that were classed or called of the household of faith.

But to have had the words direct from the Master of Masters, the Teacher of Teachers, "I do not condemn thee," *has* meant, *must* mean, in the experience of the entity, that which words cannot portray; but only the deeds of the body, the desire of the mind to bring hope, faith, *in* that Lord, that Master, who is able to *save* unto the utmost, and who hath given to all, "My peace I leave *with* you, my peace I give *unto* you."

And when the entity has experienced and does experience that consciousness by opening the door of its heart again to that voice that comes, "I condemn thee not—be thou merciful, even as I have shown and give thee mercy," then: In the life of intolerability in the experience, cannot the entity find in the heart of self to say, even as He, "They know not what they do"? and to give the cup of water, to give the healing in the hands, to give the cherishment to those that are sad?

To those that are joyous give them more joy in that the praise be given to Him who maketh life to all that seek to know His face.

How oft may the entity, if it will but cherish within the heart of self that experience, vision the experience when before those in penal law or authority, those with their pomp and glory—yet He in *all* His glory, His face shining as only from the Father-God itself!

Thus may the entity see and know that presence, "My daughter, I condemn thee not—My peace I give to thee."

Hold fast to that! For He will walk and talk with thee, if ye will but open thy mind, thy heart, to Him.

For He is nigh unto thee. For indeed in flesh, as ye will see, ye were a parent even unto Him.

Before that we find the entity was in that now known as or called the Palestine land, during those days when the sons of Jacob sought for companions; and to one of the sons of Judah (Er) the entity, Tamar, became the companion.

Owing to the *willfulness* and the sin of Er, he was taken. There was the command or the seeking that there be the fulfillment of the law of the day; and Judah—in an unknown way—failing, yet the entity sought for that as would keep the issue of the body, and went in unto her own father-in-law; and bore two sons, one becoming then later the father of the fathers of Joseph and Mary—the parent of the Master.

There the entity was condemned, yes; yet her purposes, her desires, were reckoned with by the God of mercy as being in keeping with His will and His ways.

Hence there is brought into the experience of the entity again the joys of knowing the Lord hath given, "Thy will, my will, are one with the Creative Forces."

And there is reckoned through the ages, then, that ye became as one that chose to do above the ways of men when the voice of man rose above thine own sex.

Hence in the experience, judgments are not taken away—if the entity will trust rather in the *Lord* than in the judgment of men, or the children of men.

For God is the same yesterday, today, tomorrow—yea, forever; and they that come unto Him in *humbleness* of heart, seeking to know His face and His way, may indeed find Him.

Before that we find (as has been indicated for others, the entity was born in the present during those periods when there were those coming in that are of the Atlantean age) the entity then lived during those periods of the exodus from Atlantis into the Egyptian land, and afterward.

It was during those periods when there were the correlations of those activities of the entity in correlating the teachings of the Priest Ra Ta, the teachings of Ax-Tell,' and the activities that made for the cleansing of the bodies and the minds of those that would give them in service for the Creative Forces that God be not mocked among men.

The entity then arose in power, in authority among men in the Temple of Sacrifice *first*, and then in the Temple of Beauty—the Temple Beautiful.

For there the entity gained the abilities to make for the harmonizing of colors to those extents wherein each individual was and is as yet clothed with *its* individual color—as ye call aura.

For the entity made that overture in such measures that the promises of the Divine that were and are written in the rainbow of the sky, when the cloud has passed, are the same as written in the lives of individuals; that they, too, who are in the closer walk with the Creative Forces, may see their sign, their colors, and *know* whereunto they have attained in *their* relationship with Creative energies or God.

Thus the entity in its activities through the ages of the earth as an entity, as a soul manifesting in bodily form, has given to the earth, to the world, to the children of men, that which applied in their experiences day by day in patience, in tolerance, in love, will bring the influences and forces as to bring them in closer union with and closer walks with their God.

As to the abilities of the entity in the present, then, and that to which it may attain, and how:

Say not within self, "Who shall ascend into heaven to bring me a message that I may know what I shall do?" For lo, He, thy Lord, thy God, is *within thee!* And know that the heavenly understanding or kingdom is within thee. The body is thy temple, as ye so aptly taught in those experiences in the purifying of the body that there might be no desire for the carnal forces of the natural world, the aggrandizement of self; and that as the self set it in the beauties of the divine sanction, that man might know the ways through the promises He had given.

Then He has promised to meet thee in the temple of thine own consciousness, and there ye may commune with Him.

Not *any,* then, but thy Lord, thy Master. For He hath *spoken* to thee in the *flesh!* He will speak to thee in thy mind, in thy body, in thy consciousness of His presence.

Then as to what ye may attain, it is limited only by thine own physical concepts and understanding and the willingness to be led *only* by Jesus, the Master, who hath called thee by name.

Let, then, thy ideal be set alone in Him; for in all ages, in all times, the law of one is *that*—though it may have borne many names, even as ye have borne many names in many lands, in many climes. Even in thine own individual consciousness names have only vibrated to the colors about thee, the attunement of thy material and thy mental world. Yet the *spiritual* forces must be the source of emanation, if they would be *perfected* in that as ye taught in the Temple Beautiful, as ye did before the patriarchs of old when ye commanded thy father, yea thy husband, to show thee!

"*These* signets are thine, they are the proof of my purpose, my desire"; yea, as the Master gave, "Sin no more"—keep the laws of the Lord as the signets in thy heart, thy body, thy mind, and the souls shall cry a joyful cry unto Him.

Ready for questions.

Q-1. Would it be wise for me to seek a career in the motion picture field?

A-1. As an interpreter, as a writer, this would be very well; but first attune the body again to the needs of the material world that the mental and spiritual self may have that temple, that channel, that body to the better express or manifest in. Or as given, do the first things first.

Q-2. As in presenting color shorts or as an actress?

A-2. As in that which is becoming more and more undertaken—the color photography, the color directions. For these the entity may direct in such measures as to confound many of those that are worldly wise; for were these not comprehended in the spiritual and mental world for the choice of those that were to present the laws of One by this entity?

Q-3. I have been told that I should not marry before I was 32. Please advise me regarding marriage—when should I marry and is there anyone whom I now know that I should marry?

A-3. As we find, these become not only problems in the experience but through the periods of the activities in the earth there has been that which has held the entity for a purpose.

This as we find would be nearer twenty-nine than thirty-two, as to time or period; but as we find the entity yet has *not met* the one to whom union would be made. The associations as we find would rather be in connections with its life's work.

Q-4. Along just what specific lines should I direct my studies for mental and spiritual balance?

A-4. Take that as thy God that tells of His, thy Lord's, thy God's dealings with men. Though many may pronounce same as of a questionable nature, *find*—by its study—that it is thine experience also.

Then the purpose in the experience is to present thyself holy, acceptable unto Him in the measures and in the ways that He would direct.

Know that He has *sanctioned* marriage. Know He hath not questioned thee in thy motives. Know He *will* guide and direct if ye will seek to know of Him.

Q-5. Am I fitted to do some special work in the new science of color?

A-5. As we find and as has been indicated, that so far as the commercial field is concerned, associated with the new color for the cinema—these are the fields of activity in which the entity may make the application of the abilities for the means of the world.

As for colors pertaining to life itself—as the self or the entity set in motion, *study* auras and aid *others* in knowing what they mean! There are those that interpret same in the form of spiritism. There are those that interpret same in the form of vibration. They are *all* of these and more, as the entity KNOWS and may *experience*!

Hence the studies that the entity may make will give, again, again, that leaven that leaveneth the whole, for the *use* of the masses in their *daily* experience!

Q-6. Would it be wise for me to undertake a more extensive study of metaphysics with the ultimate purpose of making this a career, as practitioner or analyst?

A-6. Rather to that of colors. Both as to their effect upon that which is the great teacher of the people (or the cinema) and as to that great understanding to those that see their fellow man.

Q-7. Should I be a lecturer?

A-7. This becomes a part of the experience in color.

Q-8. Just what is the karmic relationship with my father and what can I do to help him?

A-8. He was Er, the husband in that experience. And is there a wonder that there are those disturbing forces in the material relationships in the present? Leave these with the Lord!

Q-9. Just what is the karmic relationship with my brother Adolph? what have been the relationships in the past and what are the urges to be met in the present?

A-9. We don't find brother Adolph.

Q-10. With my mother?

A-10. These closer relationships were in the experience just previous to this, in Alsace; and as friendship during that sojourn or activity. Closer still with those members of the family, of course, before this.

We are through for the present. 1436-2

Mr. [3428] had periods of complete loss of consciousness and was diagnosed as an epileptic.

In this case we are told of "conditions of which many bodies should be warned—the opening of the centers in the body-spiritual without correctly directing same . . ." This 44-year-old highway engineer was "well versed in the study of meditation, the study of transmission of thought, with the ability to control others." He was warned, "Don't control others."

This is the only reading I have seen which gives the precise spinal vertebrae which correspond to the seven spiritual centers. The focal point of his disease was located in the seven centers, not in the brain. And question and answer #3 state that the origin of the problem was partly related to sexual expression or repression. If we seek to open the centers in meditation, we must correctly direct the energy. Know where you are going before you start out!

Responding to his reading, he wrote: "You mention: 'Don't control others.' Believe me—I have always tried to be humble—in my heart as well as in my conduct. It is true, that within me was a fierce, fire-like burning rage to try to become the head of everything I attempted. However, people sort of shunned me—or avoided me—I presume, because of my attacks." There was one period of four to six months in which he enjoyed the companionship of a woman friend during which he *never* had an attack. On this attack-free period he asked, "Was this due to the fact that I was in love with her?" Later he wrote, "I suddenly realized, out of a clear blue sky, why her comradeship proved so beneficial and that was because I never permitted the thought of lust or sex to even enter my mind—that is, in connection with her, during all that time I knew her. I forced any immoral ideas out of my mind . . ."

Mrs. Cayce: You will go over this body carefully, examine it thoroughly, and tell me the conditions you find at the present time; giving the cause of the existing conditions, also suggestions for help and relief of this body; answering the questions, as I ask them:

Mr. Cayce: Yes, we have the body here.

As we find, there are disturbances with this body. Much of these, however, are tied up with the emotional natures of the body. And here we find some of those conditions of which *many* bodies should be warned—the opening of centers in the body-spiritual without correctly directing same, which may oft lead to wrecking of the body-physical and sometimes mental.

Know where you are going before you start out, in analyzing spiritual and mental and material things.

This is not belittling the seeking of knowledge, neither is it advising individuals—or this individual—to seek knowledge. But knowledge without the use of same still remains, as in the beginning, sin. And be sure your sins will find you out!

Here we have an emotional body well versed in the study of meditation, the study of transmission of thought with the ability to control others.

Don't control others. Suppose thy God controlled thee without thy will? What would you become, or what would you have been?

But you were made in the image of thy Creator, to be a companion with Him—not over someone else, but a companion with thy brother and not over thy brother. Hence do not act that way, because ye have the greater ability or greater knowledge of control of others.

Then, as we would give for this body—for this is psychological as well as pathological—we would begin again to study—this time the Book.

Begin with Exodus 19:5.

Then read again and know thoroughly the 20th chapter of Exodus.

Study then thoroughly and apply personally the 30th of Deuteronomy, and apply it in the terms of the 23rd Psalm.

Thus ye will make thyself new.

As to physical applications:

At least once each week we would have a general hydrotherapy treatment, including first a mild cabinet sweat followed by a needle shower, and then a message using this combination of oils: olive oil (heated), 2 ounces, tincture of myrrh, 2 ounces; Calamus oil, 10 drops. Massage these oils into the spine itself, also in the areas especially of the ribs, around each rib, around the central bone or sternum or breastbone, around the collarbone, especially over the areas of the 9th dorsal, 11th and 12th dorsals, and throughout the sacral areas.

If we will do these, we will find much bettered conditions for this body.

The abilities are unlimited, but as the warnings are given in Exodus as well as in Deuteronomy, know how they may be centralized for thy brethren in "The Lord is my shepherd" and not Mr. [3428] but thy Lord, thy God.

Ready for questions.

Q-1. Is the focal center of the disease in the brain or some other part of the body?

A-1. As indicated, it is in those centers—the seven centers of the body—where sympathetic and cerebrospinal coordinate the more; 1st, 2nd and 3rd cervical; 1st and 2nd dorsal; 5th and 6th dorsal; 9th dorsal; 11th and 12th dorsal; and through the lumbar and sacral areas. These are the sources. This is not an infection—it is a lack of coordination between the impulses of the mental self and the central nerve and blood supply.

Q-2. Are there any organic changes due to the disease?

A-2. All the organic changes are due to this condition, of lack of coordination.

Q-3. Does sexual expression or repression cause this condition, or have any effect on same?

A-3. This was a part of the beginnings of it; for when the lyden (Leydig) glands are opened, which are in the gonads—or the centers through which the expression of generation begins, they act directly upon the centers through the body. Unless these find expression they disintegrate, or through thy association cause dis-association in impulse and the central or body-nerves.

Q-4. Are there any mental attitudes invdolved in the cause of this disease?

A-4. As indicated.

Do as outlined—we will have the results, according to thy faith and thy works; not by faith alone but by faith *and* works.

We are through with this reading. 3428-1

[1567] was a 52-year-old woman who was never able to marry because she had to care for her mother and father. She felt that others in the family got what they wanted; but for her, at every crucial period in her life, the door was slammed. She never believed in a personal God and, at middle age, she felt high and dry on the road.

She was given a most extraordinary reading on the purpose of life and a marvelous and instructive discourse on the mind, an excerpt worthy of repeated study and reflection. It is an excellent parallel study with Chapter Four in this book, "Mind Is the Builder."

Mr. Cayce: Yes, we have the records here of that entity now known as or called [Miss 1567].

These are we find may be said to be very beautiful records, yet in ways such that it may be questioned by some as to why one who has been so far advanced in some experiences has been so little in the limelight or in the position of prominence through the same ways in the present.

If the varied experiences are studied with an eye single to service, these may possibly be understood or comprehended. For remember that God looketh on the heart and not, as man, on the outward appearances.

Hence there are lessons to be gained by the entity from even those feelings, those innate urges that cry for expression. For in their very expression, not finding outlet they turn as it were upon those influences from within.

But we find that if these are used, the entity may yet find a peace, a manner or way of expression that will bring joy into the experience in this sojourn.

In giving the interpretations, know that these are chosen with the purpose that they are to become helpful experiences.

An experience, then, is not only a happening, but what is the reaction in your own mind? What does it do to you to make your life, your habits, your relationships to others of a more helpful nature, with a more hopeful attitude?

These are the criterions for every individual's experience—sincerity of purpose, of desire; putting the whole law into effect in the activities—which is to love the Lord thy God with all thy heart, thy mind, thy body, and thy neighbor as thyself.

This is the whole law. All the other things given or written are only the interpreting of same.

Then what does such a proclaiming preclude? From what basis is the reasoning drawn? What is the purpose of an individual experience of an entity or soul into the earth at any given period?

These answered then give a background for the interpreting of *why*.

There are urges latent and manifested in the experience of each soul, each entity, each body.

First we begin with the fact that God *is;* and that the heavens and the earth, and all nature, declare this. Just as there is the longing within *every* heart for the continuity of life.

What then is life? As it has been given, in Him we live and move and have our being. Then He, God, *is!* Or Life in all of its phases, its expressions, is a manifestation of that force or power we call God, or that is called God.

Then Life is continuous. For that force, that power which has brought the earth, the universe and all the influences in same into being, is a continuous thing—is a first premise.

All glory, all honor then, is *due* that creative force that may be manifested in our experiences as individuals through the manner in which we deal with our fellow man!

Then we say, when our loved ones, our heart's desires are taken from us, in what are we to believe?

This we find is only answered in that which has been given as His promise, that God hath not willed that any soul should perish but hath with every temptation, every trial, every disappointment made a way of escape or for correcting same. It is not a way of justification only, as by faith, but a way to know, to realize that in these disappointments, separations, there comes the assurance that He cares!

For to be absent from the body is to be present with that consciousness that we, as an individual, have worshipped as our God! For as we do it unto the least of our brethren, our associates, our acquaintance, our servants day by day, so we do unto our Maker!

What is the purpose then, we ask, for our entering into this vale, or experience, or awareness, where disappointments, fears, trials of body and of mind appear to mount above all the glories that we may see?

In the beginning, when there was the creating, or the calling of individual entities into being, we were made to be the companions with the Father-God.

Now flesh and blood may not inherit eternal life; only the spirit, only the purpose, only the desire may inherit same.

Then that error in individual activity—not of another but of ourselves, individually—separated us from that awareness.

Hence God prepared the way through flesh whereby all phases of spirit, mind and body might express.

The earth then is a three-dimensional, a three-phase or three-manner expression. Just as the Father, the Son, the Holy Spirit are one. So are our body, mind and soul one—in Him.

Now we have seen, we have heard, we know that the Son represents or signifies the mind.

He, the Son, was in the earth-earthy even as we—and yet is of the Godhead.

Hence the mind is both material and spiritual, and taketh hold on that which is its environ, its want, in our experiences.

Then mind, as He, was the Word—and dwelt among men; and we beheld Him as the face of the Father.

So is our mind made, so does our mind conceive—even as He; and *is* the builder.

Then that our mind dwells upon, that our mind feeds upon, that do we supply to our body—yes, to our soul!

Hence we find all of these are the background, as it were, for the interpreting of our experience, of our sojourns in the earth.

For the astrological or the relative position of the earth (our immediate home) is not the center of the universe, is not the center of our thought; but the kingdom of the Father or the kingdom of heaven is within! Why? Because our mind, the Son, is within us.

Then with that consciousness of His awareness, we may know even as He has given, "Ye abide in me, as I in the Father—I will come and abide with thee."

In that consciousness, then, the purposes for which each soul enters materiality are that it may become aware of its relationships to the Creative Forces or God; by the material manifestation of the things thought, said, *done*, in relation to its fellow man!

As the earth then occupies its three-dimensional phase of experience in our own solar system, and as each of those companions that are about the solar system represents as it were one of the phases of our conscience—the elements of our understanding—or our senses; then they each in their place, in their plane, bear a relationship to us, even as our desires for physical sustenance; that is: foods for the body; with all of the attributes, all of the abilities to take that we feed upon and turn it into elements for our body.

All of the elements are gathered from that upon which we have fed to build blood, bone, hair, nails; the sight, the hearing, the touching, the feelings, the expressions.

Why? Because these are *quickened* by the presence of the spirit of the Creative Force (within).

So our mind, with its attributes, gathers from that upon which we feed in our mental self; forming our concepts of our relationship with those things that are contrariwise to His biddings or in line with that Law which is all-inclusive; that is, the love of the Father, with our mind, our body, our soul, and our neighbor as self.

Then all of these influences astrological (as known or called) from without, bear witness—or *are* as innate influences upon our activity, our sojourn through any given experience. Not because we were born with the sun in this sign or that, nor because Jupiter or Mercury or Saturn or Uranus or Mars was rising or setting, but rather:

Because we were made for the purpose of being companions with Him, a little lower than the angels who behold His face ever, yet as heirs, as joint heirs with Him who *is* the Savior, the Way, then we have brought these about *because* of our activities through our EXPERIENCES in those realms! Hence they bear witness by being *in* certain positions—because of our activity, our sojourn in those environs, in relationships to the universal forces of activity.

Hence they bear witness of certain urges in us, not beyond our will but controlled by our will!

For as was given of old, there is each day set before us life and death, good and evil. We choose because of our natures. If our will were broken, if we were commanded to do this or that, or to become as an automaton, our individuality then would be lost and we would only be as in Him without conscience—*conscience*—consciousness of being one with Him; with the abilities to choose for self!

For we *can*, as God, say Yea to this, Nay to that; we *can* order this or the other in our experience, by the very gifts that have been given or appointed unto our keeping. For we are indeed as laborers, co-laborers in the vineyard of the Lord—or of they that are fearful of His coming.

And we choose each day *whom* we will serve! And by the records in time and space, as we have moved through the realms of His kingdom, we have left our mark upon same.

Then they influence us, either directly or indirectly, in the manner as we have declared ourselves in favor of this or that influence in our material experience. And by the casting of our lot in this or that direction, we bring into our experience the influence in that manner.

For this entity, then, we find these as influences:

Venus—the beauty ye enjoy; the abilities that are a part of thy whole experience. The abilities of love, yet that have in a manner been denied thee when ye consider as to thy material surroundings, thy material undertakings but in thy deeper self ye find these as a part of thy experience—apparently as yet never satisfied, or that thou hast loved, that thou hast taken to thy heart has been swept away from thee, taken to those influences or environs that to thee become as naught!

Then there must be through these very influences and channels an outlet, a manner in which these may find expression; which there is, in thy ability to *write beautiful* things that will act and react upon the minds and the hearts of others—those that may read, those that may make some to be a part of their experience by the very manner in which ye in loving care may show forth these in thy dealings with thy fellow man!

In Jupiter we find the benevolent influences. And as there is the conjunction of Venus and Jupiter, which will appear in the coming fall—or about October the 13th should be one of or *the* most glorious days, as a day, for thy experiences of wondrous things that may be an answer to thy longings in many directions; the knowledge of those very things that may bring the awareness, the consciousness of His abiding presence that is nigh unto thee ever!

In these ye may be favored with the greater comprehension.

As to thy experiences or appearances in the earth, thy sojourns among men—these have been, as indicated, beautiful in many manners, in many ways; and yet they seem so for naught in the present!

But drawing nigh unto the Father-God (within) ye may become more and more aware of thy purposes for being here. For His promise is to bring to thy remembrance all those things from the foundations of the earth!

Hence from the very activities these find expression in the present in thy love for history, historical subjects, things pertaining to influences brought because of the relationships of individuals to conditions and characters and places! These become in thy activities and in thy abilities but channels, means through which ye may bring some of that beauty, some of that joy that is in His promises to thee, and to thy fellow man in thy very activity!

Before this, then, we find the entity was in the land of the present nativity during those periods prior to and during what is known as the American Revolution.

For the entity then was among those peoples about that fort then called Dearborn, who overran the land or who prepared for the indwellings and homes for others in the land.

When the associates and companions of the entity then, as Mae Marandal, escaped and established dwellings in the hills (where there later became great orchards, above the hills of thy own present abode), the entity brought much to those peoples in the manner and the way of keeping the records. The entity brought much through the giving of the greater understanding as to how there might be the rotation of this or that in the activity to bring about conveniences in the experiences of the people.

And ye loved thy neighbors; they loved thee!

For oft many, many came to thee for counsel, for that thou had been able to give to thine own, to thine own household, to thy own neighborhood, to thy own surroundings!

And in the present, in the application of those abilities arising from that sojourn, ye may find the abilities to give to others; not to shut thyself in, either in body or mind, but *open* thy heart, *open* thy abilities to others!

Write—write—write! Though ye may tear up for a year, or for more than a year everything ye write giving expression to same, ye will find the abilities to bring into the experience and minds of others the joys that are not even comprehended in the present!

Before that we find the entity was in the Persian and Arabian land, during those periods when in the "city in the halls and the plains" that teacher Uhjltd made overtures to the experiences of men to put away their petty feelings, their petty hates, those things that made people afraid by the very power of might making right; realizing that the power of love makes right.

The entity was among the natives who were of the household of that Uhjltd, and an older—much older sister of the entity in the experience, in the name then Ujdelda.

With the establishing of the activities and the household being gathered about the entity, we find that this entity made for helpful activities with that teacher Uhjltd; and stood with the peoples against the rebellions that arose among a portion of the nomads during the early part of the activity.

Again during those periods when the Greeks and a portion of the peoples from the Persian land brought turmoils, the entity then aided in keeping that equilibrium—by what? The accounts of what had been the prices paid as it were by individuals, by those who had been cleansed in body and mind; not materially but mentally, spiritually!

Thus the beauty of such unfoldments made for experiences that brought joy and happiness to the entity in that sojourn—as it may in the applying of self in those directions associated with the activities in that experience; in spreading the gospel as it were of good tidings, by that same teacher; in being a portion of that group to aid in the publications of facts—not only of those things that may be gathered by self but that have been a part of the gatherings of others.

Before that we find the entity was in the Egyptian land, now called, when there were those activities being disseminated through the varied lands for which preparations had been made for or by individuals that might bring into the experience of material activity the greater means or manners of expression.

The entity then was among those who were in the activities of the Temple Beautiful, that made for the preparations of the many.

Thus the entity, as She-Lula-Or-Ar, made for the channels through which there arose the teachers who became especially fitted for activities or operations overseas, or the beginning of those that became the greater active upon the waves of the oceans and seas.

As to the abilities of the entity in the present, then:

Hold fast to that which is latent and may be so manifested in that love ye hold for those of princely, crowning glories in the experiences ye have enjoyed in the earth!

Study to show thyself approved unto God, a workman not ashamed; rightly divining—dividing—the words of truth, keeping thy own self in thy own good conscience unspotted from questionings within thy own self.

Write—*write*—of Him; of those experiences of thy own!

And join thyself with those things being undertaken by thy brother-teacher of old!

Thus ye shall know peace and happiness *here—now!*

We are through for the present. 1567-2

Index

Abortion 155, 156
Abstinence 58, 89, 153, 166, 256
Adam 3, 9, 11, 12, 13, 14, 27, 229
Addiction 68
Adultery 147, 164, 165–66, 167, 209
Affairs 164, 165, 167, 184
Agreement 151, 152, 153
Aggression and sex 53
Amilius 9, 13
Anger 21
Apparel 80, 102
Appetites 7, 32, 33, 44, 89, 181, 182, 185, 188
  See also Carnal desires
Archetypes 49
Atlantis 11–12
Attitudes 99–101
Automatic writing 77
Autonomic nervous system 45

Beauty of sex 149–51
Behavior, sexual 31–32, 36
Biological needs 74
Birth control 155–56, 236
Bodily desires—See Carnal desires
Body
  as temple 66–67
  as temple of God 44, 45–46, 56
  as the Father 71
  purpose of 46

Carnal desires 6, 11, 15, 21, 22, 23, 53, 65, 71, 91, 105, 154, 192, 199, 213
Carnal force 98, 192, 204
Carnality of mind 6, 11, 15
Celibacy 58, 107–8, 151–52, 167, 188
Centers, endocrine 46
  See also Glands; Endocrine glands
Chastity 151–52
Choice 16, 27, 28, 30, 98, 99, 113, 115, 164–65, 193–222
Choosing a partner 144–49
Christ 14, 27, 28–29, 37–38, 60, 174
Clothes 80, 102
Compulsions 42, 85
Conception 154, 226
Condemnation 218, 259
Conscience, spiritual 34, 35, 36
Creation 2–15, 224–27, 229
Criticism 21

"Daughters of Men" 9
Decision making 25, 27, 30, 38, 192–222
Desire 20, 23, 26, 66, 114, 192
Desires
  bodily 32, 44–45
  carnal 6, 11, 15, 21, 22, 23, 53, 65, 71, 91, 105, 154, 192, 199, 213
  loss of 152
  mental 91
  patterns 74
  physical 45
  sexual 50
  spiritualizing 91–92
  value of 88–95
Discipline 214–15

Divine origin of sex 14
Divorce 164, 168–72, 234–35
Dreams 207–12
  sex 210–12
Drives 73, 74, 96

Education 226
Ego 33, 34, 35, 200
Embarrassment 99
Emotional experiences 97
Endocrine glands 45, 65, 73, 75, 96, 250
  See also Gonads; Lyden gland; Thymus gland
Energy
  sexual/spiritual 44
  spiritual 49
Enjoyment 41
Environment 212, 227
Environmental training 96
Eve 9, 12, 13
Excitation 96
Extramarital sex 164, 165–66, 167–168

Family relationships 114–15, 116
Fantasy 83, 84–86, 108, 138
Fears 153, 190
Fetishes 101
Freedom 199–200
Free will 16, 99, 200, 212–14, 224
Freud, Sigmund 51, 113
Freud's concept of man 33
Fun, sex for fun 41–42

Glandular system purifying 250–52
Glands 64
  endocrine 45, 65, 73, 75, 96, 250
  See also Gonads; Lyden gland; Thymus gland
Gonads 49, 50, 58
  center 58, 59
Grace 217–20
Guilt 99

Habit 89, 185
Heredity 96, 212, 227
Home life 157, 163
Homemaking 157–63
Homo sapiens 15, 46, 66
Homosexual
  attraction 108
  dream 210
  fantasies 86
Homosexuality 41, 81, 101, 116–31, 210
Hypnosis 83, 119

Id 33, 34, 35
Ideal 24–28, 171, 195, 196
  Christ 60
  mental 37–39
  physical 37–39
  setting the 37–39, 43
  sexual life 39–41
  spiritual 24–26, 28, 37–39
Illegitimacy 244–48
Imagination 74
Imaginings 86
Impotence 108, 167
Inhibitions 97
Instinct 90, 185, 231
Intellect 91
Intercourse 101
  during pregnancy 157
Ire 21

Jesus 14, 27, 28–29, 37–38, 60, 174
Jung, Carl 49, 210

Karma 104, 105, 106–7, 217–19, 226
  sexual 107–10, 113, 122, 177–91, 198
Kundalini 51, 58, 62, 118, 123, 166

Leydig cells 47, 60
  See Lyden gland
Libido 51
Life force 3
Lilith 9
Lyden gland 47, 62, 118, 138, 268
  center 51

Marital relations 22–23, 36, 52–53,

115, 116, 152–53, 154, 157–60, 171–72, 195–96
Marriage 144–49, 157–63
second 172
Masturbation 41, 101, 135–40, 247–248
Mate, choosing 144–49
Meditation 74–76, 92, 122, 133, 137–38, 166, 194, 203, 205, 206, 250, 255
physiology 58
and sex 56–58
Memories 76
Mental desire 91
Mind 3
and motivation 73–74
carnal 6, 11, 15
the builder 68–95
the experiencer 78
Mire 21
Monogamy 164, 195, 234
Motivation 25, 49, 73–74, 96, 193, 195
sexual 54
Motivational centers 48
Motivative system 75
Music 80, 120, 133, 134, 195

Nature of man 2
"Normal" behavior 98–99
Normalize 18–19, 22, 99, 155
Nudism 235–36

Oedipus complex 112–13
Oral sex 101
Overemphasis 21
Oversexed 21

Partner, choosing 144–49
Past life influences 104, 105–6, 217–20, 226
sexual 106–10, 112–14, 122, 177–191, 197–98
Patience 32
Patterns of relationships 114, 115
Planetary sojourns 78–79, 97
Polygamy 195, 234
Prayer 83, 84, 203–4
Pregnancy 155, 156
illegitimate 244–48
intercourse during 157
Promiscuity 102, 127
Psychic 82–84
abilities and sex 61–62, 64
awakening 61, 62
Purpose of sex 40

Rape 53, 54
fantasies 108
Rapport 82, 83
Rebellion 3, 4, 15, 18, 43, 60, 61, 193
spirit of 67
Reincarnation 80, 86, 97, 98–99, 102, 104, 106–10, 113–14, 122, 177–91, 197
and sex 55–56
Relationships 141–49
patterns 115
Religious vs. spiritual 29
Repressions 88
Revelation of St. John 30, 43, 48, 49, 60, 204

Sacrifice, animal 57
Sadomasochism 101
Seduction 54, 173
Self-condemnation 35–39, 99, 126, 129, 130
See also Condemnation
Sensitivity 96
Sensory system 45, 123
Sensuousness 185
Separation 168–72
Sex
and psychic abilities 61–62, 64
and sustenance 58–59
beauty of 149–51
divine origin 14
dreams 210–12
education 226
extramarital 164, 165–66, 167–68
for fun 41–42
life, ideal 39–41
loss of desire 152
normal 21, 22, 28
physical, mental, spiritual 22
purpose 40

Sexes, division 9–10, 11
Sexual
  behavior 31–32, 36
  desires 50
  expression 101
  fears 153
  karma 107–10, 113, 122, 177–91, 198
  motivations 42
  oversexed 21
Siddhis 62
Sons of God 8–9, 14
Soul mates 143, 162
Spirit
  fruits of 31
  gifts of 31
Spiritual
  body 2
  vs. religion 29
Superconscious 203
Superego 33, 34, 35, 36
Sustenance 58–59

Telepathy 82–83, 84
"Thought form lover" 76–78
Thought forms 7–8, 76, 105
Thought patterns 78
Thymus gland 54
Triune 69, 71–72
Trinity 2

Venus 79–80, 81–82
Visualization 74
Vows 182, 188
  of celibacy 57, 107–8, 151–52, 167, 168

Will 3, 16, 88, 91, 97, 192–222
  free 16, 99, 200, 212–14, 224
  of God 199–201

ABOUT THE AUTHOR

HERBERT BRUCE PURYEAR is a clinical psychologist who has specialized in integrating the insights of psychical research, depth psychology, and comparative religion. This study has included an emphasis on a study of the archetypal symbolism of dreams and of religious, mystical, and psychical experiences. He has also made an intensive study of the psychic readings of Edgar Cayce.

He is the author of a number of articles and several books including *The Edgar Cayce Primer, Reflections on the Path, Sex and the Spiritual Path,* and is co-author of *Meditation and the Mind of Man*.

Dr. Puryear is currently president of Logos World University in Scottsdale, Arizona, which is dedicated to research and training in the integration of the fields of psychic research, comparative religions and holistic healing.

THE EDGAR CAYCE LEGACIES

Among the vast resources which have grown out of the late Edgar Cayce's work are:

The Readings: Available for examination and study at the Association for Research and Enlightenment, Inc. (A.R.E.®) at Virginia Beach, Va., are 14,256 readings consisting of 49,135 pages of verbatim psychic material plus related correspondence. The readings are the clairvoyant discourses given by Cayce while he was in a self-induced hypnotic sleep-state. These discourses were recorded in shorthand and then typed. Copious indexing and cross-indexing make the readings readily accessible for study.

Research and Information: Medical information which flowed through Cayce is being researched and applied by the research divisions of the Edgar Cayce Foundation. Work is also being done with dreams and other aspects of ESP. Much information is disseminated through the A.R.E. Press publications, *A.R.E. News* and *The A.R.E. Journal*. Coordination of a nationwide program of lectures and conferences is in the hands of the Department of Education. A library specializing in psychic literature is available to the public with books on loan to members. An extensive tape library has A.R.E. lectures available for purchase. Resource material has been made available for authors, resulting in the publication of scores of books, booklets and other material.

A.R.E. Study Groups: The Edgar Cayce material is most valuable when worked with in an A.R.E. Study Group, the text for which is *A Search for God*, Books I and II. These books are the outcome of eleven years of work by Edgar Cayce with the first A.R.E. group and represent the distillation of wisdom which flowed through him in the trance condition. Hundreds of A.R.E. groups flourish throughout the United States and other countries. Their primary purpose is to assist the members to know their relationship to their Creator and to become channels of love and service to others. The groups are nondenominational and avoid ritual and dogma. There are no dues or fees required to join a group although contributions may be accepted.

Membership: A.R.E. has an open-membership policy which offers attractive benefits.

For more information write A.R.E., Box 595, Virginia Beach, Va. 23451. To obtain information about publications, please direct your query to A.R.E. Press. To obtain information about joining or perhaps starting an A.R.E. Study Group, please direct your letter to the Study Group Department.